THE CONSTITUTION OF JAPAN

Japan boasts the second largest economy in the world and almost two thousand years of history. Yet, its first modern constitution, the Meiji Constitution, was not enacted until comparatively recently (1889). Since then, following World War II, Japan adopted its current Constitution, the Japanese Constitution of 1946. This book is designed to explain the outline of Japan's Constitution, together with a number of its unique characteristics and to offer an historical background and context which help explain its significance. Major topics covered include the constitutional history of Japan, fundamental principles of the Constitution, the people and the Emperor, the Diet and legislative power, Cabinet and executive power, and the Judiciary and judicial power. Also discussed is the protection of fundamental human rights, individual rights—including freedom of expression, economic freedoms and social rights—pacifism and national defence, and the constitutional amendment and reform. Although the Japanese Constitution was enacted under the strong influence of the United States Constitution, many of its features are very different. For instance the existence of an Emperor, the long dominance of a conservative party over the Government, the relatively strong power of government bureaucrats, the absence of a leadership role in the Prime Minister, the small role the judiciary play in solving constitutional disputes and the struggle over national defence. Written in an accessible style and comprehensive in content, the reader will find this account of the constitutional law of Japan both unique and stimulating.

Constitutional Systems of the World
General Editors: Peter Leyland and Andrew Harding
Associate Editors: Benjamin L Berger and Alexander Fischer

In the era of globalisation, issues of constitutional law and good governance are being seen increasingly as vital issues in all types of society. Since the end of the Cold War, there have been dramatic developments in democratic and legal reform, and post-conflict societies are also in the throes of reconstructing their governance systems. Even societies already firmly based on constitutional governance and the rule of law have undergone constitutional change and experimentation with new forms of governance; and their constitutional systems are increasingly subjected to comparative analysis and transplantation. Constitutional texts for practically every country in the world are now easily available on the internet. However, texts which enable one to understand the true context, purposes, interpretation and incidents of a constitutional system are much harder to locate, and are often extremely detailed and descriptive. This series seeks to provide scholars and students with accessible introductions to the constitutional systems of the world, supplying both a road map for the novice and, at the same time, a deeper understanding of the key historical, political and legal events which have shaped the constitutional landscape of each country. Each book in this series deals with a single country, and each author is an expert in their field.

Published volumes

The Constitution of the United Kingdom
The Constitution of the United States
The Constitution of Vietnam
The Constitution of South Africa
The Constitution of Australia
The Constitution of Finland

Forthcoming titles in this series

The Constitution of France
Sophie Boyron

The Constitution of Ireland
Colm O'Cinneide

The Constitution of the Russian Federation
Jane Henderson

Link to series website
http://www.hartpub.co.uk/series/csw

The Constitution of Japan

A Contextual Analysis

Shigenori Matsui

·HART·
PUBLISHING

OXFORD AND PORTLAND, OREGON
2011

Published in the United Kingdom by Hart Publishing Ltd
16C Worcester Place, Oxford, OX1 2JW
Telephone: +44 (0)1865 517530
Fax: +44 (0)1865 510710
E-mail: mail@hartpub.co.uk
Website: http://www.hartpub.co.uk

Published in North America (US and Canada) by
Hart Publishing
c/o International Specialized Book Services
920 NE 58th Avenue, Suite 300
Portland, OR 97213-3786
USA
Tel: +1 503 287 3093 or toll-free: (1) 800 944 6190
Fax: +1 503 280 8832
E-mail: orders@isbs.com
Website: http://www.isbs.com

British Library Cataloguing in Publication Data
Data Available

ISBN: 978-1-84113-792-6

Typeset by Hope Services Ltd, Abingdon
Printed and bound in Great Britain by
TJ International Ltd, Padstow, Cornwall

Preface

Japan is the second largest economy in the world. In its history of almost two thousand years, Japan did not have any notion of constitution, which binds the government, until 1889. After the Meiji Restoration in 1868, Japan, which used to be a country governed by samurai warriors, started modernization and introduced the Western notions of law and legal system. It was a bold attempt, since the government had to invent the Japanese word for 'freedom' or 'right' in order to introduce the Western notions of law and rule of law. The government also had to grant property rights to individuals. The Meiji Constitution, enacted in 1889, was the first modern constitution, modelled after the Prussian Constitution. It was the constitution predicated upon the sovereign and sacred power of the Emperor. Japan managed to build a powerful state under that constitution.

After the defeat in the Pacific War, Japan enacted the current constitution, the Japanese Constitution, in 1946. Modelled after the United States' Constitution, this Constitution provides for liberal democracy under the popular sovereignty principle, with an elaborate Bill of Rights. It also boldly declared the renunciation of war and a ban on armed forces, manifesting a deep commitment to pacifism. Japan has managed to rebuild the country under this constitution to become one of the leading countries of the world.

The purpose of this book is to explore the basic contours of the Constitution of Japan in its historical, societal and political contexts. This book is designed to give a brief outline of the structure of government. It is also designed to give an overview of the protection of individual rights. Although Japan managed to build a democratic state under the Japanese Constitution, there are many areas where one can question whether the Western notions of constitution and rule of law are actually accepted in Japan. Japanese people are very good at learning Western cultures and technologies and adapting them to the tradition and society of Japan. The Constitution may be said to be 'Japanized' in this sense. This book will present the image of the Constitution quite different from Western countries, adapted to the tradition and society of Japan.

I would like to thank Professor Andrew Harding and Professor Peter Leyland for their encouragement and help enabling me to finish this book. I would also like to thank my students, Victor Tsao, Anthony Seepish and Colin Trehearne, and Kerry Sloan of the University of Victoria for their editorial assistance. Special appreciation is also due to the late Professor Steve Salzberg of the Faculty of Law, University of British Columbia, who gave me the opportunity to teach Japanese constitutional law with him and also to Professor Veronica Taylor, Professor Stuart Jay and Professor Toshiko Takenaka of the University of Washington Law School, for providing me with the opportunity to teach comparative constitutional law. Finally, I would like to thank my wife Chika, and my two children, Ayana and Haruto, for allowing me to come across the Pacific Ocean to Vancouver. Without their help, I would not have been able to finish this book.

Shigenori Matsui
Vancouver

Summary Contents

Contents

Table of Cases

Supreme Court

High Court

District Court

Table of Legislation

Note on Citation of Court Decisions

It is the custom in Japan to cite the decisions of the court by common name and not by party's name (the court often does not publish the party's name in its official journal). Major decisions of the Supreme Court are published in its official journal, Supreme Court Reporter, divided into *Minshu* (Civil Cases) and *Keishu* (Criminal Cases). Some of the decisions are also published on case reporters specializing in a specific field, such as *Gyoushu* or *Shougetsu*. Some of the decisions of the Supreme Court as well as some of the decisions of the lower courts are published on commercial case reporters, such as *Hanreijihou* or *Hanreitimes*. The Supreme Court also has a website (www.courts.gov.jp) and there is a case law database where you can read the most recent decisions of the Supreme Court as well as most of its past decisions. An English translation is available for most of the famous decisions of the Supreme Court through its website as well as from the following books:

JM Maki, *Court and Constitution of Japan: Selected Supreme Court Decisions, 1948–60* (Seattle, University of Washington Press, 1964).

Hiroshi Itoh and LW Beer, *The Constitutional Case Law of Japan: Selected Supreme Court Decisions 1961–70* (Seattle, University of Washington Press, 1978).

LW.Beer and Hiroshi Itoh, *The Constitutional Case Law of Japan, 1970 through 1990* (Seattle, University of Washington Press, 1996).

However, not all decisions of the Supreme Court as well as lower courts are published. In this book, I follow the custom in Japan by citing the judgment by the court name first, judgment date second and citation last, indicating the volume number and page number.

Major Textbooks on Constitutional Law in Japan

Nobuyoshi Ashibe (supplanted by Kazuyuki Takahashi), *Kenpou* (*Constitutional Law*) 4th edn (Tokyo, Iwanamishoten, 2007) (cited as Ashibe).

Nobuyoshi Ashibe, *Kenpougaku* (*Constitutional Studies*) I, II and III (Tokyo, Yuhikaku, 1992–98) (cited as Ashibe I, II and III).

Nobuyoshi Ashibe (general editor), Toshihiko Nonaka, Hidenori Tomatsu, Takashi Ebashi, Kazuyuki Takahashi, Katsutoshi Takami and Noriho Urabe (eds), *Chuushaku Kenpou* (*Commentaries on the Constitution*) (1) (Tokyo, Yuhikaku, 2000).

Masami Ito, *Kenpou* (*Constitutional Law*) 3rd edn (Tokyo, Koubundou, 1995) (cited as Ito).

Makoto Oishi, *Kenpoukougi* (*Lectures on Constitution*) I 2nd edn (Tokyo, Yuhikaku, 2009).

Yasuo Hasebe, *Kenpou* (*Constitutional Law*) 4th edn (Tokyo, Shinseisha, 2008).

Kiminobu Hashimoto, *Nihonkokukenpou* (*Japanese Constitution*) rev edn (Tokyo, Yuhikaku, 1988) (cited as Hashimoto).

Yoichi Higuchi, *Kenpou* (*Constitutional Law*) I (Tokyo, Seirinshoin, 1998) (cited as Higuchi I).

Shiro Kiyomiya, *Kenpou* (*Constitutional Law*) I 3rd edn (Tokyo, Yuhikaku, 1979) (cited as Kiyomiya).

Yoichi Higuchi, Kouji Sato, Mutsuo Nakamura and Noriho Urabe, *Chuushaku Houritsugakuzennshuu Kenpou* (*Commentaries on the Constitution*) I–IV (Tokyo, Seirinshoin, 1994–2004).

Shigenori Matsui, *Nihonkokukenpou Japanese Constitutional Law*, 3rd edn (Yuhikaku, 2007).

Toshiyosi Miyazawa, *Kenpou* (*Constitutional Law*) II (Tokyo, Yuhikaku, 1971) (cited as Miyazawa).

Toshihiko Nonaka, Mutsuo Nakamura, Kazuyuki Takahashi and Katsutoshi Takami, *Kenpou* (*Constitutional Law*) I and II 4th edn (Tokyo, Yuhikaku, 2006) (cited as Nonaka I and II).

Kouji Sato, *Kenpou* (*Constitutional Law*) 3rd edn (Tokyo, Seirinshoin, 1995) (cited as Sato).

Hideki Shibutani, *Kenpou* (*Constitutional Law*) (Tokyo, Yuhikaku, 2007) (cited as Shibutani).

Masanori Shiyake, *Kenpou* (*Constitutional Law*) 2 2nd edn (Tokyo, Seibundou, 2001).

Yasuo Sugihara, *Kenpou* (*Constitutional Law*) I and II (Yuhikaku, 1982–89) (cited as Sugihara I and II)

Miyoko Tsujimura, *Kenpou* (*Constitutional Law*) 3rd edn (Tokyo, Nihonhyouronsha, 2008) (cited as Tsujimura).

Noriho Urabe, *Kenpougakukyoushitsu* (*Lectures on Constitution*) rev edn (Tokyo, Nihonhyouronsha, 2000) (cited as Urabe).

Yoshiaki Yoshida, *Nihonkokukenpouron* (*Japanese Constitutional Law*) 3rd edn (Tokyo, Sanseidou, 2003).

1

The Constitution: Context and History

Introduction – PART I: CONSTITUTIONAL CONTEXT – The Meaning of the Constitution – The Basic Characteristics of the Japanese Constitution – PART II: HISTORY – Prior to the Meiji Restoration – The Meiji Constitution – The Japanese Constitution – Postwar History – The Legitimacy of the Japanese Constitution – PART III: SOURCES OF CONSTITUTIONAL LAW – The Meaning of Source – Sources of Constitutional Law as Judicial Norms – PART IV: SUPREMACY OF THE CONSTITUTION – The Constitution as the Supreme Law – Laws Enacted under the Meiji Constitution – Occupation Orders – Treaties – PART V: FUNDAMENTAL PRINCIPLES OF THE JAPANESE CONSTITUTION – Popular Sovereignty – Renunciation of War and Pacifism – Protection of Fundamental Human Rights – Rule of Law – Separation of Powers – Central Government and Local Autonomy – Japanese Society and the Constitution – Conclusion

INTRODUCTION

THE CURRENT JAPANESE Constitution was enacted on 3 November 1946, and has been in force since 3 May 1947. The Constitution was enacted during the occupation after the Pacific War. Adopted under the popular sovereignty principle, it is committed to liberal democracy, with full protection of the rights of individuals as fundamental human rights and the guarantee of representative democracy.

This chapter begins with a discussion of the meaning of the Constitution and moves on to an introduction to the history of constitutionalism in Japan, especially focusing on modern history beginning with the Meiji Restoration. We then move to examine the sources of constitutional law and the supremacy of the Constitution, and then review fundamental principles of the Japanese Constitution to illustrate some of its basic characteristics. We will see that Japan has had a long history of viewing law as a means of government and that there used to be no notion of law which constrained the government. We will see that it is only when the Japanese Constitution was enacted that the notion of constitutional law which restrains the government was introduced and established. Moreover, the supremacy of the Japanese Constitution is based on the principle of individualism and the notion of human dignity, which were not concepts accepted in the past. Although there are some who argue that these concepts are alien to traditional values, nonetheless Japan has accepted them as constitutional norms.

PART I: CONSTITUTIONAL CONTEXT

THE MEANING OF THE CONSTITUTION

The term 'constitution' in Japan is defined as 'the fundamental law of the state'.[1] In this sense it is not unlike the constitutions of many other states, most of which have a single document called 'The Constitution'.

Japan enacted its first modern constitution, the Meiji Constitution, in 1889. The current Constitution was enacted in 1946 as an amendment to this Constitution. Japan therefore has a single document called the Constitution.

The concept of a constitution was developed in Europe and the United States. Even though the original ideas were developed in the United Kingdom, it was the United States that enacted the first document referred to as a constitution after independence, the Constitution of the United States, in 1787. France enacted its first constitution, the 1791 Constitution, after the French Revolution. These constitutions attempted to establish governments based on the power of the people, while at the same time restricting the power of governments. They thus provided

[1] Ashibe, 3; Sato, 3.

for the structure of government and a Bill of Rights. They were meant to be the supreme law of the land. Many other countries followed in their footsteps and enacted constitutions modelled after them. These constitutions are often called 'modern constitutions'.

The Japanese Constitution apparently followed this tradition. The Constitution has made clear that it is the supreme law of the land, it has established that the government is empowered by it and it has declared that these powers are derived from the people. It also sets limits on the power of the government by protecting a Bill of Rights.

THE BASIC CHARACTERISTICS OF THE JAPANESE CONSTITUTION

Some constitutions were enacted by kings, some by the people and others were based on the compromise between the king and the people. Overall, a majority of the modern constitutions were enacted by the people. In Japan, the first modern constitution, the Meiji Constitution, was enacted by the power of the Emperor, while the current Constitution was based on the power of the people.

Some constitutions are enacted as statutes, and can thus be amended by the legislature in the same way as any other statute. However, many constitutions have been designed to make amendment difficult. In other words, the constitution is 'entrenched'. The Japanese Constitution falls into the latter group. Any amendment to the Japanese Constitution can only be 'initiated by the Diet, through a concurring vote of two-thirds or more of all the members of each House and shall thereupon be submitted to the people for ratification, which shall require the affirmative vote of a majority of all votes cast thereon' (article 96, section 1). Compared with amendments to other ordinary legislation, this requirement is considerably more rigid. Possibly due to this rigid requirement for constitutional amendment, the Japanese Constitution has never been amended since its enactment in 1946.

In socialist countries such as the Soviet Union, the constitution used to be defined as a fundamental law of the 'state' and 'society'. In comparison, many Western democracies define the constitution only as the fundamental law of the 'state'. Consequently, in these countries, the state and society are distinguished from one another and constitutions are not designed to restrain the society. The Japanese Constitution followed this latter tradition and is defined as the fundamental law of the state. It is designed to restrain the power of the government and not private power.

The Constitution generally establishes the government, empowers it and places limits on its power. Yet, in Japan, it has been assumed that the primary purpose of the Constitution is to guarantee freedom. The Constitution is, in this sense, 'the foundational law for freedom'.[2] Although the modern Constitution consists of the structure of government and the Bill of Rights, it is the Bill of Rights that is the core part of the Constitution and the structure of government is merely a means to serve the primary purpose.[3]

PART II: HISTORY

PRIOR TO THE MEIJI RESTORATION[4]

Japan has almost two thousand years of history. Yet it is only fairly recently that the Japanese came to know the notion of the constitution and to enact such a document.

Japan's earliest history dates back to the first century AD, when it consisted of many small countries. The oldest recorded history of the Japanese state was when the '*Na*' Country of '*Wa*' sent an ambassador to China during this period. During the third century, the early state emerged: the '*Yamatai*' state, ruled by Himiko. The Yamatai government was based on the religious authority of Himiko, a female priest, while her brother controlled the mundane affairs of the state. Governmental affairs and religious beliefs were closely connected at that time.

In the fourth century, the '*Yamato*' state appeared, ruled by great kings (later called Emperors). Emperor Sujin unified the state and proclaimed himself to be the Emperor. In the official history of ancient Japan written in the eighth century, Sujin claimed to be the tenth Emperor, dating back to Emperor Jinmu, the founder of the country in 660 BC.

[2] Ashibe, 10.

[3] Nonaka I, 4, 19–20 (Takahashi).

[4] Ryosuke Ishii, *A History of Political Institutions in Japan* (Tokyo, University of Tokyo Press, 1980); C Steenstrup, *A History of Law in Japan until 1868* (Leiden, EJ Brill, 1991).

However, there is little historical evidence to support the existence of Emperors prior to Sujin. Thus, the ancient history book was regarded as a tool that created a myth to justify the legitimacy of the imperial rule.

Japanese society at that time was based on a communal lifestyle centred on rice harvesting. The people had to cooperate to plant seeds, take care of the growth and harvest the rice. People's lives were highly community-oriented. Rice harvesting relied heavily on Mother Nature, and the people thus came to respect and fear her. Gradually, a religion of worshipping various nature gods developed: *Shintoism*.

In this archaic period, the Emperor ruled the country through the system of clans, each led by a patriarchal chieftain. The government was based on religious authority—law and Shinto, a native religion of Japan, were inseparable and later Buddhism, which was introduced to Japan in 538, came to have strong influence. Law was basically customary law. The Seventeen-Article Constitution proclaimed by Crown Prince Shoutoku in 604 may be cited as showing the basic philosophy of the government. Even though it is called the Constitution, it was in reality a manifestation of moral principles for public officials. However, its first article may be said as vividly showing the cardinal principle of the Japanese society: it provided that 'harmony should be most respected'.

Gradually, the Emperors came to strengthen their powers. A highly centralized state directly governed by the Emperors emerged. However, after the Emperor Kanmu moved the state capital from Nara to Kyoto in 794, direct rule by the Emperor was gradually eroded by the rise of nobles (*kuge*). These nobles accumulated large estates (*shoen*) and eventually gained the privilege of immunity from taxes and the ability to bar court officials from entering their estates. Nobles thus came to exercise autonomous government within their estates.

The nobles then found it necessary to employ warriors to defend their estates. Gradually, warriors intermarried with nobles and came to form a new class: *bushi*. Eventually, it was these warriors who took the power, destroying the privileges of nobles, and founded the Bakufu, warriors' government. Under the rule of the warrior class, feudal relationships gradually developed. Although the Emperor retained the authority to grant the title of '*Shogun*' to the leader of the warriors, and the Imperial Court in Kyoto remained the nominal ruling government, all the political powers were exercised actually by the Shogun. The Shogun held the highest position as the leader of all warriors. All other warriors were regarded as retainers of the leader. These retainers swore loyalty to the leader and offered military service. In return, they were allotted lands and were entitled to proceeds from these lands. Unlike the medieval system in Europe, the relationship between the leader and retainers was unilateral.[5] The leader was not formally obliged to compensate his retainers. All the benefits and protection given to the retainers by the leader were regarded as favours and retainers had no legal rights against the leader.

After the battle of Sekigahara in 1600, Ieyasu Tokugawa finally established the stable Bakufu in Edo (now Tokyo), which lasted until 1867. Ieyasu received the title of Shogun from the Emperor and became the leader of the warriors. He was thus given political power to govern the country.[6]

The political system under the Tokugawa Shogunate was a combination of direct rule by the Shogunate and autonomous domains ruled by territorial lords. The Tokugawa Shogunate enacted laws dealing with fundamental issues of government and matters which required nationwide regulation. It banned Christianity and prohibited territorial lords from directly contacting the Imperial Court. In 1637, the government also implemented isolation policies that prohibited Japanese from leaving the country and also denied foreigners entry into Japan. Further, the government restricted foreign trade to the port of Nagasaki, where trade with the Netherlands and China was allowed. The government also solidified the hierarchy of social status. Aside from the Imperial Court and nobles, there were four social classes: samurai warriors were at the top, followed by peasants, artisans and merchants. Only samurai warriors were allowed to carry swords. Outside this social caste system, or rather below it, there was the class of people referred to as 'non-humans'. They were the *Buraku* people (village people).

The government consisted of senior councillors (*rojyu*), junior councillors (*wakadoshiyori*), chief censors (*ometsuke*) and commissioners (*bugyo*). Chief censors were responsible for supervising territorial lords, while three commissioners dealt with finance, supervision of temples and shrines and the administration of Edo.

The law under the Tokugawa Shogunate was largely customary law. Nevertheless, the government enacted some important codes. For

[5] Hiroshi Oda, *Japanese Law* 2nd edn (Oxford, Oxford University Press, 1999) 15; CF Goodman, *The Rule of Law in Japan: A Comparative Analysis* (The Hague, Kluwer Law International, 2003) 12–13.

[6] Ishii, above n 4, 59–89; MB Jansen, *The Making of Modern Japan* (Cambridge, Belknap Press, 2000) 32–62.

instance, in 1615, the government enacted the Law on the Imperial Court and Nobles and the Law on Military Households (*buke-sho-hatto*). The Law on the Imperial Court and Nobles was designed to severely limit the political power of the Imperial Court and nobles: both were prohibited from leaving Kyoto. On the other hand, the Law on Military Households was aimed at controlling territorial lords: it prohibited territorial lords from forming political alliances, moving troops outside their territory, maintaining more than one castle and marrying without the approval of the Shogunate. The code also mandated that they spend alternative years living in Edo and their local territory.

There was no comprehensive code regulating the general public at the beginning of the Tokugawa Shogunate period. Disputes were adjudicated based on precedents and on individual bases. However, in 1742, a comprehensive code was enacted, the *Kujikata Osadamegaki*. The code was a compilation of Acts and precedents and consisted of two volumes: the first volume was a compilation of various Acts and the second was a compilation of civil and criminal law. The second volume was not published.

Therefore, until the end of the Tokugawa period, law used to be primarily a means used by government officials to govern the people. There was no notion of superior law that constrained the Emperor or the government. The relationship between the government and local lords or the government and the people was not governed by notions of rights and obligations. Indeed, there were no Japanese words corresponding to 'rights', 'freedom' or 'liberty' until the end of the Tokugawa period. It is noteworthy that the Tokugawa government emphasised Confucianism as the most fundamental philosophy for samurai warriors.

THE MEIJI CONSTITUTION

The Tokugawa Bakufu lasted almost three centuries. In 1853, Commodore Matthew Perry of the United States Navy came to Japan and demanded that Japan should open to foreign trade or face the threat of attack. Fearing an attack, the Tokugawa Shogunate decided to sign a commerce treaty. The treaty was grossly unfair to Japan, as it granted extraterritoriality to foreigners and denied Japan the power to impose customs duties. Many people felt uncomfortable with the treaty. The Tokugawa Shogunate sought imperial sanction over the commerce treaty but the Imperial Court declined. The Tokugawa Shogunate had to ratify the commercial treaty on its own and such direct conflict with the Imperial Court severely impaired its prestige. Consequently, some of the lords came to demand the overthrow of the Bakufu and the restoration of political power back to the Emperor in order to cope with the threat of foreign powers.

In 1867, imperial permission to attack the Tokugawa Bakufu was issued and the fifteenth Tokugawa Shogun, Keiki Tokugawa, surrendered his power to the Emperor and resigned as Shogun. On 3 January 1868, Emperor Mutsuhito declared the restoration of imperial rule.[7] Although some supporters of the Tokugawa Bakufu refused to obey the Imperial Court, they were ultimately defeated by its supporters. In the same year, the commemorative year[8] was changed to Meiji. As a result, these events were generally referred to as the Meiji Restoration (1868).

Territorial lords surrendered their lands to the Emperor and were appointed as governors in their domains. In 1871, the system of domains was replaced by the system of prefecture, directly ruled by the Emperor through officials appointed by him.

On 5 April 1868, the government announced a new fundamental law attempting to revamp the governmental system[9] and restored the archaic *dajokan* system, which dated back to the eighth century.[10] Under this system, the Emperor was assisted by the Prime Minister (*dajo-daijin*), ministers and councillors. However, it was not long before leaders of the government realized that a modernization of the government and society, accepting Western technology, knowledge and culture, was necessary.

The Meiji Government set out to build a modern society ruled by a modern legal system, accepting a Western-style legal system.[11] This

[7] Ishii, above n 4, 91–126; Jansen, above n 6, 294–413.

[8] The commemorative year is used in Japan to denote the period of reign of the Emperor. Although the Emperors used to change the commemorative year quite often in the old days, the Meiji Government established the system of using just one commemorative year to denote the entire reign of one Emperor. The government followed this tradition even under the Japanese Constitution. All public documents are written using the commemorative year.

[9] Jansen, above n 6, 337–41 (Charter Oath).

[10] Ishii, above n 4, 98, 101–06.

[11] *Ibid*, 117–18. See also Kenzo Takayanagi, 'A Century of Innovation: The Development of Japanese Law 1869–1961' in AT von Mehren (ed), *Law in Japan: The Legal Order in a Changing Society* (Cambridge, MA, Harvard University Press, 1963) 5–40.

modernization was necessary to cope with the threat of colonization by Western countries and to renegotiate the unfair commerce treaties. The government thus invited French scholars to draft codes for Japan. The government must have believed that France was a leading European country, which had comprehensive legal codes, and that it could enact codes modelled after those in France, with necessary modifications. It therefore enacted major codes, such as the Civil Code and the Criminal Code, modelled after the French codes. The drafters had to invent the Japanese words for 'right', 'freedom' and 'liberty'. The government also had to create the notion of property rights over land in order to introduce a modern tax system.

However, the Civil Code, especially its family law part, triggered strong criticism from conservative scholars, who thought it was destroying the tradition of Japan; thus, the government decided to postpone its enforcement. Then, the government decided to rely more on German law. Ultimately, Japan established the whole legal system modelled on Germany, while retaining some influences from French legal codes. Japan has thus become a civil law country.

The Meiji Government initially did not have any plan of enacting a constitution. However, the government gradually came to be criticised as too despotic and, in 1874 a call for establishment of the legislature was voiced by opposition groups and received support chiefly from former samurai warriors who had come to feel dissatisfaction with the government. The rising demand for the establishment of a representative body ultimately forced the government to announce the establishment of the Diet. The government thus decided to enact a constitution in order to establish the Diet.

Hirohumi Itoh, the leader of the new government, went to Europe to research the subject of constitutions. He came back particularly impressed with the Prussian Constitution in Germany, where the king had a very strong hold on power. Ito decided to enact a constitution based on the Prussian Constitution.

When the Meiji Constitution was enacted in 1889, it was premised upon the sovereignty of the Emperor.[12] The Emperor had the power to govern Japan (article 1) based on the imperial prescript given by the ancient sun goddess Amaterasu. The power to govern Japan had been

[12] Ishii, above n 4, 114–16. See also W Rohl, 'Public Law' in W Rohl (ed), *History of Law in Japan since 1868* (Leiden, Brill 2009) 29.

inherited by Emperors in unbroken lineage. By enacting the Constitution, the Emperor merely proclaimed his will to abide by it. According to the provisions of the Constitution, the Emperor had all the governmental powers (article 4) and he was sacred and inviolable (article 3). His power derived from religious authority and he himself was a living god. His status was closely related to Shinto. As a result, Shinto was treated as the de facto state religion and played a major role as religious justification for the Emperor and his rule.

Even though the Constitution introduced some mechanisms for separation of powers and parliamentary democracy, there were serious limitations. According to the Constitution, the Diet was supposed to assist the Emperor in enacting legislation (article 5). Yet, the Emperor had the power to veto any Bill and to regulate the public by emergency orders (article 8) or independent orders (article 9) without the Diet's authorization. In addition, ministers of state were obligated to assist the Emperor in his exercise of administrative power (article 55). Working within a Cabinet formed under such a Constitution, the Prime Minister was viewed just as one of of the ministers of state, and did not exercise any real leadership power. Moreover, as the supreme advisory body to the Emperor, which was supposed to give opinions regarding amendments to the Constitution, affiliated statutes and other important matters, the Privy Council was set up (article 56), consisting mostly of former senior bureaucrats. Even though the Prime Minister and other ministers of state were allowed to participate in the decisions, the Privy Council often interfered with Cabinet decisions. Furthermore, the Emperor had certain sovereign prerogatives, such as commanding the military (article 11), which could be exercised without the Cabinet's authorization. The judiciary was supposed to exercise judicial power in the name of the Emperor (article 57). However, there was no fully guaranteed judicial independence and courts' powers were severely limited.

The Meiji Constitution did protect some individual rights. Yet these rights were merely granted to the 'subjects' of the Emperor by his benevolence. The people did not have any inherent constitutional rights against the government. Moreover, these rights were protected merely within the confines of statute. When the Imperial Diet enacted statutes to restrict rights, the public could not therefore argue for the unconstitutionality of the restriction. Furthermore, the judiciary did not have any power to review the constitutionality of a statute. As a consequence, the protection of individual rights was severely restricted.

Voting rights were granted to a limited number of adult male citizens who had sufficient wealth. Freedom of expression was severely restricted by statutes such as the Publications Act and Newspapers Act, as well as by a ban in the Criminal Code on insult against the Emperor. Freedom of religion was protected only so far as the obligation of subjects to the Emperor was not infringed (article 28) and Shinto was accorded the status of de facto state religion. Women were subjected to various forms of sexual discrimination, especially in the family, since the Meiji Family Law was premised upon the supremacy of the 'house' headed by a male 'housemaster'.

Legal control of the government was also seriously limited. The people could not challenge administrative actions before the judicial court, since judicial courts were granted jurisdiction only in civil and criminal and not in administrative cases. There was an Administrative Court to hear complaints, yet only one court was established and the public could file complaints based only on listed grounds. Moreover, the Administrative Court was supposed to be an administrative organ. The people could not seek damages in the judicial courts against the government for illegal exercise of power.

Even under the Meiji Constitution, there existed a possibility that it could be construed to vest political power in the Imperial Diet and the Cabinet, thus practically depriving the Emperor of his political power. In particular, after the death of the Meiji Emperor on 30 July 1912, when his son Yoshihito became the next Emperor and the commemorative year was changed to Taisho, there were increasing calls for democratization and liberalization, and demands for major political reform. In 1918, the Cabinet came to rely on the majority support among the political parties in the Diet for the first time. Despite such potential, however, the government generally used the Emperor's power to secure social stability and to build a 'strong and wealthy state'. The Diet passed many statutes restricting political freedoms of the people. Even after the introduction of universal male suffrage in 1925, the government never allowed the public to actively participate in politics. It thus enacted the notorious Public Peace Preservation Act to tightly regulate public gatherings. In order to maintain a strong military, the government introduced mandatory military service requirements and allotted a large budget to military spending. Moreover, the prerogatives of the Emperor to command the military came to be construed very broadly so as to exclude Diet and Cabinet supervision over the military.

As a result, military forces had practically free reign over their decision making process.

The economy was also heavily dependent on the government. Since there was no modern industry at the time of the Meiji Restoration, the government had to establish such industry, especially heavy industry, in order to develop a strong state. After successfully developing major industries, the government sold them to a small number of economic giants, the so-called '*Zaibatsu*'. The labour movement and socialist advocates were rigorously suppressed. Most of the lands were owned by a limited number of landowners and most of the farmers simply did not own farmland. There was no social basis for creating citizen support for a modern society.

Japan's victory in the Sino–Japanese War (1894–95) gave it control over the territories of Korea and Taiwan. Subsequent victory in the Russo–Japanese War (1904–05) solidified Japanese control over Manchuria and further helped to promote militarism in Japan. Japan annexed Korea in 1910. After the death of the Taisho Emperor in 1926, his son Hirohito became the next Emperor and the commemorative year was changed to Showa. During Hirohito's reign, Japan became an increasingly militaristic state. Japan walked out of the League of Nations in 1933, allied itself with Germany and Italy in 1940 and concluded a neutrality treaty with the Soviet Union in 1941. Meanwhile, the terrorist attack by the radical militarists against the Prime Minister, Tsuyoshi Inugai, who was in favour of limitation of military power, on 15 May 1932 and the attempted coup d'état by radical military officers on 26 February 1936, totally undermined parliamentary democracy.

Subsequently, Japan started a war against China in 1937, invaded other Asian countries and finally attacked the United States to start the Pacific War in 1941. During wartime, the Constitution was almost meaningless. The military government mobilised all available manpower for war purposes through the Total Mobilization Act and did not tolerate any resistance or criticism against it, under such statutes as the Public Peace Preservation Act.

Although the military invasion was successful at the beginning, the Allied Powers gradually came to dominate the battles. In the end, most of the major Japanese cities were burned down by repeated bombings and Japan was devastated by two atomic bombs in Hiroshima and Nagasaki, which killed several hundred thousand civilians. Fearing the near certain destruction of the entire country, and faced with attacks by the Soviet Union despite the neutrality treaty, the government was forced to accept the Potsdam Declaration and surrendered unconditionally on 15 August 1945.

THE JAPANESE CONSTITUTION

After the Pacific War, Japan was placed under occupation by the Allied Powers. General Douglas MacArthur arrived in Atsugi to head the occupation as the Supreme Commander for the Allied Powers (SCAP) on 30 August 1945.[13]

The purpose of the occupation was to democratise Japan and to ensure that Japan would never become a threat to the world as a military power. Thus, the SCAP dismantled the imperial military (November 1945), abolished legislation that restricted individual rights (Direction on Removal of Restrictions on Political, Civil and Religious Liberties, October 1945), dismantled *Zaibatsu* to democratise the economy (November 1945) and implemented large scale land reform to take lands from landowners and redistribute them to individual farmers (1947).[14] The SCAP also made the Emperor proclaim that he was a human being, not a living god (January 1946) and prohibited any governmental support for Shinto (December 1945).

The SCAP also purged all ultra-militarists from governmental positions in January 1946. The International Military Tribunal for the Far East was established in Tokyo in 1946 to prosecute those responsible for the invasions. Twenty-eight political leaders and leading soldiers were prosecuted as Class A war criminals for war crimes and crimes against peace. Most were found guilty and seven were sentenced to death. More than 10,000 soldiers were prosecuted and found guilty as Class B and C war criminals for war crimes and crimes against humanity, and some 1000 were sentenced to death. Despite the strong opinion outside Japan calling for criminal prosecution of the Emperor, MacArthur defended him as an essential person to implement the occupation policy and he was thus never prosecuted.

The SCAP also started wholesale legal reforms of all major laws.[15] The SCAP was convinced that in order to accomplish democratization,

[13] Ishii, above n 4, 127.

[14] Ishii, above n 4, 128–29; Jansen, above n 6, 667–69.

[15] AC Oppler, *Legal Reform in Occupied Japan: A Participant Looks Back* (Princeton, Princeton University Press, 1976).

amendments to the Meiji Constitution were inevitable. They thus urged the Japanese government to prepare such amendments, but the government was reluctant. The leaders of the government at the time were convinced that a change in interpretation of the Meiji Constitution would be sufficient. Pressured by the SCAP, the Japanese government decided to establish the Research Committee on Constitutional Issues headed by Jouji Matsumoto. This committee was established, however, merely based on the agreement of the Cabinet, not by an Imperial Order or by an official decision of the Cabinet, and its objective was merely to study the necessity of constitutional amendment. The committee ultimately concluded constitutional amendment was necessary, yet it believed that some minor changes to the Meiji Constitution should suffice. According to Matsumoto's statement to the Finance Committee of the House of Representatives on 8 December 1945, he would not change any underlying principle that the Emperor had full governmental powers, but would increase the power of the Diet, expand the power of ministers of state and expand the freedoms and rights of the people. The committee therefore prepared a draft amendment, which would have only changed the wording of the Meiji Constitution slightly and would essentially have preserved imperial governance.[16]

The SCAP was not informed of this development on the Japanese side. When the draft was published in a newspaper without authorization, on 1 February 1946, the SCAP was shocked by the draft's conservative content.[17] The SCAP felt that such a draft would thwart the aim of occupation and that the SCAP might be subjected to wide criticism from abroad. Moreover, the Far Eastern Commission was to be established on 25 February. The SCAP feared that their judgement on constitutional reform might be restricted after its establishment and the SCAP decided therefore to prepare a new draft of the Constitution and present it to the Japanese government for consideration.[18] The document, entitled 'Reform of Japan', issued on 27 November 1945, from the State-War-Navy Coordinating Committee (SWNCC-228) provided the basic framework for reform.[19] MacArthur insisted on three fundamental

[16] Shoichi Koseki (trans RA Moore), *The Birth of Japan's Postwar Constitution* (Boulder, Westview Press, 1998) 56–60; JW Dower, *Embracing Defeat: Japan in the Wake of World War II* (New York, W.W. Norton, 1999) 353–54.

[17] Koseki, *ibid*, 61.

[18] Koseki, *ibid*, 77; Dower, above n 16, 360.

[19] State-War-Navy Coordinating Committee, Reform of Japan (SWNCC-228): www.ndl.go.jp/constitution/shiryo/03/059/059_002l.html.

principles: popular sovereignty, renunciation of war and dismantling of the feudal system.[20] MacArthur wanted to maintain the imperial system because he believed that its existence was essential for implementation of occupation policy, but he also wanted the establishment of popular sovereignty, the renunciation of war and prohibition of the maintenance of armed forces as a condition for keeping the Emperor. He believed that if Japan renounced war and prohibited armed forces, other Asian countries might not object to the preservation of the Emperor.

The draft of the new Constitution was thus prepared in eight days between 4 and 12 February by SCAP's staff members.[21] This draft was handed over to Japanese officials on 13 February, when they visited the SCAP in order to hear the approval for their draft. They were simply aghast to be informed that their draft had been rejected and that they were being given a new draft of the Constitution. The leaders of the government were deeply astonished as well.[22] They tried to persuade the SCAP to accept their draft but to no avail. The SCAP warned the leaders of the government that if they did not accept this new draft, the SCAP

[20] Koseki, above n 16, 79. The three principles are as follows:

I

Emperor is at the head of the state.

His succession is dynastic.

His duties and powers will be exercised in accordance with the Constitution and responsive to the basic will of the people as provided therein.

II

War as a sovereign right of the nation is abolished. Japan renounces it as an instrumentality for settling its disputes and even for preserving its own security. It relies upon the higher ideals which are now stirring the world for its defense and its protection.

No Japanese Army, Navy, or Air Force will ever be authorized and no rights of belligerency will ever be conferred upon any Japanese force.

III

The feudal system of Japan will cease.

No rights of peerage except those of the Imperial family will extend beyond the lives of those now existent.

No patent of nobility will from this time forth embody within itself any National or Civic power of government.

Pattern budget after British system.

Three basic points stated by Supreme Commander to be 'musts' in constitutional revision: www.ndl.go.jp/constitution/e/shiryo/03/072/072tx.html.

[21] Koseki, above n 16, 82, 98; Dower, above n 16, 364–70.

[22] Koseki, *ibid*, 99–101: Dower, *ibid*, 375.

would publish it to the general public.[23] The leaders of the government feared that such publication would make the issue of the enactment of the Constitution the focus of the next election, and that they might lose the election to socialist forces. The government therefore decided to accept the draft on 26 February 1946[24] and published it as its own draft of the Constitution after some minor modifications on 6 March 1946.[25] The official draft was published on 17 April 1946.

Subsequently, amendments to the Constitution were accomplished according to article 73 of the Meiji Constitution. The draft of the new Constitution was submitted to the Privy Council on 22 April 1946 and was approved on 8 June 1946. It was then submitted to the Imperial Diet after the first postwar election, in which women were given the right to vote for the first time, on 20 June 1946. On 24 August 1946, the House of Representatives passed the amendment and on 6 October 1946 the House of Peers passed it after some revisions. The House of Representatives passed the revised Bill on 7 October 1946. After examination by the Privy Council, the Emperor approved it on 29 October 1946. It was then promulgated on 3 November 1946 and took effect on 3 May 1947. This is the current Constitution: the Japanese Constitution.

The Japanese Constitution is a modern constitution premised upon the popular sovereignty principle. It establishes liberal democracy, even though it maintains the Emperor as a symbol without any political power, and protects a panoply of individual rights as fundamental human rights. It is based on individualism, placing individuals over society and the state. It is generally believed that human dignity lies as the basis of this individualism principle. Moreover, the Constitution has a unique clause which renounces war and prohibits the maintenance of armed forces (article 9).

POSTWAR HISTORY

Japan's major cities were devastated by repeated bombings and the two atomic bombs dropped on Hiroshima and Nagasaki. After the Pacific War, there were no industries left and the people had to endure extreme food shortages. Demonstrations calling for a better life were a common scene.

[23] Koseki, *ibid*, 104–05.
[24] *Ibid*, 108.
[25] *Ibid*, 129.

In 1950, the Korean War erupted and provided an opportunity for Japan to start rebuilding its economy. At the same time, the Korean War brought significant changes in occupation policy. MacArthur had to move his troops to Korea and allowed the Prime Minister, Shigeru Yoshida, to establish the National Police Reserve.[26] The SCAP banned strikes by public employees, and made local governments enact public safety ordinances to strictly regulate public demonstrations. The SCAP also allowed previously purged ultra-militarists to return to government posts and instead pushed out communists and their sympathisers from the government and major industries (the Red Purge). The United States' government had apparently decided to make Japan one of its allies in the fight against communist forces.

In 1951, Japan finally managed to sign a peace treaty in San Francisco with most of the countries of the world.[27] The occupation ended when this treaty took effect on 28 April, 1952, and the Japanese Constitution became the supreme law of the land (except for Okinawa, where the United States had maintained occupation because of the military bases, until it was returned to Japan in 1972). Despite all this, Japan and the United States concluded the Japan-United States Mutual Security Treaty (Treaty of Mutual Cooperation and Security between the United States and Japan) to oblige the United States to cooperate in defence of Japan and to allow the United States to station military forces in Japan even after the end of the occupation. The government changed the National Police Reserve to the National Safety Force and then to the Self-Defence

[26] RB Finn, *Winners in Peace: MacArthur, Yoshida, and Postwar Japan* (Berkeley, University of California Press, 1992) 263.

[27] The Soviet Union never signed the Peace Treaty because of dissatisfaction with the non-participation of the People's Republic of China. The island dispute between the two countries thereafter has prevented the conclusion of a peace treaty. There is still no peace treaty between Japan and Russia. Japan and the Republic of China (Taiwan) signed a separate Treaty of Peace in 1952. Yet, Japan and the People's Republic of China issued the Joint Communiqué of the Government of Japan and the Government of the People's Republic of China in 1972 and recognized the government of the People's Republic of China as the sole legal government of China, thus terminating official diplomatic relations with Taiwan and starting diplomatic relations with the People's Republic of China. Korea did not sign the Peace Treaty because Korea was not among the Allied Powers. However, Japan and the Republic of Korea (South Korea) signed the Treaty on Basic Relations between Japan and the Republic of Korea in 1965 and normalized diplomatic relations between their two countries. There is still no diplomatic relation with the People's Republic of Korea (North Korea).

Force (SDF). Japan became one of the liberal allies of the Western nations in the fight against communism.

This was not accomplished without opposition. In particular, when the government attempted to renew the Japan-United States Mutual Security Treaty in 1960, more than five million people participated in the nationwide protest, and more than three hundred thousands protesters surrounded the Diet building in order to prevent Diet approval. Even though the Shinsuke Kishi Cabinet managed to renew the treaty, it had to cancel the planned visit of the United States' president amid the chaos and resign en masse. The succeeding Hayato Ikeda Cabinet had to focus the attention of the public on economic development rather than on security issues.

Japan has successfully developed its economy under this new Constitution. In particular, after the 1960s, the government adopted various policies to facilitate economic development. During the 1960s and 1970s, Japan recorded an unprecedented rate of economic growth and became one of the largest economies in the world. Japan was even hailed as the number one country in the world during the 1980s.[28] Although Japan's economy suffered from recession after the economic bubble burst in the early 1990s, it started to gain stability and strength in the 2000s.

Meanwhile, Emperor Hirohito died in 1989 and the current Emperor Akihito succeeded the throne. The commemorative year was changed from 'Showa' to 'Heisei'.

THE LEGITIMACY OF THE JAPANESE CONSTITUTION

Ever since its enactment, the legitimacy of the Japanese Constitution has been the subject of heated debate.

It is generally agreed that there is a limit to the power of constitutional amendment.[29] The Meiji Constitution was premised upon the sovereign power of the Emperor while the Japanese Constitution was premised upon the popular sovereignty principle. It is beyond the scope of permissible constitutional amendment to alter the sovereignty principle.

[28] EF Vogel, *Japan as No. 1: Lessons for America* (New York, Harper, 1979).

[29] See below, ch 9, n 5. A few argued that there was no limit to constitutional amendment, and, according to this view, the Japanese Constitution could be valid as an amendment to the Meiji Constitution.

This leads to the conclusion that the Japanese Constitution was invalid as an amendment to the Meiji Constitution.

It is truc that thc Japanese Constitution fundamentally altered the sovereignty principle of the Meiji Constitution and went beyond the permissible limits of the power of constitutional amendment. Yet the Potsdam Declaration, outlining the terms for surrender, clearly stipulated that '[t]he Japanese Government shall remove all obstacles to the revival and strengthening of democratic tendencies among the Japanese people. Freedom of speech, of religion, and of thought, as well as respect for the fundamental human rights shall be established' (article 10) and that Japan should be placed under occupation until these objectives 'have been accomplished and there has been established in accordance with the freely expressed will of the Japanese people a peacefully inclined and responsible government' (article 12). Japan accepted these terms of surrender in August 1945. Professor Toshiyoshi Miyazawa thus argued that the sovereignty of the Emperor of the Meiji Constitution had already been abandoned via the acceptance of the Potsdam Declaration and thus the popular sovereignty principle had been established.[30] In a legal sense, therefore, there was revolution in the constitutional order: the 'August Revolution'. The Japanese Constitution was legitimised by this 'August Revolution'. It was a new constitution based on the popular sovereignty principle already established, even though it was enacted as an amendment to the Meiji Constitution. Despite some strong criticisms against the August Revolution theory, it is widely supported in Japan.[31]

Some critics also claimed that this constitution was forced on Japan by the occupation forces, and should therefore be invalid. They urged the enactment of a new constitution that was based on the history and tradition of Japanese society. These critics were particularly offended by the renunciation of war and the prohibition of military forces under article 9.

There is no question that the Japanese Constitution was enacted during the occupation. It is also true that it was drafted by officers working in the SCAP and subsequently handed over to the Japanese government. The SCAP, while allowing the Japanese government to make minor changes, did not allow the fundamental principles of the

[30] Toshiyoshi Miyazawa, 'Nihonkoku Kenpou Seitei no Houri' ('Theory on the Birth of the Japanese Constitution') in *Kenpou no Genri* (*Principle of Constitution*) (Tokyo, Iwanamishoten, 1967) 375.

[31] Ashibe, 30–31.

draft to be altered in any way. These facts were never disclosed during the enactment process. When the draft was handed over to the Japanese government, Courtney Whitney, the chief of the government section in charge of constitutional amendment, made remarks to the Japanese delegates, indicating that while General MacArthur had been defending the Emperor, there was a limit to what he could do; and although the Japanese government was by no means forced to enact this draft, it would be most appropriate for them to do so, if the government wished to protect the Emperor.[32] Leaders of the Japanese government might have taken his remarks as a threat to prosecute the Emperor for war crimes if the government were to refuse the draft. The Japanese government was, therefore, 'forced', in the minds of critics, to accept the draft and enact the Japanese Constitution.

However, the Potsdam Declaration clearly stipulated as a term of surrender that the new government must be 'established in accordance with the freely expressed will of the Japanese people' and must be a 'peacefully inclined and responsible government'. Japan accepted these terms of surrender, and it was quite clear from that point on that the sovereign power of the Emperor under the Meiji Constitution was no longer sustainable.

The Japanese government was given ample opportunity to enact a new constitution in conformity with these terms but failed to do so. Moreover, the draft prepared by the SCAP officers was influenced by various proposals for a new constitution published after the Pacific War in Japan,[33] although we can find a strong influence of the United States' Constitution. Furthermore, the most important reason for the Japanese government to accept the SCAP's draft was the fact that the SCAP indicated its willingness to publish its draft if the government refused to accept it. The leaders of the government feared that if the draft were to be published and receive widespread support, it could become an issue during the coming election, endangering their chances of winning.[34] Indeed, when the draft was published as an official government Bill, it did receive widespread support from the public.[35]

[32] Koseki, above n 16, 101; Dower, above n 16, 374–75.

[33] The draft published on 26 December 1945, by the Study Group on Constitution, headed by Iwasaburou Takano, had a great influence on the draft prepared by the SCAP.

[34] Dower, above n 16, 377.

[35] *Ibid*, 387.

The Bill was examined by the Diet after the general election, which was conducted with universal male and female suffrage, together with political freedom for the first time in the history of Japan. The examination and deliberation in the Diet also took almost 50 days and there were significant revisions during these examinations. [36] The Japanese Constitution was adopted by a two-thirds majority in both the House of Representatives and the House of Peers, according to article 73 of the Meiji Constitution.

Lastly, the MacArthur gave the Japanese government an opportunity to re-examine the Constitution one year after its enactment, but the government decided not to do so, a decision made without any outside influence.

In light of these circumstances, it would be unfair to say that the Constitution was 'forced' upon the Japanese people and was thus invalid.[37]

PART III: SOURCES OF CONSTITUTIONAL LAW

THE MEANING OF SOURCE

'Source of law' usually refers to different forms of law.[38] In general, sources of law can be divided into textual documents, customs and precedents.

If we use the phrase 'source of law' to mean different forms of law, then 'constitutional law' can consist of many forms of law. Aside from the document called the Japanese Constitution, there are many statutes and treaties that have constitutional relevance. The Diet Act, the Cabinet Act and the Judiciary Act are such examples. Moreover, some statutes, such as the Fundamental Act on Education, are closely related to constitutional law. The Japan-United States Mutual Security Treaty has a close relationship with the national defence issue. We may even be able to include some unwritten forms of constitutional law, such as customary law, as sources of constitutional law.

36 *Ibid*, 388–89.
37 Sato, 77.
38 Ashibe, 32.

However, if we use the term 'source of constitutional law' as a norm, which can be invoked by the judiciary to evaluate the constitutionality of government conduct, there is no doubt that other statutes or treaties cannot be a source of constitutional law. It is the textual document, the Japanese Constitution, which should be the authoritative source of constitutional law. However, there are questions as to whether some parts of the Constitution could be properly referred to as sources of constitutional law. Moreover, there exists a significant issue as to whether custom or precedent could be considered a 'source of law' in this sense.

SOURCES OF CONSTITUTIONAL LAW AS JUDICIAL NORMS

The Japanese Constitution is the single most important source of constitutional law in Japan. Yet, there are some ambiguities that exist in parts of this document. The preamble is one of these parts.

The preamble of the Japanese Constitution proclaims that it is the people of Japan who enacted the Constitution and show strong commitment to world peace. It is generally believed that this preamble is a part of the Constitution, but could the courts invoke this preamble to evaluate the constitutionality of government actions? The general assumption is no. The preamble is an interpretive provision of the main text and not an independent source that could be relied on by the courts during an evaluation of constitutionality.[39]

Some provisions of the Constitution may pose unique challenges for courts. For instance, article 9 of the Constitution provides for the renunciation of war and prohibition of military forces. Is article 9 a constitutional norm or merely a political principle? The general assumption is that it is a constitutional norm, which binds the government.[40] Could the courts then enforce this provision, or is it merely a declaration of constitutional principle to be enforced in the political process? The Japanese Supreme Court appears to believe that this provision is an enforceable judicial norm.[41] Nevertheless, it has refused to rule on the constitutionality of the SDF and the Japan-United States Mutual Security Treaty.

[39] Ashibe, 38. This issue is mostly debated in relation to whether the courts should enforce the right to live in peace mentioned in the preamble as an individual right. See below, ch 8, n 25.

[40] Nonaka I, 159 (Takami).

[41] See below, ch 8, n 33.

Article 25 of the Constitution provides for a welfare right. Is this really an individual right which can be enforced by the courts, or is it merely a declaration of the duty of the government, which cannot be judicially enforced? The Supreme Court apparently thinks that article 25 does not vest individual constitutional rights in citizens so as to allow them to challenge government actions.[42] On the other hand, if the Diet enacts a welfare statute that entitles an eligible citizen to receive welfare benefits, then, based on this entitlement, that citizen should be able to claim that any infringement on his or her welfare right is unconstitutional.[43]

There are also disputes as to whether custom could be a source of constitutional law as a judicial norm. Many believe that it could be a secondary source of law when followed with uniformity and backed by public support.[44] They do not consider, however, any customs or practices which violate the text of the Constitution to be a source of constitutional law.[45] Unlike in the United Kingdom, no convention is admitted as distinct from customary law, which is admitted.

Precedents are not legally binding in the civil law countries and therefore they have only de facto binding power.[46] Each court can independently interpret the text of the Constitution to solve a dispute. Therefore, precedents have not been regarded as a source of law. Yet, a constitutional holding of the Supreme Court has a tremendous amount of influence over the lower courts. It is quite rare for the lower courts to disregard the holding of the Supreme Court. Usually, a party can seek appeal to the Supreme Court if the High Court decision is against the precedents of the Supreme Court. The Supreme Court can therefore overturn lower court decisions that disregard its precedents. Consequently, it has been argued that precedents should be viewed as legally binding and as a source of law.[47]

The opinions of scholars or academics are not a source of law. However, since Japan is a civil law country, the opinions of scholars or academics have strong authority (they used to have stronger authority

[42] See below, ch 7, nn 110–11.
[43] Nonaka I, 479, 483 (Nonaka).
[44] Ashibe, 33.
[45] Ashibe, 34; Sato, 24. The establishment of the SDF might be interpreted as establishing customary constitutional law to change the meaning of art 9. Yet many doubt whether the SDF is supported by the majority of people as an armed force and many refuse the possibility of changing the meaning of art 9 by unconstitutional custom.
[46] Ashibe, 374.
[47] Sato, 27–29.

over judicial precedents). The judges usually look to opinions of scholars or academics when they face suits before writing judgments. The law clerks of the Supreme Court usually research academic opinions in their memoranda to the Supreme Court. When the government prepares the legislation, it usually hears opinions from scholars or academics. Scholars and academics are also invited by the government to join or chair the study committee or advisory group for giving recommendations to the government. The Justice Minister asks the opinion of the Legal Council, consisting of many academics, for advice on criminal and civil law matters. Therefore, opinions of academics are very important for understanding law in Japan. The opinions of academics are also useful for understanding the meaning of the general structure of the Constitution as well as the meaning of particular provisions, especially when there is no judicial precedent.[48] Quite often, the opinions of scholars or academics are split. In such circumstances, it is the custom in Japan to distinguish a dominant view or prevailing view among scholars or academics from a minority or dissenting view. Usually, the dominant or prevailing opinion is more important than the minority or dissenting view. However, sometimes the minority or dissenting view might prompt the changes in legislation or judicial interpretation. It is impossible to understand Japanese law without references to opinions of scholars and academics; I have therefore, in this book, also made frequent references to the opinions of scholars and academics.

PART IV: SUPREMACY OF THE CONSTITUION

THE CONSTITUTION AS THE SUPREME LAW

The Japanese Constitution made clear that it is the supreme law of the land and any legislation or acts of the government that would violate the Constitution are invalid. In Chapter X: Supreme Law, the Constitution thus provides that '[t]his Constitution shall be the supreme law of the nation and no law, ordinance, imperial rescript or other act

[48] Even though the Japanese Constitution was enacted under the strong influence of the United States' Constitution, constitutional academics still retain the very strong influence of German constitutional jurisprudence. The majority of constitutional academics thus look to Germany for guidance on interpretation of the Constitution.

of government, or part thereof, contrary to the provisions hereof, shall have legal force or validity' (article 98, section 1). It also provides that '[t]he Emperor or the Regent as well as Ministers of State, members of the Diet, judges, and all other public officials have the obligation to respect and uphold this Constitution' (article 99).

The supremacy of the Constitution is a natural result of its entrenchment. Yet, the supremacy of the Constitution is believed to be derived from the fact that it is the foundational law for freedom.[49] The Bill of Rights, the constitutional provisions protecting freedoms, is the core of the Constitution, since it was meant to protect as positive rights natural rights deriving from human dignity. These provisions are the basic norms which support and constrain the Constitution.[50]

LAWS ENACTED UNDER THE MEIJI CONSTITUTON

What about the legal effect of all the statutes and orders enacted under the Meiji Constitution? It is generally believed that article 98, section 1, allows the statutes and orders enacted under the Meiji Constitution to retain their legal validity so long as they do not violate the Japanese Constitution. Of course, any statutes and orders which substantively violate the Constitution should be declared void. As a result, the Family Law and Inheritance Law of the Civil Code[51] were completely rewritten and the Code of Criminal Procedure was newly enacted.[52] Some of the provisions of the Criminal Code, such as those concerning insulting the Emperor[53] and adultery,[54] were repealed in 1947. There were some questions as to the validity of statutes and orders that were enacted in violation of the procedural provisions of the Constitution. The government believed that all the statutes passed by the Imperial Diet could retain their validity. On

[49] Ashibe, 12.

[50] *Ibid*, 10.

[51] The Family Law and Inheritance Law were premised upon the supreme power of the housemaster to control the internal matters of the house, to be succeeded by the first-born boy. See below, ch 7, pp 178–79.

[52] The previous Code of Criminal Procedure did not grant sufficient rights to suspects and defendants. Torture was also widely used.

[53] The insult against the Emperor was believed to violate freedom of expression.

[54] The adultery provision punished adultery as sexual relationships only with married women, and it was believed that this was unreasonable sexual discrimination. The government could have retained the adultery provision by amending it to be a gender neutral provision. Yet, it decided that this provision should be repealed.

the other hand, the Diet passed a statute on the validity of orders which were enacted without legislative delegation on matters to be decided by the Diet, extending their validity until 31 December 1947, and then enacted a statute in 1947 authorizing their legal validity, specifically listing 23 orders. As a result, those orders not specifically authorized by this statute lost effect.[55] Yet, some of the orders and regulations which were not enacted by the Diet still retain their legal validity.[56]

An interesting question was raised in the *Placard Case*.[57] The defendant in that case participated in a rally demanding food, carrying a placard saying that 'Emperor Hirohito said, "The body politic was saved. I am full of food. You, the poor people, die of hunger"'. He was then prosecuted for an insult against the Emperor. The District Court held that the insult provision lost effect after the acceptance of the Potsdam Declaration and found the defendant guilty of defamation and not for an insult against the Emperor. After the District Court's judgment, the Japanese Constitution was promulgated and the government gave pardons to all prisoners and defendants accused of committing insult against the Emperor. Yet the High Court believed that the insult provision was still legal and found the defendant guilty for the insult against the Emperor. It dismissed the prosecution, however, because the government pardoned all defendants who were prosecuted for the insult against the Emperor. The defendant appealed to the Supreme Court arguing that he should be acquitted because the insult provision was unconstitutional. The Supreme Court, believing that since the prosecution for the insult lost effect because of the pardon, overturned the guilty verdict of the High Court, holding that the court should dismiss the prosecution without reaching a decision on whether the defendant was guilty as charged. It thus refused to rule that the defendant should be acquitted because the insult provision was unconstitutional and lost effect.

[55] Supreme Court, grand bench, 24 December 1952, 6 *Keishu* 1346 (Gun and Fire Arms Control Regulation, which punished violations without legislative authorization, lost effect).

[56] There is no statute, for instance, on the method of execution of the death penalty. The Proclamation of Dajokan issued prior to the Meiji Constitution stipulates hanging as the method of execution and the government has relied on this proclamation to execute the death penalty. This proclamation was treated as equal to statute under the Meiji Constitution and is still valid even under the Japanese Constitution. Supreme Court, grand bench, 19 July 1961, 15 *Keishu* 1106.

[57] Supreme Court, grand bench, 26 May 1948, 2 *Keishu* 529.

OCCUPATION ORDERS

During the occupation, the orders of the SCAP had superior power over the Constitution. It was only after the end of occupation that the Constitution came to occupy the status of the supreme law of the land. Therefore, the Supreme Court has rejected constitutional attack on an order issued by the SCAP during the occupation. It thus rejected the constitutional attack against the Red Purge under article 14.[58]

The most interesting question was raised in the *Cabinet Order 325 Case*.[59] During the occupation, the SCAP used two different measures to implement its occupation policy. One was to use an individual national law, such as a statute passed by the Diet. The second was a general authorization under the national law. The Japanese government thus enacted Imperial Order 542, which authorized the government to issue an order to punish criminal violation of all orders enacted to implement the policy of the SCAP. The government then enacted Cabinet Order 325 to punish any conduct which prevented the implementation of occupation policy. These orders were unconstitutionally delegated, since they did not specifically define the crimes to be punished. The Supreme Court upheld the orders, however, since SCAP orders had superior authority over the Constitution during the occupation.[60]

The question was then raised as to the legality of these orders after the end of occupation. When the occupation ended, the Diet repealed Imperial Order 542 and extended the validity of orders issued under this Order for an additional 180-day period. Then the Diet enacted a statute repealing Cabinet Order 325, while authorizing the criminal punishment of violations that took place prior to its repeal. In this case, the defendant was prosecuted under Cabinet Order 325 for a violation of the order of the SCAP prohibiting the publication of the leftwing newspaper *Red Flag* and similar papers. During the proceedings, the occupation ended. The defendant thus argued that Imperial Order 542 and Cabinet Order 325 were unconstitutional, that the SCAP order was an unconstitutional violation of freedom of expression stipulated in article 21 and that the prosecution should be dismissed since both Imperial Order 542 and Cabinet Order

[58] Supreme Court, grand bench, 2 April 1952, 6 *Minshu* 387; Supreme Court, 3rd petty bench, 3 December 1963, 156 *Hanreitimes* 205. See below, ch 7, n 7.

[59] Supreme Court, grand bench, 22 July 1953, 7 *Keishu* 1562.

[60] Supreme Court, grand bench, 8 April 1953, 7 *Keishu* 775.

325 lost effect when the occupation ended. The Supreme Court upheld the validity of Imperial Order 542 and Cabinet Order 325 during the occupation since they had superior authority over the Constitution. Yet, the majority of the Supreme Court dismissed the prosecution by a 10 to 4 vote. Six members of the Court believed that the Cabinet Order lost effect when the occupation was ended and it was unconstitutional for the Diet to extend its validity after the occupation under article 39, which prohibits retrospective punishment on legal conducts. Four members of the Court did not believe that the punishment under Cabinet Order 325 after the end of occupation was totally precluded. Yet they believed that the SCAP order was an unconstitutional violation of article 21 and criminal punishment for violation of this order under Cabinet Order 325 after the end of occupation was thus unconstitutional.

TREATIES

There is a dispute over which is superior, the constitution or a treaty. Article 98, section 1, is not clear whether a treaty contrary to the Constitution is void and, in section 2, it stipulates that '[t]he treaties concluded by Japan and established laws of nations shall be faithfully observed'. Some have thus argued that treaties should have superior authority over the Constitution.

The relationship between domestic law and international law has been subjected to continuing discussion. The monists argue that domestic law and international law belong to the same legal system. The dualists argue, however, that domestic law and international law belong to different legal systems, and that international law cannot have domestic legal effect unless it is transformed into Japanese state law. The dualists hold the predominant view in Japan. According to the dualist theory, a treaty is international law and does not have any legal effect unless it is transformed into domestic law or is somehow self-executing and could be enforced directly by the courts as a domestic law.

Even when it has effect as domestic law, a treaty may be concluded by the Cabinet with the approval of the Diet (article 73). The House of Representatives is allowed to approve it even when the House of Councillors rejects it (article 61) while, with respect to statute, a two-thirds majority of the House of Representative is required to override the rejection of the House of Councillors (article 59, section 2). A treaty can be concluded far more easily than a constitutional amendment, which requires a two-thirds majority in both Houses and majority support in a public referendum (article 96). It is thus hard to allow that a treaty has superior authority over the Constitution.[61]

This issue has been debated in the context of the Japan-United States Mutual Security Treaty. If we allow the superior authority of treaties over the Constitution, it may be possible to argue that the Japan-United States Mutual Security Treaty overrides article 9 of the Constitution. Yet, such an override was rejected by many academics.

PART V: FUNDAMENTAL PRINCIPLES OF THE JAPANESE CONSTITUTION

POPULAR SOVEREIGNTY

The first fundamental principle of the Japanese Constitution is the popular sovereignty principle. The first paragraph of the preamble of the Japanese Constitution declares that '[w]e, the Japanese people, acting through our duly elected representatives in the National Diet . . . do proclaim that sovereign power resides with the people and do firmly establish this Constitution'. Therefore, it is abundantly clear that it is the people who have sovereign power in Japan.

Yet, there have been controversies as to the precise meaning of this popular sovereignty principle and its implications. The Emperor is no longer sovereign. He is merely a symbol and does not have any political powers. Yet, his existence presents some complicated issues regarding the relationship between his own role and the popular sovereignty principle. We will discuss these issues in chapters two and three.

RENUNCIATION OF WAR AND PACIFISM

The second principle of the Constitution is the renunciation of war and prohibition of the maintenance of military forces. It is the pacifism principle.

[61] Kiyomiya, 451. It is generally believed that a treaty has superior authority over a statute as domestic law.

The international community had struggled for a long time in the attempt to prohibit war and secure peace. However, before the Japanese Constitution was proclaimed, most attempts were aimed at deterring countries from invading others. No attempt was ever made to prohibit war itself, regardless of its possible justifications. The Japanese Constitution was therefore a bold attempt in this regard, since it could be interpreted as prohibiting war and the maintenance of military forces, even for the purposes of self-defence. Interpreted this way, the so-called 'pacifism clause' of the Japanese Constitution may have made a highly significant contribution to constitutionalism.

Despite this clause, the government established the National Police Reserve, and ultimately the SDF. The government also concluded the Japan-United States Mutual Security Treaty, allowing American military forces to be stationed in Japan after the end of the occupation. As a result of these decisions, Japan has, in reality, maintained one of the strongest military forces in the world. These developments have very serious constitutional implications, and we will discuss these issues in chapter eight.

PROTECTION OF FUNDMENTAL HUMAN RIGHTS

The Japanese Constitution also protects the rights of individuals as 'fundamental human rights', as set out in Chapter III: Rights and Duties of the People.

The fundamental human rights guaranteed by the Constitution are generally construed as rights inherent in all human beings, as rights accorded to all human beings by the law of nature. Thus, according to the prevailing interpretation, they are not first granted by the Constitution. The Constitution merely affirms the existence of these rights.

This is a radical departure from the Meiji Constitution, under which rights of individuals were merely granted by the benevolent grace of the Emperor to his 'subjects'. Moreover, constitutional protection of individual rights under the Meiji Constitution was limited only within the confines of statutes. Therefore, if the Diet and the Emperor enacted statutes to restrict individual rights, no constitutional violation claim was possible.

On the other hand, under the Japanese Constitution, these rights are constitutionally protected. Since the Constitution is the supreme law of the land, the Diet cannot enact a statute that violates the Constitution.

Therefore, even though the Diet can still pass legislation that restricts individual rights, such restrictions cannot be unreasonable, otherwise the legislation must be viewed as invalid. The Constitution vests the power of judicial review in the judiciary to determine whether individual rights are unjustifiably infringed (article 81).

We will discuss the mechanisms of constitutional protection of individual rights in chapter six, and specific protections afforded to each right in chapter seven.

RULE OF LAW

Rule of law is a constitutional principle which requires the government to be restrained by impersonal rule. The Constitution can be viewed as embodying this principle. As stated above, the Constitution is the supreme law and any legislation or other governmental acts which violate the Constitution are invalid.

Moreover, in order to provide a remedy when the legislature or the executive branch infringes upon the Constitution, the Japanese Constitution entrusts the courts with the power of judicial review (article 81). The Supreme Court can review the constitutionality of legislation or any other governmental act and invalidate it if it is found to be infringing upon the Constitution. The system of judicial review is vital to compliance with the Constitution. Yet, if judges use this power to strike down legislation based on their personal values, then the courts will be acting above the law. We will explore the delicate issue of conditions and limits placed on the court's power of judicial review in chapter five.

The rule of law also demands that government action be authorized by a statute passed by the legislature and that it obeys the statute. It also stipulates that governmental action is subject to judicial review. Under the Meiji Constitution, the Emperor could enact independent orders and emergency orders without authorization by the Imperial Diet and he also had sovereign prerogatives, which were not subject to any legislative scrutiny. Moreover, the courts did not have any authority to review the legality of governmental exercise of power. On the other hand, the Japanese Constitution clearly assumes that the executive branch must be authorized by a statute passed by the Diet and that the executive must obey the statute. The Japanese Constitution also ensures that executive action is subject to judicial review. We will review these requirements in detail in chapter four.

SEPARATION OF POWERS

The separation of powers principle divides the governmental powers into separate categories and entrusts them to different branches of the government. The Japanese Constitution is premised upon this principle. It vests legislative power in the Diet (article 41), executive power in the Cabinet (article 65) and judicial power in the courts (article 76).

There are some ambiguities regarding the precise nature of this separation of powers principle and its implications. Japan's political system is based on the Westminster model and adopts the Cabinet system. As a result, the Prime Minister is chosen from the Diet members and he or she appoints other ministers of state to form the Cabinet. The Cabinet is jointly responsible to the Diet for its exercise of executive powers. The ties between the Diet and the executive branch are much closer in Japan than in other countries where the president is the head of the executive branch chosen by the people.

Moreover, the executive power of the Cabinet has been construed to mean all the governmental powers except legislative power and judicial power. As a result, the executive branch in Japan enjoys wide-ranging powers to govern the country. Moreover, the separation of powers principle was sometimes invoked to preclude judicial interference with the executive power.

We will discuss the precise meanings of the separation of powers in chapter four.

CENTRAL GOVERNMENT AND LOCAL AUTONOMY

Japan is not a federal state. The Japanese government is a centralised government. The Constitution guarantees local autonomy and provides for local government. The Constitution provides, in Chapter VIII: Local Self-Government that '[r]egulations concerning organization and operations of local public entities shall be fixed by law in accordance with the principle of local autonomy' (article 92). Local public entities shall establish assemblies as their deliberative organs, in accordance with law. The chief executive officers of all local public entities, the members of their assemblies, and such other local officials as may be determined by law shall be elected by direct popular vote within their several communities (article 93). According to article 94, '[l]ocal public entities shall have the right to manage their property, affairs and administration and to enact their own regulations within law'. 'A special law, applicable only to one local public entity, cannot be enacted by the Diet without the consent of the majority of the voters of the local public entity concerned, obtained in accordance with law' (article 95).

There are 47 prefectures and some 1720 cities, towns and villages in Japan and each prefecture as well as municipal government is granted the power of local autonomy under the Local Government Act.

The power of local government is seriously limited, however, and its power to tax is also seriously limited. Despite the attempt to decentralise by the Decentralization Act and to promote further decentralization through the Decentralization Reform Promotion Act, the fact still remains that many of the tasks of the local government are the tasks of the central government, and local governments are performing these tasks under the supervision of the central government. With a total population of more than 127 million, Japan is one of the countries that maintains highly centralised government. In this book, I will focus on the structure of the central government.

JAPANESE SOCIETY AND THE CONSTITUTION

Japanese society is generally believed to be a more group-oriented society than Western societies, with more emphasis on harmony and cooperation due to the strong influence of Confucian tradition, and less on individual autonomy. The relationships between people were not regulated by the concepts of rights and obligations. Rather, favours (*on*) and debts (*giri*) meant much more to ordinary people. One can thus wonder whether the concept of a constitution with full protection of individual rights fits with traditional Japanese societal norms.

It is true that there was no tradition in Japan of creating a constitution to restrain the government. Rather, law used to be a means by which the government governed the public. Moreover, individualism and protection of human dignity, the core substantive principles underlying the Japanese Constitution, were alien to traditional Japanese society. Japanese society used to place more emphasis on groups rather than on individuals. Yet, the Japanese people came to support the principles of individualism and protection of human dignity under the Japanese Constitution.

There are conservative people who still believe that the Constitution protects individual rights to the detriment of public welfare and common interests, thus ignoring Japanese tradition. The notion of the constitution, with its strong protection of individual rights, is, for them, rooted in the Western, Judaeo-Christian tradition and is not suited to Japanese society, which is regulated by Shintoism and Buddhism. Human dignity, the core value of individualism, may be unfamiliar to Shintoism and Buddhism. Yet, respect for the living can be also found in Buddhism and there is no reason to believe that the commitment to human dignity should be limited to the Christian tradition. Moreover, the tradition of giving priority to the group over individual autonomy does not necessarily mean that this is better than individualism. In light of the international protection of human rights, it may be better to discard the old tradition to accomplish individual dignity and autonomy.

Nevertheless, Japanese society still seems to be oriented to group harmony rather than individual autonomy. There are many restrictions on individual freedoms under statutes passed by the Diet. In particular, there are hundreds of statutes requiring government permits or licences to engage in any kind of business, and the public must obey government regulations as well as administrative guidance. These restrictions have been upheld by the courts in almost every instance. Japanese society does not facilitate development of individual autonomy or tolerate much diversity. In light of the actual implementation of the Constitution, therefore, Japan has shown unique development. These issues will be covered in chapters six and seven.

CONCLUSION

Japan did not have a notion of constitution or any notion of law which constrained the Emperor or the government. The first modern constitution, the Meiji Constitution, modelled on the Prussian Constitution, was premised upon the sovereign power of the Emperor, giving all governmental powers to the Emperor and providing only limited protection of individual rights. Yet, the current Constitution, the Japanese Constitution, is an entirely modern constitution premised upon the popular sovereignty principle, committed to liberal democracy, with the codification of the rule of law and the separation of powers principle and giving full protection to individual rights as 'fundamental human rights'. Individualism and human dignity are basic foundational principles of the Japanese Constitution.

Even though these principles are alien to traditional Japanese society, the Japanese people came to accept them. Moreover, although the Japanese Constitution was enacted under the strong influence of the United States' Constitution, strong German influence also remained. The modern constitutional history of Japan can be said to be an implantation of American jurisprudence on a German foundation, modified by Japanese tradition. Furthermore, during the 60 years after its enactment, the Constitution showed development quite unique to Japan.

FURTHER READING

R Benedict, *The Chrysanthemum and the Sword: Patterns of Japanese Culture* (Boston, Houghton Mifflin Company, 1946).

Takeo Doi, *The Anatomy of Dependence: The Key Analysis of Japanese Behavior* (Tokyo, Kodansha International, 1971).

A Gordon (ed), *Postwar Japan as History* (Berkeley, University of California Press, 1993).

DM Hellegers, *We the Japanese People: World War II and the Origins of the Japanese Constitution* (Stanford, Stanford University Press, 2001).

Tetsuya Kataoka, *The Price of a Constitution: The Origin of Japan's Postwar Politics* (New York, Crane Russak, 1991).

T McNelly, *The Origins of Japan's Democratic Constitution* (Lanham, University Press of America, 2000).

RA Moore and DL Robinson, *Partners for Democracy: Crafting the New Japanese State under MacArthur* (New York, Oxford University Press, 2002).

Chie Nakane, *Japanese Society* (Middlesex, Penguin Books, 1970).

EO Reischauer and MB Jansen, *The Japanese Today: Change and Continuity* enlarged edn (Cambridge, Belknap Press, 1995).

RJ Smith, *Japanese Society: Tradition, Self and the Social Order* (Cambridge, Cambridge University Press, 1983).

Yoshio Sugimoto, *An Introduction to Japanese Society* (Cambridge, Cambridge University Press, 1997).

2

The Constitution, the People and the Emperor

Introduction – PART I: THE POPULAR SOVEREIGNTY PRINCIPLE – The Meaning of the Popular Sovereignty Principle – The Power of the People to Choose their Representatives – PART II: THE PEOPLE – The Scope of the People – The Special Status of Resident Koreans and Taiwanese – PART III: ELECTION AND POLITICAL PARTY – The Electoral System – Public Participation in Politics – The Role of the Political Parties – PART IV: THE EMPEROR – The Status of the Emperor – The Power of the Emperor – Conclusion

INTRODUCTION

THE JAPANESE CONSTITUTION is premised upon the popular sovereignty principle. The opening sentence of its Preamble declares that '[w]e, the Japanese people, acting through our duly elected representatives in the National Diet, . . . do proclaim that sovereign power resides with the people and do firmly establish this Constitution'. It continues: '[g]overnment is a sacred trust of the people, the authority for which is derived from the people, the powers of which are exercised by the representatives of the people, and the benefits of which are enjoyed by the people. This is a universal principle of mankind upon which this Constitution is founded. We reject and revoke all constitutions, laws, ordinances, and rescripts in conflict herewith'. Further, in article 1, regarding the status of the Emperor, the Constitution makes clear that the Emperor shall be 'the symbol of the State and of the unity of the People, deriving his position from the will of the people with whom resides sovereign power'.

This is a radical departure from the Meiji Constitution, under which the Emperor was sovereign and had all governmental powers. In this chapter, we will see the meaning of the popular sovereignty principle. We will also examine the requirements for becoming Japanese citizens and what kinds of power the people actually have under the Constitution. Special attention will be paid to the electoral system by which the people elect their representatives and to the question whether the people actively participate in politics. Then, we will review the status and power of the Emperor under the Constitution.

PART I: THE POPULAR SOVEREIGNTY PRINCIPLE

THE MEANING OF THE POPULAR SOVEREIGNTY PRINCIPLE

Even though there is an almost unanimous consensus that the Japanese Constitution is premised upon the popular sovereignty principle, there have been heated debates over its specific meanings. It is fair to say that there is no consensus on this latter point.

This issue was of course debated during the course of the enactment of the Japanese Constitution. The government was reluctant to alter the sovereign power of the Emperor. Even after they decided to enact the Constitution based on a draft provided by the Supreme Commander for the Allied Powers (SCAP), the government resisted the use of the phrase 'sovereign power resides with the People' contained in the draft. Yet, the SCAP steadfastly resisted the government's attempts to alter this phrase. Still, the government was reluctant to admit that the status of the Emperor would be altered by the new Constitution. When asked about whether the Japanese Constitution would alter the sovereign power of the Emperor, the government insisted that it would not alter the political system within which the Emperor was governing Japan.[1] The Emperor used to be and continues to be the centre of respect and nothing will change this principle. The leading scholar in constitutional law, Professor Miyazawa, criticised this view and argued that the Japanese Constitution is clearly based upon the popular sovereignty principle and body politics

[1] Nonaka I, 83 (statement of State Minister Tokujirou Kanamori).

has changed.[2] He argued that 'the people' meant all the people of Japan (excluding the Emperor) and the popular sovereignty principle meant that all governmental powers derived from the people.

His view came to be supported by many. It is now well settled that the Japanese Constitution radically altered the Meiji Constitution and adopted the popular sovereignty principle. Nevertheless, there are various conflicting views as to the precise meaning of the popular sovereignty principle.

One influential view argues, based on the French theory of popular sovereignty, that the popular sovereignty principle means that the people have the power to enact the constitution and all governmental powers are derived from the people.[3] It is thus a principle about the legitimacy of the government. According to this view, after the people enacted the constitution based on this sovereign power, they no longer had any sovereign power. The sovereign power was therefore 'eternally frozen' after the enactment of the constitution. 'The people' in this sense includes all Japanese citizens, including those who are ineligible to participate in election, such as minors and people who are mentally disabled.

The other influential view argues, based on a different French theory of popular sovereignty, that the popular sovereignty principle means that the people have actual power to govern themselves.[4] Even after the enactment of the constitution (which is based on the people's sovereign power), the people can still participate in elections as sovereigns. The people who are sovereign in this view are citizens who can participate in elections, thus excluding minors and the mentally disabled.

These two views both rely on the discussion of the popular sovereignty principle in France, since the popular sovereignty principle was first established there. The other influential view, criticizes the reliance on the French discussion and argues that the popular sovereignty principle should be viewed as having dual elements: the legitimacy element and the power element. First, this means that the people have sovereign

[2] Toshiyoshi Miyazawa, 'Kokuminshuken to Tennnousei' ('Popular Sovereignty and the Imperial System') in *Kenpou no Genri* (*Principle of Constitution*) (Tokyo, Iwanamishoten, 1967) 281–344.

[3] Higuchi I, 78–79; Yoichi Higuchi, *Kindairikkenshugi to Gendaikokka* (*Modern Constitutionalism and the Contemporary State*) (Tokyo, Keisoshobou, 1973) 287–303.

[4] Sugihara I, 195–97; Yasuo Sugihara, *Kokuminshuken no Kenkyuu* (*A Study on Popular Sovereignty*) (Tokyo, Iwanamishoten, 1971); Yasuo Sugihara, *Kokuminshuken no Shitekitenkai* (*Historical Development of Popular Sovereignty*) (Tokyo, Iwanamishoten, 1985).

power to enact the constitution and that all the governmental powers derive from the people. The popular sovereignty principle in this sense is the legitimacy principle. Even after the enactment of the constitution, however, the people retain some limited sovereign power to approve constitutional amendments.[5] According to the provision of the Constitution, a constitutional amendment can be made only after initiation by the Diet, through a concurring vote of two-thirds or more of all the members of each House and ratification by the people, 'which shall require the affirmative vote of a majority of all votes cast thereon, at a special referendum or at such election as the Diet shall specify' (article 96). The power to approve a constitutional amendment can be said to be an institutionalised power to make the constitution; this is in contrast to the original power to enact the constitution. Therefore, the popular sovereignty principle also has a power element. The people in the legitimacy element refers to all the people of Japan, while the people in the power element refers to the electorate, who have the power to participate in constitutional amendment.

Another influential view argues that the popular sovereignty principle has both a legitimacy aspect and an institutional aspect.[6] In its legitimacy aspect, the popular sovereignty principle will hold that the people have a power to enact the constitution and all the governmental powers derive from the people. This legitimacy aspect is closely tied to the power of the people to approve constitutional amendment. Moreover, the popular sovereignty principle has an institutional aspect which demands that the public be allowed to participate in politics. Freedom of public expression and freedom of information are necessary elements of this institutional aspect.

It may be useful to make a distinction between the constitutional politics regarding the enactment of the constitution and ordinary politics regarding the exercise of governmental powers under the enacted constitution. According to the first view, once the constitution was enacted by the people, the people did not have any sovereign right to participate in ordinary politics. According to the second view, the people have a sovereign right to enact the constitution and to participate in ordinary politics, but the sovereign people are limited to those who have voting rights. The third view, in contrast, grants sovereign power to all

[5] Ashibe, 41–43.
[6] Sato, 98–101.

the people to enact the constitution and also grants the quasi-sovereign right to amend the constitution to those who have voting rights. The fourth view would further require universal suffrage and freedom of expression in ordinary politics as an institutional aspect of popular sovereignty.

Although the popular sovereignty principle means that the people have a power to enact the constitution and that all governmental powers are derived from the people, it would be inappropriate to deny the power of the people in ordinary politics: the people also have a quasi-sovereign power to approve the constitutional amendment as well as the constitutional power to govern themselves in ordinary politics. The Japanese Constitution established representative democracy and vested voting rights in all adult citizens and guaranteed citizens' rights to political participation. Therefore, it would be better to interpret the Constitution not only as mandating the popular sovereignty principle, but as establishing democracy as a guiding political principle for ordinary politics.

THE POWER OF THE PEOPLE TO CHOOSE THEIR REPRESENTATIVES

In accordance with the democracy principle, the Japanese Constitution guarantees people's voting rights. The Constitution stipulates that the people have 'the inalienable right to choose their public officials and to dismiss them' (article 15, section 1) and that '[u]niversal adult suffrage is guaranteed with regard to the election of public officials' (article 15, section 3). Moreover, the Constitution protects the secrecy of the voting by providing that '[i]n all elections, secrecy of the ballot shall not be violated. A voter shall not be answerable, publicly or privately, for the choice he has made' (article 15, section 4).

Although the Constitution protects citizens' inalienable right to choose 'public officials', it merely guarantees that both Houses of the Diet 'shall consist of elected members, representative of all the people' (article 43). Therefore, the people only have a right to choose their representatives to the Diet. The Public Office Election Act enacted by the Diet provides voting rights to all Japanese adult citizens (article 9, section 1). Even though the Constitution also mentions the right to dismiss public officials, the Public Office Election Act does not allow voters to dismiss their representatives. This portion of article 15 has been treated largely as irrelevant.[7]

The Constitution also gives a full panoply of political rights to its citizens. These include the right to petition,[8] the right to seek redress against the Government[9] and the right against slavery and servitude.[10] The Constitution also protects other rights essential for political participation, including freedom of thought, religious freedom, freedom of expression and academic freedom (these topics are covered in chapter seven). Citizens, by exercising these rights, can participate in politics and decide government policies through their representatives.

Essentially, all adult citizens are granted the right to vote by the Public Office Election Act. The age of majority in Japan is 20.[11] However, those who have committed crimes and are imprisoned are denied the right to vote (article 11, section 1). Those who have committed election law violations are also disenfranchised (articles 11 and 252). The Supreme Court has upheld this disenfranchisement as a proper penalty for election law violation.[12] The voting right is generally viewed as having a dual nature: it is an individual right and a performance of official duty. The people are thus not only exercising their rights when they vote[13] but

[7] There are some who argue that citizens should be allowed to dismiss their representatives if the latter violate mandates of the voters. Sugihara II, 168. However, most academics tend to believe that since the Diet members are representatives of all the people, they should not be dismissed by voters from a single election district, even if the district is their own.

[8] 'Every person shall have the right of peaceful petition for the redress of damage, for the removal of public officials, for the enactment, repeal or amendment of laws, ordinances or regulations and for other matters; nor shall any person be in any way discriminated against for sponsoring such a petition' (art 16).

[9] 'Every person may sue for redress as provided by law from the State or a public entity, in case he has suffered damage through illegal act of any public official' (art 17).

[10] 'No person shall be held in bondage of any kind. Involuntary servitude, except as punishment for crime, is prohibited' (art 18).

[11] The Popular Referendum Act (Act Concerning the Procedure for Amendment to the Japanese Constitution) enacted in 2007 gave the right to participate in the referendum on constitutional amendment to every citizen over the age of 18 on the condition that the Public Office Election Act was amended to give voting rights to 18-year-olds. See below, ch 9, p 259. This prompted the reconsideration of the age of majority in Japan. The Legal Council of the Ministry of Justice recommended the change of the majority age from 20 to 18 in October 2009: www.moj.go.jp/SHINGI2/091028-2-1.html.

[12] Supreme Court, 3rd petty bench, 27 April 1954, 8 *Keishu* 568; Supreme Court, grand bench, 9 February 1955, 9 *Keishu* 217.

[13] The people have a right not to participate in elections. Therefore, unlike in Australia, there is no penalty for failure to vote in Japan.

are also fulfilling their official duty as electors under the Public Office Election Act. As a result of this dual nature, restrictions on voting rights have been tolerated so long as they are reasonable to secure the performance of official duty. Yet, since the voting right is an essential right of the people, the restriction on voting rights should be subjected to more rigorous scrutiny. Deprivation of all prison inmates' voting rights will be hard to justify.

Moreover, even though voters have the right to vote, some may have difficulties going to the polling station on election day. Persons with severe physical handicaps are among them. There once was a system that allowed these voters to vote at home, but the system was abolished after various abuses were discovered. As a result, many physically handicapped voters could not cast their votes because of difficulties visiting the polling station. The Supreme Court rejected a constitutional challenge filed by a voter in the *Voting at Home Case*.[14] In that case, a voter who could not vote in elections due to disability sought a damages award from the government. He argued that the Diet unconstitutionally infringed his right to vote when it abolished the voting-at-home system and failed to reinstate it. In rejecting his claims, the Supreme Court asserted that it could only order the government to pay damages when the Diet unequivocally violated the provisions of the Constitution, and such was not the case when the Diet abolished the voting-at-home system and failed to reintroduce it.[15]

On the other hand, Japanese citizens living abroad who had no address in Japan were deprived of any opportunity to participate in elections before 1998. As will be explained below, the election for both members of the House of Representatives and House of Councillors is a combination of election in election districts and proportional representation, but, after an amendment to the Public Office Election Act in 1998, overseas voters were allowed to participate in proportional representation elections, although they were still shut out of elections in election districts. In a suit filed by overseas voters, the *Overseas Voters Case*,[16] the Supreme Court held that the Diet had an obligation to provide opportunities to these overseas voters so that they could participate in elections, unless there were exceptional circumstances that could justify

[14] Supreme Court, 1st petty bench, 21 November 1985, 39 *Minshu* 1512.

[15] The government later decided to allow severely physically handicapped voters to cast their votes by mail: Public Office Election Act, art 49, s 2.

[16] Supreme Court, grand bench, 14 September 2005, 59 *Minshu* 2087.

deprivation necessary to accomplish compelling interests. In this case, the Supreme Court found no compelling interests to justify the failure to provide the opportunity to overseas voters before the amendment. It also held that the failure to allow overseas voters to participate in elections in election districts after the amendment infringed their right to vote. The Supreme Court therefore affirmed the overseas citizens' status as voters and their eligibility to vote. It also held that the government should be liable when there was a clear and serious infringement of their constitutional rights. Applying this standard, the Court concluded that the failure to provide an opportunity to vote to overseas voters was a clear and serious infringement of their constitutional rights and ordered the government to pay damages awards to the overseas voters.

This decision is remarkable, for it stands for the requirement that the government must grant voting rights to all adult citizens unless there are compelling reasons for refusing to do so. The government finally amended the Public Office Election Act in 2006 to allow overseas voters to participate in elections in election districts (articles 30-2 to 30-16, 49-2).

PART II: THE PEOPLE

THE SCOPE OF THE PEOPLE

Who are the Japanese people? Nowhere in the Japanese Constitution is the scope of 'the people' defined. The 'people' means all the people of Japan, that is to say, all Japanese citizens. The Japanese Constitution, however, does not define citizenship. Instead, it provides that '[t]he conditions necessary for being a Japanese national shall be determined by law' (article 10). The Diet passed the Nationality Act to define 'Japanese citizens'.

The most significant characteristic of the Japanese Nationality Act is that it gives Japanese nationality only to children born to Japanese parents (*jus sanguinis*). This is quite different from countries where citizenship is granted when the child is born inside its territory (*jus soli*). According to article 2 of the Nationality Act, a child is given Japanese nationality:

1. if the father or mother is Japanese at the time of the child's birth;
2. if the father, who had died before the child's birth, was Japanese at the time of his death; or

3. if a child is born in Japan when both father and mother are unknown or have no nationality at all.

It is believed that the Diet has a broad discretion in designing the nationality system. As a result, it is commonly regarded as constitutional for the Diet to vest Japanese nationality only in children of Japanese parents.

Yet, there is a constitutional restriction on the discretion of the Diet. In the 2008 landmark decision in the *Illegitimate Child Nationality Case*,[17] the Supreme Court invalidated a provision of the Nationality Act, which was discriminatory against illegitimate children with respect to Japanese nationality. According to article 2 of the Nationality Act, a child born to a Japanese mother was granted Japanese nationality at birth. Yet, a child born to a foreign mother and a Japanese father could not obtain Japanese nationality when the parents were not married. In such a case, if the father acknowledged the child before birth, then the child would be given Japanese nationality. According to article 3, section 1 of the Nationality Act, however, after the child's birth, the child could obtain Japanese nationality only after his or her parents married. While the Supreme Court held it was reasonable to require marriage as evidence of connection between the father and the child at the time this provision was inserted, it came to the conclusion that the times had changed and there were no longer reasonable grounds to require marriage of the parents as exclusive evidence for such connection. As a result, the Supreme Court struck down the provision as being unreasonably discriminatory and in violation of the equality right in article 14 and granted Japanese nationality to the child. The Nationality Act was amended to conform to the judgment of the Supreme Court.

THE SPECIAL STATUS OF RESIDENT KOREANS AND TAIWANESE

The definition of 'citizen' raised unique issues for resident Koreans and Taiwanese. Before the Pacific War had ended, Japan had territorial control over Korea and Taiwan, and treated Koreans and Taiwanese as Japanese citizens. They were deprived of their own nationalities and were forced

[17] Supreme Court, grand bench, 4 June 2008, 2002 *Hanreijihou* 3. See below, ch 7, n 21.

to carry Japanese names, obey the command of the Emperor and go to war for Japan. Many Koreans and Taiwanese came to Japan, either on their own to seek success or were forced to come as labourers. After the Pacific War, Japan lost control over Korea and Taiwan and the Japanese government started treating these resident Koreans and Taiwanese as foreigners. The Japanese Government then officially abandoned any authority over Korea and Taiwan in the Peace Treaty.

There were approximately two million Koreans living in Japan at the end of the Pacific War. Many Koreans returned to their home countries after the Pacific War. However, a significant number remained in Japan and many who went back to Korea returned to Japan because of economic despair at home. They lived and worked in Japan just like their fellow Japanese citizens, but were treated as foreigners[18] and were subjected to regulations under the Immigration Control Act (Immigration Control and Refugee Act). The Foreigner Registration Act required foreigners living in Japan to register at local municipalities (article 3), carry their foreign registration certificates at all times and produce them to police officers on request (article 13). Moreover, it required foreigners to submit fingerprints at the time of registration and their renewal. Even though they could become Japanese citizens through naturalization, the government required them to adopt Japanese names in order to do so, thus making it difficult for many Koreans to apply for naturalization. Furthermore, since they were considered foreigners, their children were denied Japanese citizenship as well. As further discussion below will show, foreigners do not have voting rights or the right to receive welfare.

The Japanese Supreme Court upheld the deprivation of citizenship of these resident Koreans as being a natural consequence of the end of the Pacific War.[19] In this case, a formerly Japanese woman who married a Korean and became Korean herself, still a Japanese citizen, according to the statute at that time, challenged the deprivation of her Japanese nationality. The Court held that the loss of Japanese nationality was a

[18] Some have citizenship of South Korea. Yet, Japan has no diplomatic relationship with North Korea. As a result, those resident Koreans who came from regions of North Korea currently have no established nationality. Most of these resident Koreans were given a 'special permanent resident status' under article 3 of the Act Concerning Special Treatment for the Immigration Control of Those Who Lost Japanese Nationality Based on the Peace Treaty with Japan as distinguished from regular permanent resident status and were guaranteed stronger protection against deportation than that granted to foreign visitors (article 9).

[19] Supreme Court, grand bench, 5 April 1961, 15 *Minshu* 657.

result of change of territory based on the Peace Treaty and thus it did not violate the Constitution. Moreover, the Supreme Court has rejected all discrimination challenges by foreigners, including resident Koreans.[20]

There has been an attempt to redress the plight of these resident Koreans. It has been proposed, for instance, to distinguish 'long-term resident foreigners' from foreign visitors and grant much wider constitutional protection to the former, including resident Koreans.[21] Despite the laudable intention, it is difficult to define 'long-term resident foreigners' and provide a reasonable explanation why long-term resident foreigners should be distinguished from foreign visitors merely based on the length of stay. The origin of the problem is actually rooted in the deprivation of Japanese nationality of these former citizens and the government's failure to provide them with an opportunity to retain their citizenship. These resident Koreans and Taiwanese should be treated as Japanese citizens, at least when they stay in Japan, even if they regain their original nationalities.

PART III: ELECTION AND POLITICAL PARTY

THE ELECTORAL SYSTEM

According to the Constitution, the Diet shall consist of two Houses, namely the House of Representatives and the House of Councillors (article 42). Both Houses shall consist of elected members, representative of all the people (article 43, section 1) and the number of the members of each House shall be fixed by law (article 43, section 2). The Japanese Constitution leaves the design of the election system to the discretion of the Diet by providing that '[t]he qualifications of members of both Houses and their electors shall be fixed by law. However, there shall be no discrimination because of race, creed, sex, social status, family origin, education, property or income' (article 44) and that '[e]lectoral districts, method of voting and other matters pertaining to the method of election of members of both Houses shall be fixed by law' (article 47).

[20] See below, ch 6, nn 23–25.

[21] See below, ch 6, n 26.

The Constitution apparently gives stronger power to the House of Representatives: it could override the decision of the House of Councillors by two-thirds majority, and it could approve treaties and budgets even when the House of Councillors disapproves them (article 59, section 2). The term of office for members of the House of Representatives is shorter than for members of the House of Councillors (articles 45 and 46). Furthermore, there is a possibility of dissolution of the House of Representatives (article 69). Clearly, the Constitution anticipates that the House of Representatives should be comprised of representatives much closer to the people.

The Diet passed the Public Office Election Act to regulate the election system. The election of the members of both Houses is a combination of election in election districts and of proportional representation.

The number of the House of Representatives is set at 480: 300 members are elected from single-member election districts and the remaining 180 members are elected through proportional representation (Public Office Election Act, article 4, section 1) from 11 blocks all around Japan. The voter votes on two ballots: one for a candidate in the election district and another for a political party in proportional representation (Public Office Election Act, article 36). The candidate who receives the highest votes in the district will be elected as a representative (Public Office Election Act, article 95). The vote for a political party is calculated in each of the 11 blocks and each political party will receive a corresponding number of seats. Candidates on the list published by a political party will obtain House seats according to their priority on the list (Public Office Election Act, article 95-2). A candidate officially endorsed by the political party can run for both the election in his or her district and proportional representation. As a result, even if a candidate is defeated in the election district, he or she can still obtain a seat based on proportional representation.

The number of the House of Councillors is set at 242: 146 members are elected in election districts and the remaining 96 members are elected by proportional representation at the national level (Public Office Election Act, article 4, section 2). Unlike the members of the House of Representatives, election districts for members of the House of Councillors are demarked by 47 prefectures. Since the term of office for the members of the House of Councillors is six years, and one-half of its members are chosen every three years, each prefecture has an even number of Councillors: two to 10 members. Therefore, in any given election, one to five members are elected in each prefectural constituency. Yet, regardless of the numbers of members to be elected in a single district, the voter has only one vote. The Councillors will be elected based on the number of votes each candidate receives in the district (Public Office Election Act, article 95). Each political party submits the list of its candidates for proportional representation. Each voter then casts an additional ballot for a party or a particular candidate listed in the proportional representation system. Votes are calculated all around Japan. Political parties will receive seats according to their votes and votes for listed candidates, and the candidate who has the highest number of votes will obtain his or her seat first (Public Office Election Act, article 95-3).[22]

The current election system for the members of the House of Representatives was introduced in 1994 as a result of political reform. Before that, the members of the House of Representatives were chosen in election districts where three to five seats were allotted to each district, yet the voter had only one vote. As a result, multiple candidates from the same party often ran in the same district, and voters chose a candidate based on his or her ability or willingness to 'bring back the pork barrel' rather than based on party platform. The 1994 reform was designed to allow voters to choose candidates based on the political platform of each party.

Yet, the introduction of the single-member election district was controversial and some even questioned its constitutionality. Since the single-member district would allow candidates to be chosen by relative majority among voters, thus potentially allowing the biggest party to dominate the legislature, critics argued that the single-member district violates the Constitution.[23] These critics instead supported the proportional representation system. The Supreme Court, however, held that the Constitution does not mandate the Diet to choose any particular election system and that the choice of election system is at the discretion of the Diet.[24] The Supreme Court therefore upheld the constitutionality

[22] Since a vote for a listed candidate is automatically calculated as a vote for the political party that endorsed that candidate, thus allowing that party to give seats to other candidates, this system was attacked as an infringement of the right to vote. Yet, the Supreme Court rejected the attack: Supreme Court, grand bench, 14 January 2004, 58 *Minshu* 1.

[23] Hiroyuki Kamiwaki, Blog: blog.livedoor.jp/nihonkokukenpou/archives/50917817.html.

[24] Supreme Court, grand bench, 10 November 1999, 53 *Minshu* 1704.

of the 1994 reform and held that the Diet is free to adopt the single-member districts system, the proportional representation system, or a combination of the two.

The 1994 reform also introduced significantly different treatment towards candidates of a political party versus independent candidates. Candidates belonging to political parties can run for seats in election districts for the House of Representatives election and can also be listed as candidates for proportional representation (Public Office Election Act, article 86-2, section 4), while independent candidates are not allowed to run for both elections (Public Office Election Act, article 87, section 1). Nevertheless, the Supreme Court upheld this different treatment, on the assumption that the reform was intended to allow political parties to play a bigger role in elections.[25]

PUBLIC PARTICIPATION IN POLITICS

Despite the guarantee of universal suffrage and freedom of expression, it is difficult to say that people actively participate in politics.

First, the election system is not well suited to encourage citizens to actively participate in elections. Voting is not mandatory, but all eligible voters are registered on a list compiled by the local Public Election Commission. Before the voting day, voters will receive a voting notice along with a certificate to vote. The Public Office Election Act requires voters to go to the polling station on election day and vote by writing down the name of the particular candidate the voter chooses. The Act does not allow voters to cast their votes prior to voting day unless voters have other conflicting business or social engagements on voting day.[26]

[25] Supreme Court, grand bench, 10 November 1999, 53 *Minshu* 1577. Similarly, the Public Office Election Act allows the political party to engage in election campaigning in addition to a candidate running in his or her election district for the House of Representatives election (Public Office Election Act, art 141, s 2 and art 142, s 2) and allows political parties to use TV to deliver the message of the party (Public Office Election Act, art 150, ss 1 and 3), while denying such opportunity to each candidate. The Supreme Court upheld these different treatments of candidates running as members of political parties and independent candidates: Supreme Court, grand bench, 10 November 1999, 53 *Minshu* 1704.

[26] In 2003, the voting system was reformed to facilitate voter participation. Those voters who have conflicting business can vote prior to election day (Public Office Election Act, art 48-2) or cast an absentee vote (art 49, s 1) and those voters who have difficulty coming to the polling station due to disability can vote via the post (art 49, s 2).

Secondly, the Public Office Election Act tightly regulates election campaigns.[27] The Act limits election campaigns to a very short period of time after the announcement of the candidacy (5 to 17 days depending on the type of election) to a day before the election day (article 129) and prohibits any election campaigning prior to the announcement date. There is a strict ban on door-to-door canvassing (article 138, section 1) and visiting of private residences, either to ask for votes or to announce candidate meetings (article 138, section 2). There is also very tight regulation on distribution of documents (article 142). Candidates are allowed to put up a limited number of posters at designated spaces on public announcement boards, but are otherwise almost totally prohibited from distributing any documents or materials. It is, therefore, very difficult for average citizens to actively participate in election campaigns.

Thirdly, there is a gross mal-apportionment among election districts in that voters living in urban districts are often underrepresented. The number of seats assigned to each election district was initially determined according to the population of each district. The Public Office Election Act required the number of seats allocated to each district to be readjusted every five years based on the newest national census (later every ten years after the national census). Yet, the rapid economic growth during 1960s and 1970s brought a rapid influx of workers from rural areas into urban centres, thus causing gross disparity between the population and the number of seats allocated to these districts. As a result, voters in rural districts are overrepresented, while voters living in urban districts are underrepresented. The government, occupied by the conservative Liberal Democratic Party (LDP), had been reluctant to adjust this gross disparity, since the party enjoys overwhelming support from rural voters.

When such gross mal-apportionment was challenged in court, the Supreme Court initially showed tremendous reluctance to intervene. Yet, in the first *Reapportionment Case*[28] in 1976, the Supreme Court, for the first time, acknowledged that the effectiveness or worth of each vote should be equal regardless of where the vote is cast and this equality is constitutionally mandated in light of article 14, article 15 and article 44. This case was filed by voters from underrepresented districts, challenging the validity of elections under article 204 of the Public Office Election Act. They alleged that the discrepancy between the most underrepresented district

[27] See below, ch 7, p 200.

[28] Supreme Court, grand bench, 14 April 1976, 30 *Minshu* 223.

and the most overrepresented district was of the ratio of 1 to 4.99, and that such gross underrepresentation in certain districts was unconstitutional. Even though the Supreme Court had accorded wide discretion to the Diet in terms of apportioning seats among different electoral districts, the Court held that there is a limit to this discretion. If a representation discrepancy cannot be viewed as reasonable in light of the all the factors to be considered by the Diet, and if the Diet fails to adjust the apportionment scheme within a reasonable period, then the Court must hold such gross malapportionment unconstitutional. In this case, the Supreme Court concluded that the representation discrepancy ratio of 1 to 4.99 was unreasonable and the Diet failed to remedy the discrepancy; therefore, the entire apportionment provision was declared unconstitutional.

Nevertheless, the Supreme Court declined to invalidate the election result after considering the impracticality of such action. The Court held that not only apportionment in a challenged district, but the apportionment provision as a whole was unconstitutional. The Court thus feared that the invalidation of the election result and the deprivation of the qualification of all the members of the House of Representatives would not only undermine the validity of all legislation passed by the Diet, but would make it impossible for the Diet to amend the underlying apportionment provision. The Court relied on the provision in the Administrative Case Litigation Act, which enables the courts to decline invalidation of administrative action in the public interest, even when they find the action illegal (article 31), and applied the general principles of law behind that provision, holding that the election result obtained under the unconstitutional apportionment provision should not be disturbed. Therefore, even though the Court declared the unconstitutionality of the apportionment provision, it rejected the invalidation claim of the voters.

Further, the Supreme Court declined to specify a maximum limit for the discrepancy, and this issue had to be clarified in subsequent suits filed by voters in later elections. The Supreme Court in the second *Reapportionment Case*[29] held that the maximum discrepancy of 1 to 4.40 was unconstitutional. Yet, it appears that the Supreme Court will accept

[29] Supreme Court, grand bench, 17 July 1985, 39 *Minshu* 1100. The Court once again refused to invalidate the election result, while declaring the unconstitutionality of the apportionment provision.

a discrepancy ratio of up to 1 to 3[30] and is not willing to invalidate the underlying apportionment provision unless it concludes that the Diet failed to amend the provision within a reasonable period of time. As a result, voters in rural districts are allowed to have as much as three times more effective voting power than their urban counterparts.

Moreover, because of the limitation of the election campaigning to such a short period between the announcement of the election and a day before the election and a ban on election campaigning prior to the announcement, it is hard to attract voters after the announcement of an election. At the time of the announcement, therefore, the winner and loser are already fairly apparent (but of course, since many voters do not have a favourite political party, the outcome of the election is always unpredictable). This system is undoubtedly beneficial for the incumbents. Many candidates therefore have supporters organizations called '*koenkai*,' which solicit votes between elections through various services to the voters, including making calls to agency bureaucrats to do small favours for voters. Through such services and personal networking, the candidate can attract votes in an election. It is no wonder that many politicians in Japan are children of politicians, since their father's name is already well known in the district and they can simply succeed the *koenkai* and supporters to win the election.

After the announcement of an election, candidates will drive around the district in a car with a loudspeaker, waving hands with white gloves and calling for votes by simply repeating the name of the candidate from morning to evening. Sometimes, they rush into the crowds to shake hands with supporters and make public speeches. The local Public Election Commission will distribute papers describing the personal history and campaign promises of the candidates and NHK, the public broadcast station, will air programmes describing the personal history of the candidates and will provide free airtime for candidates and political parties to deliver their messages to voters. Major political parties also run television advertisements (but there is not much negative campaigning). The voters will decide who to vote for by relying on this kind of information and it is rare for ordinary voters to participate in election campaigning.

Lastly, aside from participating in election, the people do not have an opportunity to participate in politics directly. The Constitution

[30] Supreme Court, 2nd petty bench, 21 October 1988, 42 *Minshu* 644; Supreme Court, 1st petty bench, 8 June 1995, 49 *Minshu* 1443; Supreme Court, grand bench, 10 November 1999, 53 *Minshu* 1441; Supreme Court, grand bench, 13 June 2007, 61 *Minshu* 1617.

guarantees public referendum on constitutional amendment (article 96) and local referendum on statute specifically applicable to a particular local government (article 95). It also authorizes the public review of Supreme Court Justices upon appointment (article 79). But the Constitution does not have any provision for direct public participation in politics. Although some of the local government occasionally employ referendum on particular local issues, no referendum has ever been conducted on national level. Although the Local Government Act allows local residents to request the enactment of local ordinance (article 74), dissolution of local assembly (article 76), dismissal of local legislator (article 80), and dismissal of head of the local government (article 81), no such system exist for national politics. Therefore, the permissible scope of public participation in politics is considerably narrow in Japan.

THE ROLE OF THE POLITICAL PARTIES

The Japanese Constitution does not have any specific provision regarding political parties. Therefore, political parties exist in Japan as associations whose freedom is guaranteed by the Constitution under article 21.

There is likewise no statute which specifically regulates political parties. The Act to Regulate Political Expenditure defines a 'political organization' as an organization whose primary purpose is to promote, support or to oppose a particular political theory or policy and organization whose primary purpose is to endorse, support or to oppose particular candidates for election' (article 3, section 1), and defines the 'political party' 'as a political organization which has more than five affiliated members of the House of Representatives or the House of Councillors, or which received at least 2% of all legal votes in the most recent election' (article 3, section 2). It thus attempts to regulate the contribution to such political parties and requires them to publish income. The Political Party Public Funding Act requires political parties to satisfy similar requirements in order to receive public funding (article 2). Most of the major political parties do receive public funding and therefore must satisfy these requirements.[31]

[31] However, the Japan Communist Party (JCP) has criticized this Act as unconstitutional since it would force taxpayers to support a political party they do not support. The JCP also refused to receive public funding.

The Act to Regulate Political Expenditure limits the amount of money one can contribute to the political party (article 21-3). Yet, its provisions are not strictly enforced and there exists a great deal of leeway when it comes to political contributions. Indeed, the LDP has received huge political contributions from major enterprises and business associations. In *Yahata Steel Political Contribution Case*,[32] shareholders challenged the company's decision to make political contributions to the LDP. The Supreme Court upheld the legality of the contribution because it was within the legitimate power of the company and within the freedom of political contribution as protected by the Constitution.[33]

Political parties play a significant role in elections. This is particularly true when political parties participate in proportional representation. If members of a political party were elected to the Diet based on proportional representation, however, they are representatives of all the people. Thus, even when they resign their membership from one political party to join another, they do not lose their seats. However, the Public Office Election Act provides that members of the Diet elected based on proportional representation would lose their seats if they joined other political parties that participated in the election (article 99-2). Therefore, members who wish to leave their party can create a new party to join but will not be allowed to join any pre-existing parties that participated in the election. The constitutionality of this provision is thus questionable, since it will deprive those who leave a political party to join a pre-existing political party after an election of their status as representatives.

The Japanese government has long been dominated by conservatives. The first government after the War was a socialist coalition Cabinet, yet it did not take long before the conservatives took over again. Ever since the Japan Liberal Party and Democratic Party joined forces and created the LDP in 1955, in response to the creation of the Japan Socialist Party (JSP), the LDP has controlled the government exclusively except for a short period of time in 1993–94, when some influential members of the LDP left the party to join the opposition and formed a new government under Morihiro Hosokawa. However, this coalition was short-lived: the JSP left it to help the LDP to come back to power. Since then, the LDP,

32 Supreme Court, grand bench, 24 June 1970, 24 *Minshu* 625.

33 The Supreme Court concluded, however, that the Tax Attorneys' Association, a compulsory organization for tax attorneys, acted ultra vires when it forced its members to pay special dues for political contributions: Supreme Court, 3rd petty bench, 19 March 1996, 50 *Minshu* 615. See also below, ch 7, n 34.

together with the Komei Party, the third largest political party, which is backed by one of the largest religious organizations, the Souka Gakkai, used to control the government. In 2009, however, the LDP suffered a devastating loss in the House of Representatives election and lost the government to the Democratic Party of Japan (DPJ). The DPJ formed the coalition government with the Social Democratic Party (SDP) and the People's New Party (PNP). Yet, in 2010, the SDP left the coalition and the current government is a coalition government between DPJ and PNP.

The LDP is a conservative party, which avows to maintain a liberal and democratic society. It is backed by large corporations, and the *Keidanren*, the Federation of Economic Organizations, the largest interest group representing the economic interests of all corporations, has managed to obtain political contributions from major corporations. It has also received support from farmers and fishermen in rural districts, who are generally conservative and need government help to compete against foreign imports. One of the important issues in its platform is the enactment of the new Constitution or the total amendment of the Japanese Constitution. Yet, in reality, the LDP is a collection of various factions which have different views and policy orientations. It is sometimes said that the LDP is a political party for all those politicians who want to remain within the ruling party to form the government. Some of them favour a free market economy but others strongly argue for government regulation of the economy to help farmers or small businesses. Some are in favour of rearmament and expansion of the military capability, but some are more pacifist.

The DPJ was created in 1996 by some members of the JSP and the Democratic Socialist Party, which split off from the JSP. Later, the Liberal Party, headed by Ichirou Ozawa, who used to be one of the leaders of the LDP, joined the DPJ. The DPJ has a very close relationship with the *Rengo*, the largest union organization in Japan. Similar to the LDP, the DPJ is also a mix of politicians who have quite different political ideologies. Some of the DPJ politicians, in particular those who belonged to the former Liberal Party, are conservative, and are in favour of constitutional amendment, but others are social democrats, who strongly oppose constitutional amendment.

There are other smaller parties, like the PNP, which split from the LDP over the privatization of the postal service, the SDP, which is a successor of the JSP, and the Japan Communist Party (JCP).

The JSP used to be the biggest opposition party and played a significant role in opposing the rearmament of Japan. It joined other opposition parties to form the government in 1993 under Hosokawa, the Prime Minister. Yet, because of internal disputes, it left the coalition in 1994 and joined its archrival LDP to form a new coalition government under Tomiichi Murayama, the socialist Prime Minister. The JSP then abandoned its previous stance against the Self-Defence Force (SDF) and the Japan-United States Mutual Security Treaty. The JSP suffered a devastating loss in the 1995 election and lost a significant number of its members to the DPJ. After its name change to the SDP, it has returned to the position of opposing the SDF and the Japan-United States Mutual Security Treaty and opposing amendment of the Constitution. In the first Hatoyama DPJ government, it was a partner of the coalition but it left the coalition over the issue of American base in Okinawa.

In the 2005 election of the House of Representatives, the LDP, together with the Komei Party, obtained a two-thirds majority in the House over the issue of privatization of the postal service. The two-thirds majority was particularly important since a two-thirds majority in the House of Representatives is required to override a decision of the House of Councillors. Yet, in the 2007 election of the House of Councillors, the LDP lost control of the House of Councillors. As a result of the 2009 House of Representatives election, the DPJ occupied the majority seats in the House of Representatives.[34] It was the first time that the voters consciously chose to bring a change in government. Since the DPJ did not have a majority of seats in the House of Councillors, it decided to form a coalition government together with the SDP and PNP. Yet, since the SDP left the coalition and the DPJ suffered a significant loss in the 2010 House of Councillors' election,[35] the DPJ lost control of the House of Councillors.

It must be added that Japanese political parties tend to propose their general commitments as campaign promises. They do not usually promise that specific policy choices will be achieved if they are given

[34] The seats were 308 for the DPJ; 119 for the LDP; 21 for the Komei Party; 9 for the CJP; 7 for the SDP; 3 for the PNP; and 12 for others. The DPJ is a little bit shy of a two-thirds majority, which could override the decision of the House of Councillors.

[35] The seats are 106 for the DPJ, 3 for the PNP, 84 for the LDP, 19 for the Komei Party, 6 for JCP, 4 for SDP, 9 for others. The Your Party, lead by Yoshimi Watanabe, who left the LDP before the election, surprisingly obtained 11 seats.

a chance to form the government. This makes sense because the LDP used to hold the government almost continuously and did not have to stick to its campaign promises if elected. Opposition parties had virtually no chance of occupying the government and there was no need for them to promise specific achievement. Recently, the DPJ started to adopt the achievement promise as a 'manifesto' and the other parties began to join this movement. Yet, political parties still tended to attract the vote more by promoting their general commitments than by promising specific achievements. After winning the 2009 election, Yukio Hatoyama, DPJ Prime Minister, vowed to accomplish the agenda on his party's manifesto over four years and he will ask voters to evaluate the party's achievements in the next election. But, after Hatoyama stepped down, Naoto Kan became the second DPJ Prime Minister and it looks like that the DPJ is beginning to admit that it is impossible to accomplish all the promises of the previous manifesto.

PART IV: THE EMPEROR

THE STATUS OF THE EMPEROR

Under the Japanese Constitution, '[t]he Emperor shall be the symbol of the State and of the unity of the People, deriving his position from the will of the people with whom resides sovereign power' (article 1). As discussed before, the Emperor was sovereign under the Meiji Constitution and he possessed all governmental powers. He was also sacred and inviolable. However, the Japanese Constitution radically altered the Emperor's status and power. He is now merely a 'symbol of the State and of the unity of the People'. His status also depends on 'the will of the people with whom resides sovereign power'. He 'shall perform only such acts in matters of state as are provided for in this Constitution and he shall not have powers related to government' (article 4). Moreover, '[t]he advice and approval of the Cabinet shall be required for all acts of the Emperor in matters of state, and the Cabinet shall be responsible therefor' (article 3).

There is some controversy about whether the Emperor is a king. The Japanese Emperor closely resembles the British Queen in some ways. Therefore, there are those who argue that the Emperor is a king and Japan is a constitutional monarchy. However, under the Constitution, the Emperor does not have any power related to government and merely performs acts in matters of state as directed by the Cabinet. He thus has no political power at all. It is, therefore, questionable whether the Emperor can be regarded as a king. Consequently, Japan should be viewed as a constitutional republic.

More than 80 percent of the population supports the current Emperor system. It is only roughly 10 per cent of the public who argue for the abolition of the Emperor system. Unlike the Emperor under the Meiji Constitution, the current Emperor and the Imperial Family have been accepted simply as celebrities by most of the public.[36]

'The Imperial Throne shall be dynastic and succeeded to in accordance with the Imperial House Law passed by the Diet' (article 2). The Diet passed the Imperial House Act and provided for the eligibility and the order of succession. Basically, it provided that the first-born son of the Emperor will succeed the throne (Imperial House Act, articles 1 and 2). No female members of the Imperial Family are eligible for succession. There are debates as to the constitutionality of exclusion of female members from succession in light of the equality right provision of article 14. The current Crown Prince Naruhito, a first-born son of current Emperor Akihito, has only a daughter and his younger brother, Prince Fumihito (generally known as Akishinomiya), second in line to the throne, has only daughters as well. There were concerns that there might be no one to succeed the throne in the future and some pushed to amend the Imperial House Act to allow females to succeed the throne. However, with the birth of Prince Hisahito to Fumihito in 2006, the calls for amendment subsided.

THE POWER OF THE EMPEROR

Under the Japanese Constitution, the Emperor performs only such acts in matters of state as are provided for in the Constitution and he does not have powers related to government (article 4, section 1), and the advice

[36] Yet, it must be noted that there are some taboos among the mass media against reporting public critiques of or unfavourable stories about the Imperial Family. Moreover, the Imperial House Agency often attempts to control the media by threatening to refuse to cooperate with interviews or provide pictures. When the Showa Emperor was dying of cancer in 1989, most of the Japanese media did not report the true nature of his illness.

and approval of the Cabinet are required for all acts of the Emperor in matters of state and the Cabinet is responsible for them (article 3).

The important role of the Emperor includes the appointment of the Prime Minister as designated by the Diet (article 6, section 1) as well as appointment of the Chief Judge of the Supreme Court as designated by the Cabinet (article 6, section 2). The Emperor, with the advice and approval of the Cabinet, shall also perform the following acts in matters of state on behalf of the people (article 7):

1. Promulgation of amendments of the constitution, laws, cabinet orders and treaties;
2. Convocation of the Diet;
3. Dissolution of the House of Representatives;
4. Proclamation of general election of members of the Diet;
5. Attestation of the appointment and dismissal of Ministers of State and other officials as provided for by law, and of full powers and credentials of Ambassadors and Ministers;
6. Attestation of general and special amnesty, commutation of punishment, reprieve, and restoration of rights;
7. Awarding of honours;
8. Attestation of instruments of ratification and other diplomatic documents as provided for by law;
9. Receiving foreign ambassadors and ministers;
10. Performance of ceremonial functions.

Some of these acts may have political implications. For instance, the power to dissolve the House of Representatives may indicate the power of the Emperor to determine the dissolution. Yet, as will be explained below, it is the Cabinet, through the Prime Minister, that has the power to decide whether to dissolve the House of Representatives and the Emperor merely proclaims the dissolution as directed by the Cabinet.[37] Therefore, all these acts should be interpreted as merely ceremonial in their nature and it is the Cabinet that decides how these acts should be conducted.

Could the Emperor perform other public functions? This issue was debated regarding the delivery of speech in the opening session of the Diet.[38] Such acts are not listed in the Constitution. By strictly interpreting

[37] See below, ch 4, pp 101–102.

[38] The Emperor does not read the government policy proposal of the Cabinet as a 'throne speech' in the Diet. The Emperor's delivery of the speech is merely a ceremonial and non-political one.

the text of the Constitution, it is likely that one will conclude that the Emperor is not allowed to perform such acts. Yet, many people believe that the Emperor can perform other public functions, either as the Emperor of Japan or simply as a public figure, so long as he is acting within the advice and approval of the Cabinet. In any case, since the Emperor has no political power, all the details of such public functions must be decided by the Cabinet and the Emperor should refrain from interfering with politics.

The Japanese Constitution also strictly regulates the financial power of the Imperial House. Under the Meiji Constitution, the Imperial House had vast amounts of land and independent financial resources. However, after the Pacific War, all properties of the Imperial House were confiscated and now '[n]o property can be given to, or received by, the Imperial House, nor can any gifts be made therefrom, without the authorization of the Diet' (article 8). Also, '[a]ll property of the Imperial Household shall belong to the State. All expenses of the Imperial Household shall be appropriated by the Diet in the budget' (article 88).

CONCLUSION

Despite the popular sovereignty principle, it is hardly plausible to say that Japanese citizens actually control the government decision-making process. Citizens have only the right to choose their representatives but do not have any power to directly participate in politics. Even with regard to the right to choose their representatives, the Public Office Election Act imposes very strict restrictions on citizen participation and there exists gross malapportionment. Many citizens do not support any particular political party[39] and they do not participate in politics

[39] According to a March 2009 survey, 23.3% of voters support the LDP; 22.7% support the DJP, while 42.1% replied that they do not support any particular party. JNN public opinion survey (7 and 8 March, 2009): http://news.tbs.co.jp/newsi_sp/shijiritsu/. After the 2009 election, 43.4% of voters support the DPJ; 16.7 % support the LDP and 28.6% replied that they do not support any particular party. JNN public opinion survey (3 October 2009): news.tbs.co.jp/newsi_sp/shijiritsu/. According to the most recent survey, 28.5% of voters support the DPJ, 18.3% support the LDP, and 31.9% replied that they do not support any political party. JNN public opinion survey (7 July, 2010): http://news.tbs.co.jp/newsi_sp/yoron/backnumber/20100717/q1-2.html/.

except on voting day. Moreover, the participation ratio is generally not high[40] and citizens tend to show no particularly strong interest in politics.

The 2009 election was a landmark in this regard. Before and during the election, the DPJ strongly argued for the change of government. The LDP asked the voters to trust an experienced LDP government over an inexperienced DPJ. With quite a high participation ratio, the voters went to polling stations to choose the DPJ over the LDP. This may indicate the possibility of change of government despite many restrictions on public participation and general apathy of citizens about politics. We will have to wait and see how this election will change the scope and effectiveness of public participation in politics.

Sixty years have passed since the introduction of liberal democracy in Japan, yet there is still a long way to go before the popular sovereignty principle and the ideal of democracy are truly accomplished.

FURTHER READING

GD Allinson and Yasunori Sone (eds), *Political Dynamics in Contemporary Japan* (Ithaca, Cornell University Press, 1993).

HP Bix, *Hirohito and the Making of Modern Japan* (New York, Harper Collins, 2000).

GL Curtis, *The Japanese Way of Politics* (New York, Columbia University Press, 1988).

——, *The Logic of Japanese Politics: Leaders, Institutions, and the Limits of Change* (New York, Columbia University Press, 1999).

LD Hayes, *Introduction to Japanese Politics* 5th edn (Armonk, M.E. Sharpe, 2009) 67–39.

Takeshi Ishida and ES Krauss (eds), *Democracy in Japan* (Pittsburgh, University of Pittsburgh Press, 1989).

Purnendra Jain and Takeshi Inoguchi, *Japanese Politics Today: Beyond Karaoke Democracy?* (New York, St Martin's Press, 1997).

Masaru Kohno, *Japan's Postwar Party Politics* (Princeton, Princeton University Press, 1997).

[40] The voter turnout rate for the general election in 2005 for members of the House of Representatives was 66.29%. It was 59.86% in 2003. The voter turnout in the 2009 election was 69.2%

B Richardson, *Japanese Democracy: Power, Coordination, and Performance* (New Haven, Yale University Press, 1997) 1–94.

JAA Stockwin, *Governing Japan* 4th edn (Oxford, Blackwell Publishers, 2008) 135–78.

3

The Diet and the Legislative Power

Introduction – PART I: THE DIET – The Status of the Diet – The Organization of the Diet – PART II: POWERS OF THE DIET – Legislative Power – What Kind of State is Envisaged by the Constitution? – Budget and Treaty Approval – Power over Finance – Delegation of Legislative Power – PART III: LEGISLATIVE PROCESS – Introduction of a Bill – Examination of a Bill – Voting – Diet Sessions – Power of the House to Investigate Governmental Affairs – Privileges of Diet Members – PART IV: LEGISLATORS AND BUREAUCRATS: REALITY OF THE LEGISLATIVE PROCESS – Who are Legislators?–Reality of Legislative Process – Legislators or Bureaucrats? – Conclusion

INTRODUCTION

THE CONSTITUTION, IN its Chapter IV: The Diet, vests legislative power in the Diet. The Diet is the highest organ of the state and its sole law-making organ. Consisting of representatives chosen by the people, it is supposed to decide the fundamental government policies to be enforced by the Cabinet.

In this chapter, we will see the powers of the Diet and its status in the constitutional system. We will examine the legislative process and then examine the power of bureaucrats and legislators to see which one of the two is more powerful in Japan. Even though it is the Diet that has legislative power, most of the Bills enacted by the Diet are government Bills and it is the bureaucrats working in the executive departments that have a strong influence on their content. It is as though the Diet is simply rubber-stamping Bills prepared by these bureaucrats. We will see to what extent the Diet has actually achieved the status of the highest and sole legislative organ of the state.

PART I: THE DIET

THE STATUS OF THE DIET

Under the Meiji Constitution, the Imperial Diet was established in 1890 in response to an increasing call for establishment of the representative body. The Emperor was the head of the state and had all the government powers (article 4). Therefore, the Emperor had a legislative power and the Imperial Diet assisted the Emperor in exercising the legislative power (articles 5 and 37). The Emperor had a power to veto the Bill passed by the Imperial Diet (article 6) and the Emperor could issue imperial orders (emergency orders) in time of emergency when the Imperial Diet was in recess (article 8). The Emperor could also issue imperial orders (independent orders) to implement the statutes or to assure the public safety (article 9).

In contrast, under the Japanese Constitution, the Diet shall be the 'highest organ of state power, and shall be the sole law-making organ of the State' (article 41). Even though the Diet is characterised as the 'highest organ of state power', this does not mean that the Diet is sovereign in Japan. It is the people of Japan who have sovereign power and the Diet must obey the Constitution enacted by the Japanese people. Even among the three branches of the government, the Diet is not literally the highest organ. The judiciary could strike down legislation passed by the Diet if it believes it to be unconstitutional (article 81).

It is generally believed, therefore, that this characterization merely pays lip service to the Diet.[1] The Diet is proclaimed to be the highest organ of state power since it consists of members elected by the citizens and represents them, and has the most important powers of government, including legislative power.

The Diet consists of 'elected members, representative of all the people' (article 43). Therefore, all Diet members are representative not only of the voters who elected them, but of all the people. They are

[1] Ashibe, 279.

also not bound by the wishes of their electorate. They can participate in deliberation in the Diet and vote freely without directives from their voters. Members of both Houses shall not be held liable outside the House for speeches, debates or votes cast inside the House (article 51). This immunity is an essential element of modern democracy.

Yet, as in France, where the principle of popular sovereignty originally developed, it has been assumed that the legislators in the Diet should reflect the division of various opinions in the society. Representation in this sense thus requires sociological representation. Many academics in Japan believe that article 43 also requires this kind of sociological representation.[2]

THE ORGANIZATION OF THE DIET

The Diet shall consist of two Houses; the House of Representatives and the House of Councillors (article 42). The Japanese Constitution is thus based on bicameralism. This was an important change from the original draft of the Constitution prepared by the Supreme Commander of Allied Power (SCAP), since the original draft had adopted a unicameral model. The Japanese side was strongly opposed to unicameralism and the SCAP conceded this revision to a bicameral model.

However, on the face of the Constitution, the difference between the House of Representatives and the House of Councillors is not clear. Both Houses shall consist of elected members, representative of all the people (article 43, section 1). The number of the members of each House shall be fixed by law (article 43, section 2). The qualifications of members of both Houses and their electors shall be fixed by law (article 44). Electoral districts, the method of voting and other matters pertaining to the method of election of members of both Houses shall be fixed by law (article 47). The Diet is thus given the power to adopt different qualifications and different election systems.

The only difference can be found in the different terms of office. Members of the House of Representatives shall have a term of four years, unless the House of Representatives is dissolved prior to the end of the four-year period, in which case the term shall end when the House is dissolved (article 45). On the other hand, the term of office for members

[2] *Ibid*, 278–79.

of the House of Councillors shall be six years, and election for half the members shall take place every three years (article 46). No person shall be permitted to be a member of both Houses simultaneously (article 48).

We have already seen that the Diet has created different election schemes for members of the House of Representatives and members of the House of Councillors. However, the difference is quite minor and many people doubt whether this difference is sufficient to justify the existence of the second House. Some even argue that the House of Councillors is no longer needed. Yet, many still believe that the House of Councillors could provide another opportunity for sober reflection on a Bill passed by the House of Representatives, and there is thus a need for the second House.

When both Houses are controlled by the same ruling party, the House of Councillors does not play much of a significant role. In the 1989 election for the members of the House of Councillors, however, the Liberal Democratic Party (LDP) registered an unprecedented loss because of the introduction of a controversial sales tax and because of the involvement of Sousuke Uno, the Prime Minister, in a sex scandal—and lost control of the House of Councillors for the first time. In the 2007 election of the House of Councillors, the LDP again similarly encountered a devastating loss due to continuing scandals of Cabinet members and maladministration in the pension office, and lost control of the House of Councillors. Because the LDP lost control of the House of Councillors, the LDP Government could not pass legislation unless it had a two-thirds majority in the House of Representatives. Thanks to its unprecedented victory in the 2005 general election, the LDP had a two-thirds majority in the House of Representatives and the government was able to pass legislation despite the rejection in the House of Councillors. Nevertheless, the government had to resort to this override cautiously because, in the next election, voters might have reacted negatively to its increased use, especially if they viewed the inclination to resort to override as arrogant. The government therefore had some difficulty in implementing its policy. As a result of the 2009 House of Representatives election, the coalition government of the Democratic Party of Japan (DPJ), the Social Democratic Party (SDP) and the People's New Party (PNP) occupied the majority in both houses. Yet, after the 2010 House of Councillors election, the coalition government between the DPJ and PNP lost control of the House of Councillors. It is expected that the coalition government will face a tremendous difficulty in coming years since it does not have two-thirds majority in the House of Representatives to override the rejection in the House of Councillors.

PART II: POWERS OF THE DIET

LEGISLATIVE POWER

The Diet is the sole legislative organ of the government and, as such, enjoys exclusive legislative authority.[3] No one or branch of the government other than the Diet has legislative power. The Emperor does not have power to enact independent orders or emergency orders without the approval of the Diet. The Cabinet does not have the power to enact orders without delegation from the Diet.

That the Diet is the sole legislative organ of government also means that it is entitled to exercise its legislative authority without the involvement or interference of other governmental institutions or actors. A Bill becomes a law on passage by both Houses, except as otherwise provided by the Constitution (article 59, section 1).[4] The Emperor no longer holds veto power. After passage, the Prime Minister, as well as the minister of state who is responsible for enforcement of that statute, is supposed to sign the statute (article 74). Yet, the statute is valid and binding even without their signatures. The signatures are merely symbolic of taking responsibility for the statute's enforcement. After the signing, the statute will be sent to the Emperor for promulgation (article 7, item 1). Although the statute is supposed to be valid and binding, it has to be promulgated before it can be enforced. Of course, the Emperor does not have any power to refuse promulgation; it is merely a symbolic act of publishing the statute in the *Official Gazette* in the name of the Emperor.[5]

[3] Exceptions to this rule are the rule-making power of each of the Houses (art 58, s 2) and the rule-making power of the Supreme Court (art 77, s 1).

[4] Exception is art 95, which provides that '[a] special law, applicable only to one local public entity, cannot be enacted by the Diet without the consent of the majority of the voters of the local public entity concerned, obtained in accordance with law'. In order for such a statute to be enacted, therefore, a local referendum has to be conducted.

[5] Does promulgation have to be made through publication of the statute in the Official Gazette? During the Meiji Constitution, the Order for Promulgation provided for promulgation through publication in the Official Gazette, yet this Order lost its effect when the Japanese Constitution took effect and there is now

What is the appropriate subject matter for legislation? Unlike the constitutions of some other nations,[6] the Japanese Constitution does not limit the subject matter of legislation. The Diet can thus enact legislation on whatever subject it may find appropriate. Even with respect to local matters, it has been assumed that the Diet can enact legislation despite promises and guarantees of local government.

Does the Cabinet have the power to conduct public affairs without delegation from the Diet? Traditionally, it had been assumed that the Diet had exclusive power to legislate on matters that infringe liberty and property rights. Therefore, the Cabinet was allowed to conduct public affairs unless they infringed on the liberty and property of the public. Yet, this traditional view has been subject to increasing criticism. The critics argue that the Diet should be the sole organ to enact legislation on any subject,[7] including administrative organization, the non-governmental exercise of power, the vesting of benefits in the public, or even de facto acts of government. Some argue that, at a minimum, the most important decisions should be left to the Diet. Yet, it may be difficult to argue that the Cabinet is not allowed to conduct any public affairs without explicit delegation from the Diet.

This issue is especially significant since in Japan administrative guidance without any explicit statutory authorization plays quite an important role.[8] Many administrative agencies promote desirable conduct by issuing memorandums or delivering oral messages to the public concerned. This is merely guidance and is not legally binding. It can be issued without explicit statutory authorization. Nevertheless, it has a very strong de facto binding power over the public. There is a heated dispute about whether such practices should be allowed, or whether the administrative agencies must have explicit statutory authorization to issue such guidance.

For example, Japan used to have the Large Scale Store Act (an Act

no statute on promulgation. As a result, the Supreme Court held that promulgation does not have to be made through publication in the Official Gazette, but that is the usual method: Supreme Court, grand bench, 28 December 1957, 11 *Keishu* 3461. Sometimes, a question was raised as to when a statute was promulgated, since some of the statutes took effect upon promulgation. The Supreme Court held that promulgation took place when it first became possible for the public to look at the Gazette, ie, when the Gazette was delivered to the National Printing Office or sales office: Supreme Court, grand bench, 15 October 1958, 12 *Keishu* 3313.

[6] US Constitution, art I, s 8.

[7] Ashibe, 280.

[8] See below, ch 4, pp 107–108.

Concerning Adjustment of Retail Business at Large Scale Stores), which obliged the owners of certain big retail stores to apply to the Minister of International Trade and Industry (MITI), a predecessor to the current Ministry of Economy, Trade and Industry (METI), for registration through municipal governments. Registration was not a permit or licence and the system was designed to accept the application unless it failed to satisfy the statutory criteria. The Act authorized the minister to recommend scaling down or limiting store hours and ultimately to order the owner to obey these recommendations. The minister is supposed to hear the opinion of a consultative body before issuing these recommendations and this consultative body is supposed to hear the opinion of a local consultative body. Yet, under this statute, the MITI developed the practice of requiring advance consultation with local merchants before filing an application. Practically speaking, in order to open a large scale supermarket, for instance, the applicant must receive an approval from the opposing local merchants. Some of the municipalities boldly declared that they would not accept any applications. As a result, opening large retail stores became extremely difficult.[9] If the agency needed legislative authorization for administrative guidance, these practices would be held to be illegal.

Does legislation have to be general or is a statute targeting specific persons allowed? Although some argue that legislation has to be general, since statutes directed to individual persons can be arbitrary,[10] actual practice allows statutes targeting specific persons. The Japan Tobacco Company Act is one example. This Act was passed to privatise the public corporation, which had exclusive authority to manufacture and sell tobacco products in Japan and to regulate the activities of the new company. The Act Providing Special Treatment for Debts to the Government in the Bankruptcy Proceeding of Aum Shinrikyo, which was designed to give preferential treatment to victims of crimes of the Aum Shinrikyo, is another example. Almost certainly, a specific statute imposing criminal penalty on specific persons should not be allowed as a Bill of Attainder,[11] but the Diet should be allowed to enact statutes

[9] Shigenori Matsui, 'Lochner v New York in Japan: Protecting Economic Liberties in a Country Governed by Bureaucrats' in PSC Lewis (ed), *Law and Technology in the Pacific Community* (Boulder, Westview Press, 1994) 199, 224–26. The Large Scale Store Act was abolished in 2000.

[10] Ashibe, 280.

[11] See US Constitution, art I, s 9; cl 3 and s 10.

targeting specific persons.[12] In Japan, however, the Diet does not accept private Bills, giving benefits or exemptions to individual persons or corporations. All the enactments passed by the Diet are public laws even when they are directed toward specific persons or corporations.

WHAT KIND OF STATE IS ENVISAGED BY THE CONSTITUTION?

The Constitution does not have a provision concerning the kinds of legislative goals to be achieved through the Diet, aside from the pacifism principle and the restraint imposed by the Bill of Rights. In other words, the Constitution does not specify the kind of state it envisions. Since most of the provisions of the Bill of Rights are supposed to preclude the government from interfering with the freedom of the public, the Diet can decide whatever policy it chooses unless it infringes on such individual freedoms. The Constitution, however, obliges the government to guarantee the welfare right, the right to receive education and the rights of workers. In particular, article 25, section 1, guarantees that '[a]ll people shall have the right to maintain the minimum standards of wholesome and cultured living' and section 2 provides that '[i]n all spheres of life, the State shall use its endeavours for the promotion and extension of social welfare and security, and of public health'. As a result, many believe that the Constitution is committed to a welfare state or social state, in which the government is obliged to guarantee social welfare and public health care. Since the Diet has broad discretion as to the specific shapes of these welfare programmes, however, the Diet is able to adopt whatever social policy or economic policy it wants.

The LDP is committed to liberal democracy, and is grounded on capitalist principles, while the DPJ is committed to moderate social democracy, the SDP is committed to left-wing social democracy principles and the Japan Communist Party (JCP) is committed to communist principles. Therefore, generally speaking, the LDP represents the interests of industries, in favour of economic development, while the DPJ, SDP and JCP represent the interests of unions and workers, in favour of the welfare state. However, there are conflicting opinions within the LDP. Some LDP members are in favour of the market economy, with the goal of a minimal state, whereas other LDP members

[12] Shibutani, 480.

represent the interests of farmers, fishermen and small business owners, thus favouring protectionist measures rather than a free market economy. The Komei Party is committed to the welfare of working people and to peace, but it is largely supported by the Buddhist religious organization Souka Gakkai.

Since the government had a very close relationship with industries during the Meiji period, that strong relationship remains the most prominent characteristic of Japanese society even after the end of the Pacific War. During 1950s to the 1970s in particular, when industry needed government support for rapid economic development, the Diet passed many statutes authorizing broad government regulation of the economy and allowed the government to set goals to be achieved together with industry, while it passed many protectionist statutes designed to protect farmers, fishermen and small businesses. Japanese society is a highly egalitarian society closely regulated by the government. When these regulations were criticised as preventing the entry of foreign companies into the Japanese market during the 1980s, and when excessive economic regulations were criticised as stifling economic development during the 1990s, the Diet liberalised many government regulations relying on the market economy. Now, with the growing division between rich and poor, many are criticising the market economy as a culprit which is destroying egalitarian society and are calling for more government regulations. It is likely that this is one of the reasons for the success of the DPJ in the 2009 House of Representatives election.

BUDGET AND TREATY APPROVAL

The Diet also has two significant powers controlling the executive branch.

The first is the power to approve the budget. According to article 73, item 5, the Cabinet has the authority to prepare the budget and present it to the Diet. The budget must first be submitted to the House of Representatives (article 60, section 1). According to article 60, section 2, the decision of the House of Representatives shall be the decision of the Diet when, on consideration of the budget, the House of Councillors makes a decision different from that of the House of Representatives and when no agreement can be reached even through a joint committee of both Houses, as provided for by law. This is also the case in the event of failure by the House of Councillors to take final action within 30 days, the period of recess excluded, after the receipt of the budget passed by the House of Representatives.

The second power is the treaty approval power. According to article 73, the Cabinet has the power to 'manage foreign affairs' (item 2) and to 'conclude treaties' (item 3). However, the Cabinet must obtain 'prior or, depending on circumstances, subsequent approval' of the Diet. The superior power of the House of Representatives outlined in article 60 applies also to the Diet approval required for treaties (article 61). When Japan attempted to renew the Japan-United States Mutual Security Treaty in 1960, the House of Councillors could not give approval to the Treaty because of strong opposition. As a result, the Treaty was given approval 30 days after the House of Representatives gave approval to it without the participation of opposition parties.

POWER OVER FINANCE

The Diet also has the power to tax and to decide on spending. Chapter VII: Finance is devoted to public finance. The power to administer national finances shall be exercised as the Diet shall determine (article 83). This principle is generally called the principle of democratic control over finance.

No new taxes shall be imposed or existing ones modified except by law or under such conditions as the law may prescribe (article 84). The Japanese citizen has a constitutional duty to pay tax (article 30). Yet, the imposition of tax is allowed only when the Diet has passed a law. This provision derives from the age-old doctrine: 'no taxation without representation'.

'Taxes' as stipulated in article 84 used to be thought of as including not only the typical tax, but all monetary impositions on the public, including government permit fees, examination fees, postal charges and prices of products sold exclusively by state corporations.[13] The Supreme Court took a somewhat different view in the *Asahikawa City National Health Insurance Ordinance* Case.[14] Japan has a mandatory national health

[13] Kiyomiya, 262. Some distinguish, however, the imposition of tax from imposition of fees or charges for a particular service or product and limit the applicability of art 84 to the former. Ashibe, 344.

[14] Supreme Court, grand bench, 1 March 2006, 60 *Minshu* 587.

insurance system. In order to implement it, the Asahikawa City had an ordinance, which imposed an obligation to pay an insurance premium on its residents. At issue was whether this insurance premium was a 'tax' in the sense of article 84 and whether the standard for calculating this tax was specified in the ordinance as required by article 84. The Court held that this premium was a monetary charge for certain services and not a 'tax' in the sense of article 84. It nevertheless applied the 'basic philosophy' of article 84 to this premium since it was mandatory for residents and it resembled a tax.

The Diet must decide who has the obligation to pay tax, the subject matter of taxes, the standards for tax, the tax rate and procedures to impose and collect tax.[15] The Supreme Court has allowed the government, however, to change its internal interpretation of the tax statute by issuing new administrative letters and imposing tax on products which had been previously construed as exempt from taxation.[16]

To what extent must the Diet enact specific standards for taxation? The Supreme Court faced this issue in the *Asahikawa City National Health Insurance Ordinance Case*. As explained above, the Court examined whether the mandatory premium for all residents complied with the 'basic philosophy' of article 84, while it was not a tax in the sense of article 84. Yet, it concluded that the ordinance did not violate the 'basic philosophy' of article 84, even though the ordinance did not provide a specific rate in itself but allowed the city to calculate the premium based on the estimate of total costs and decide the specific rate in the form of a public announcement.

No money shall be expended, nor shall the State obligate itself, except as authorized by the Diet (article 85). As explained above, government spending must be based on a budget submitted by the Cabinet. The Cabinet shall prepare and submit to the Diet for its consideration and decision a budget for each fiscal year (article 86). The fiscal year starts on 1 April and the general budget is submitted to the Diet in January. The general budget estimates the revenue and specifies how much each agency can spend on specific items over the course of one fiscal year. If there is a need to spend additional money, the government must submit a revised budget to the Diet. In order to provide for unforeseen deficiencies in the budget, a reserve fund may be authorized by the Diet

[15] Supreme Court, grand bench, 23 March 1955, 9 *Minshu* 336.
[16] Supreme Court, 2nd petty bench, 28 March 1958, 12 *Minshu* 624.

to be expended under the Cabinet's authority. The Cabinet must get subsequent approval of the Diet for all payments from the reserve fund (article 87).

No public money or other property shall be expended or appropriated for the use, benefit or maintenance of any religious institution or association, or for any charitable, educational or benevolent enterprises not under the control of public authority (article 89). The first half is of course a separation of Church and State provision. The original intent behind the latter is somewhat ambiguous, yet it is believed that this provision was inserted to maintain fiscal health by prohibiting unnecessary spending in the name of benevolent contributions.

This provision has raised a difficult issue with respect to government funding of private universities. Many tend to believe that private universities are under the general supervision of the Ministry of Education, Technology and Science (under the School Education Act and the Act to Assist the Development of Private Schools), and this is sufficient to place private universities 'under the control of public authority'. Yet, critics view the term 'under the control of public authority' as requiring more direct involvement of the government in managing the enterprise or personnel decisions and argue that private universities are not 'under the control of public authority' in this sense.[17]

Final accounts of the expenditures and revenues of the State shall be audited annually by a Board of Audit and submitted by the Cabinet to the Diet, together with the statement of audit, during the fiscal year immediately following the period covered. The organization and competency of the Board of Audit shall be determined by law (article 90). The Board of Audit is the organ of the state established under the Constitution to audit government spending.

At regular intervals and at least annually, the Cabinet shall report to the Diet and the people on the state of national finances (article 91).

[17] Even if private universities are not 'under the control of public authority', it might be argued that public funding can be justified based on the right to receive education as stipulated in art 26. Urabe, 551.

DELEGATION OF LEGISLATIVE POWER

Although there is no explicit provision allowing the Diet to delegate legislative power to administrative agencies, it has been assumed that such delegation is permissible under the Constitution.[18] Article 73, item 6, while authorizing the Cabinet to enact Cabinet Orders in order to execute the provisions of the Constitution and of the law, provides that 'it cannot include penal provisions in such cabinet orders unless authorized by such law'. This may be construed as assuming the delegation of legislative power. (Article 11 of the Cabinet Act thus provides that a Cabinet Order cannot impose any duties or provide for restriction of rights without delegation by statute.) In a modern democracy, the government must play substantial roles in many fields. The need for expertise and technical knowledge will naturally increase. The government is often forced to act promptly. As a result, it would be better for the Diet to enact statutes providing only the general framework and to allow the government to enact orders to implement the statute. The delegation of legislative power is quite common in modern countries.

However, it has been assumed at the same time that there are limits to the delegation of legislative power. The Diet is not allowed to give carte blanche to the executive. The Diet must make fundamental value judgements and specify the criteria to be used by administrative agencies when it delegates legislative power.[19]

Yet the Supreme Court has been very reluctant to overturn the delegation of broad discretion to the administrative agencies. For instance, the National Public Workers Act prohibits public workers from engaging in 'political activities' and relegates the power to define prohibited 'political activities' to the National Personnel Authority, an independent agency which is in charge of personnel administration concerning public workers (article 102, section 1). The Supreme Court quite summarily rejected a constitutional attack against this broad delegation.[20]

On the other hand, the Supreme Court has occasionally found that the administrative agencies went beyond the scope of the delegated power

[18] Shibutani 491.

[19] Sato, 147.

[20] Supreme Court, 1st petty bench, 1 May 1958, 12 *Keishu* 1272; Supreme Court, grand bench, 6 November 1974, 28 *Keishu* 393 (*Sarufutsu Case*).

or violated the statute. For instance, article 4, section 1, of the Child Support Benefit Act vested child support benefits in 'children of divorced parents', 'children who lost their fathers' and 'other children designated by the Cabinet Order as similarly situated'. Articles 1–2 of the Order to Implement the Child Support Benefit Act listed the 'children born from mothers who were not in matrimonial relation', yet it exempted a child if the father acknowledged him or her. The Supreme Court held that the Child Support Benefit Act gave the power to designate a child who could not expect support from the person responsible and concluded that the Order was in conflict with the Act since the child could not expect support from a father even when he acknowledged the child.[21]

PART III: LEGISLATIVE PROCESS

INTRODUCTION OF A BILL

A Bill is introduced by a member of the Diet. In order to introduce a Bill, there must be sufficient support from the legislators as stipulated in the Diet Act.[22] Moreover, there is a custom requiring the approval of affiliated 'factions' in the Diet in order to introduce a Bill.[23]

Yet, the Japanese Constitution is based on the Westminster model and therefore it has been considered appropriate for the Cabinet to introduce a Bill in the Diet (Cabinet Act, article 5).[24] As a matter of fact, most of

[21] Supreme Court, 1st petty bench, 31 January 2002, 56 *Minshu* 246.

[22] There must be at least the support of 20 members in the House of Representatives or 10 members in the House of Councillors to introduce a Bill, while there must be the support of 50 members in the House of Representatives or 20 members in the House of Councillors to introduce a Bill which requires budgetary spending (Diet Act, art 56, s 1).

[23] The 'factions' are groups inside the Diet, usually consisting of political parties. This custom was designed to prevent the introduction of a Bill by minority members of the political party without endorsement of the party leaders. It was upheld by the lower court out of deference to the autonomy of each House. Tokyo High Court, 18 June 1997, 1618 *Hanreijihou* 69.

[24] Ashibe, 281; Sato 150. Some deny the power of the Cabinet to introduce a Bill. Urabe, 538. It must be noted that Cabinet Bills are introduced into the Diet by the Prime Minister, representing the Cabinet, and not by individual ministers.

the Bills introduced in the Diet are Cabinet Bills and these Cabinet Bills occupy the majority of statutes passed by the Diet every year.[25]

A Bill is submitted to the Cabinet Legal Bureau for legal examination prior to Cabinet approval. The Cabinet Legal Bureau, consisting of legal experts, examines the legal terms, the structure of the Bill and possible conflicts with other statutes, and prepares an official bill together with necessary amendments to other relevant statutes. Then the Bill will be submitted to the Cabinet for official approval. The Cabinet thereafter submits the Bill to one of the Houses of the Diet.

EXAMINATION OF A BILL

Once a Bill is submitted, it will be referred to one of the committees for review. Each House has many standing committees and ad hoc committees. When the relevant committee has passed the Bill, the Bill will be transferred to a plenary session of the House. When the Bill is approved by the majority of the House, it will then be forwarded to the other House for review. A similar procedure will be followed in the other House. It is only when both Houses agree on the same Bill that the Bill will be passed into law.

Business cannot be transacted in either House unless one-third or more of the total membership is present (article 56, section 1).

Deliberation in each House shall be public. However, a secret meeting may be held if a majority of two-thirds or more of those members present passes a resolution therefor (article 57, section 1). This openness requirement has been construed to be applicable only to plenary sessions and the Diet Act gives discretion to the chairperson of the committee to close the committee hearing (Diet Act, article 52). Each House shall keep a record of proceedings. This record shall be published and given general circulation, except for such parts of proceedings of secret sessions as may be deemed to require secrecy (article 57, section 2). On demand of one-fifth or more of the members present, members' votes on any matter shall be recorded in the minutes (article 57, section 3).

[25] During the 166th Diet in 2007, 97 Cabinet Bills were introduced in the Diet and 89 were passed, while 68 Bills were introduced by Diet members and 22 were passed. During the 169th Diet in 2008, 80 Cabinet Bills were introduced in the Diet and 63 were passed, while 59 Bills were introduced by Diet members and 17 were passed.

Each House shall establish its own rules pertaining to meetings, proceedings and internal discipline, and may punish members for disorderly conduct. However, in order to expel a member, a majority of two-thirds or more of those members present must pass a resolution thereon (article 58). Each House is therefore given autonomous power regarding its internal affairs.[26] Each House shall also judge disputes related to qualifications of its members. However, in order to deny a seat to any member, it is necessary to pass a resolution by a majority of two-thirds or more of the members present (article 55).

The Prime Minister and other ministers of state may, at any time, appear in either House for the purpose of speaking on Bills, regardless of whether they are members of the House or not. They must appear when their presence is required in order to give answers or explanations (article 63).

VOTING

According to article 59, a Bill becomes a law on passage by both Houses, except as otherwise provided by the Constitution (section 1). A Bill which is passed by the House of Representatives, and on which the House of Councillors makes a decision different from that of the House of Representatives, becomes a law when passed a second time by the House of Representatives by a majority of two-thirds or more of the members present (section 2). Failure by the House of Councillors to take final action within 60 days after receipt of a Bill passed by the House of Representatives (time in recess excepted) may be determined by the House of Representatives to constitute a rejection of said Bill by the House of Councillors (section 4). The House of Representatives thus has greater power than the House of Councillors.

All matters shall be decided, in each House, by a majority of those present, except as elsewhere provided in the Constitution, and in case of a tie, the presiding officer shall decide the issue (article 56, section 2).

Since most of the Bills submitted to the Diet are Cabinet Bills approved by the Cabinet after approval of the ruling parties, they are most likely to be passed with the support of the ruling parties. It is

[26] The Diet has enacted the Diet Act, however, and regulates internal matters of each House.

thus unlikely that these Bills will be rejected or modified in the Diet. However, occasionally, strong opposition can be successful in blocking their passage. For instance, in 1987, the opposition parties conducted an 'ox walk' (deliberately walking too slowly like an ox to cast votes in order to prevent the passage of a Bill during the Diet session) during voting in the House of Representatives and successfully blocked the passage of a controversial sales tax Bill during the ordinary session.

Sometimes, the opposition parties use physical force to attempt to block the passage of controversial Bills. For instance, in 1954 the Cabinet introduced a controversial Police Act Bill, which was designed to reorganise the police force, stripping from municipalities the power over the police and giving it to prefectures and establishing the central police organization. The opposition parties strongly opposed the Bill's passage because it was regarded as overturning the democratization introduced after the Pacific War during the occupation. Members of the ruling party and members of the opposition parties clashed over the extension of the Diet session and the police force were called into the Diet. This Diet session was often referred to as the 'fighting Diet session'. The DPJ has adopted the policy of not using such physical force to block the passage of a Bill and, as a result, it has been rare to see such use of physical force. We must wait and see whether the LDP is willing to resort to such physical forces.

As explained above, when the LDP controlled both Houses, the House of Councillors did not usually play a significant role. Yet, sometimes, there were exceptions. For instance, in 2005 the House of Councillors rejected a Bill to privatise the postal service, passed by the House of Representatives. The Bill was strongly supported by Koizumi, the Prime Minister, over the strong objection of some LDP members. The Bill failed. Koizumi dissolved the House of Representatives to seek a general election on the issue of privatization of the postal service. The LDP did not approve the candidates who argued against the privatization and chose new candidates as 'assassins' against the LDP incumbents who could not receive official endorsement. The result was an overwhelming victory for Koizumi, and many LDP incumbents who were against the privatization lost seats. Afraid of the same fate, LDP members in the House of Councillors who voted against the privatization Bill changed their stance to support the Bill when the new House of Representatives passed roughly the same Bill after election. This episode illustrates the power of the House of Councillors and its limit.

After the 2007 election, the opposition parties controlled the House of Councillors and rejected many Bills passed by the House of Representatives. The LDP Government did manage to pass some of the more important Bills by a two-thirds majority in the House of Representatives, but the total number of Bills passed by the Diet is significantly lower than before.[27] It will be interesting to see what kind of role the House of Councillors will play under the DPJ coalition government following the 2010 House of Councillors election.

DIET SESSIONS

The Diet will be convened only during a designated period of time. This period is generally called a 'session'. The Constitution distinguishes three different sessions: ordinary sessions, extraordinary sessions and special sessions.

An ordinary session of the Diet shall be convoked once per year (article 52). The ordinary session is convoked in January. When opening the ordinary session, the Emperor delivers his speech in the House of Councillors, with all the members of the Diet present. Unlike in the UK, the Emperor does not read a 'throne speech'. Instead, the Prime Minister will usually deliver a speech outlining the government policy to be implemented during that year. The ordinary session can be extended only once (Diet Act, article 12) and the House of Representatives has superior power over the House of Councillors in making this decision.

The Cabinet may determine when to convoke extraordinary sessions of the Diet. When a quarter or more of the total members of either House makes the demand, the Cabinet must submit and order such a convocation (article 53).

When the House of Representatives is dissolved, there must be a general election of members of the House of Representatives 40 days from the date of dissolution, and the Diet must be convoked within 30 days from the date of the election (article 54, section 1). This session is generally referred to as a special session.

It is assumed that a Bill must be passed during a session of the Diet (Diet Act, article 68). If it is not passed, it will have failed. Otherwise,

[27] During the 166th Diet in 2007, 111 Bills were passed, while only 80 Bills were passed during the 169th Diet in 2008.

the House must decide to review the Bill even after the end of the session (Diet Act, article 68 proviso). However, this principle is not constitutionally mandated and therefore it may be permissible to allow the Diet to consider the Bill during the period between general elections.[28] Could the same Bill be reintroduced during the same session after it is defeated? Probably not.[29] Yet, this is not regarded as a constitutional rule.

When the House of Representatives is dissolved, the House of Councillors is closed at the same time. However, the Cabinet may in time of national emergency convoke the House of Councillors in an emergency session (article 54, section 2). Measures taken at such a session shall be provisional and shall become null and void unless agreed to by the House of Representatives within a period of 10 days after the opening of the next session of the Diet (article 54, section 3). In the past, this emergency session was held only twice, even though it could hardly be said that the nation was 'in time of national emergency'.

POWER OF THE HOUSE TO INVESTIGATE GOVERNMENTAL AFFAIRS

Each House may conduct investigations in relation to government, and may demand the presence and testimony of witnesses and the production of records (article 62).

This power of the House to investigate governmental affairs is theoretically a very significant power of control over the government. Although it is assumed that this power can be exercised only to assist the legislative power of the House,[30] apparently the House has a very broad power to call all kinds of witnesses and subject them to questioning and ask for the presentation of documents and files for inspection so long as they are relevant to its business. Refusal to testify can be punished under the House Investigation Act (Act Concerning Solemnization and Testimony of Witness before the House).

Of course, the House is not allowed to ask personal questions related to privacy. Witnesses have also the privilege against self-incrimination and should not be forced to answer incriminating questions.

[28] Shibutani, 505–06.

[29] Kiyomiya, 249.

[30] Ashibe, 302; Sato,197. Some argue that the House should be allowed to exercise this power to inform the public of governmental affairs.

There must also be some limits on the House's ability to investigate specific cases, which are handled or decided by the courts. When the defendant Mitsuko Urawa killed her three children and attempted to commit suicide out of despair for her husband's failure to work and habitual gambling, the District Court sentenced her to three years of imprisonment but suspended the sentence's enforcement for three years. The Judiciary Committee of the House of Councillors picked up this case, called the defendant, defendant's husband and prosecutor as witnesses and resolved that this sentence was too lenient. The Supreme Court strongly protested.[31] Consequently, it came to be believed that the investigative power of the House should not be exercised in the handling of a specific case by a court or regarding the adequacy of the judgment in a specific case.[32]

There might be also a limit on investigating prosecutors regarding specific cases. It is believed that the House should not be allowed to investigate a specific case in order to influence the decision of a prosecutor whether to file prosecution, to inquire into the specifics of prosecution or to prevent the proper pursuit of prosecution.[33]

Yet, other than these limitations, the House can invoke this power quite broadly.[34] Despite its theoretical importance, the power to investigate governmental affairs has not been widely used in Japan, because the

[31] Urawa case: www.cc.matsuyama-u.ac.jp/~tamura/urawajikenn.htm.

[32] Ashibe, 303; Sato,198.

[33] Ashibe, 303. Although the justice minister can supervise the Public Prosecutors Office, the Public Prosecutor Office Act mandates the justice minister to supervise the agency in general and allows him or her to direct only the Prosecutor General with respect to individual cases (art 14). This power was exercised only once when Ken Inugai, the Justice Minister under the Liberal Party Yoshida Cabinet, blocked the request for an arrest of a Diet member, Eisaku Sato, the Secretary General of the Liberal Party at that time, and ended further criminal investigation of his involvement with scandals in 1954. Inugai's action was widely condemned and he had to resign the next day. No justice minister ever resorted to using this power again.

[34] Public officials can refuse to answer questions regarding official secrets without permission from the agency (House Investigation Act, art 5, s 1). When the agency refuses to grant permission, invoking official secrets, the House can request an explanation and ultimately a declaration of the Cabinet that the testimony would impair significant public interests (House Investigation Act, art 5, s 3). When Ken Inugai the Justice Minister exercised his supervisory power to block the request for an arrest of Eisaku Sato, the finance committee of the House of Representatives called the Prosecutor General and other high-ranking prosecutors as witnesses but they refused to answer all relevant questions. The committee requested an official explanation from the justice minister and ultimately a declaration of the Cabinet.

majority and the government belong to the same party and the ruling party is unwilling to investigate scandals of its own government. It has thus been proposed to allow the minority party to call witnesses and ask questions, for instance, by a one-third vote. The absence of change of government has certainly prevented the effective use of this power.

PRIVILEGES OF DIET MEMBERS

In order for Diet members to exercise power free from intimidation or interference, the Constitution provides them with several privileges.

First, except in cases provided by law, members of both Houses shall be exempt from apprehension while the Diet is in session, and any members apprehended before the opening of the session shall be freed during the term of the session upon demand of the House (article 50). When a member is arrested for committing crimes outside the House and when the House gives permission to arrest, members of the Diet may be arrested even while the Diet is in session.

Secondly, members of both Houses shall not be held liable outside the House for speeches, debates or votes cast inside the House (article 51). Legal immunity is extended to all official activities of the members of the Diet but no violence is allowed. This provision will only give legal immunity in criminal and civil proceedings; it will not prevent a political party from disciplining its members who violate the party line.[35] Even when a Diet member makes a defamatory speech during the deliberation of the Diet, he or she will not be held liable for defamation. Yet, the Supreme Court has held that the person defamed can seek damages from the government in exceptional circumstances such as when a Diet member illegally makes defamatory remarks with an illicit motive and without any relevance to his or her official duty.[36]

Members of both Houses shall receive appropriate annual payment from the national treasury in accordance with law (article 49).

[35] Ashibe, 277; Sato, 142.

[36] Supreme Court, 3rd petty bench, 9 September 1997, 51 *Minshu* 3850.

PART IV: LEGISLATORS AND BUREAUCRATS: REALITY OF THE LEGISLATIVE PROCESS

WHO ARE LEGISLATORS?

There is no established path to becoming a Diet member. Some members are former bureaucrats (93 out of some 740 as of 2007), and some were once business leaders or union leaders. Many would-be members run for local assemblies before running for the Diet (204 out of 740). Some members worked as secretaries for Diet members before running for election. Some are graduates of prestigious universities (133 are graduates of Tokyo University, 94 are graduates of Waseda University) but some do not have a university diploma.[37] Some of the members of the Diet who are appointed via proportional representation are those representing special interest groups, like the Japan Medical Association.

One of the prominent characteristics of Japanese politics is the fact that a significant number of legislators are children of politicians. Roughly over 102 among a total of some 740 members of the Diet are children or grandchildren of former Diet members or relatives of politicians. The election system and the importance of *koenkai* surely contributes to this large number.

Unlike in the United States Congress, the number of lawyers is very small. Therefore, most Diet members do not have a sufficient knowledge of law. They do not have sufficient drafting skills. Moreover, they do not have sufficient personal staff.

REALITY OF THE LEGISLATIVE PROCESS

Cabinet Bills are prepared by bureaucrats working in one of the executive departments. Bureaucrats thus play a leading role in legislation. They draft legislation and submit Bills for approval by the minister of state.

In Japan, there are some agencies that have a supervisory power over a particular industry. If it is the construction or transportation industry, it is the Ministry of Land, Infrastructure, Transport and Tourism. If it is the manufacturing or retail industry, it is the Ministry of Economy, Trade and

[37] Publistella: www.publistella.net (2007).

Industry. If it is medicine or pharmaceuticals, it is the Ministry of Health, Labour and Welfare. If agency bureaucrats find it necessary to enact legislation or to amend it, then they will start drafting. Often the agency has an advisory board or expert study groups and often their advice will help them draft a Bill.[38] These advisory boards or study groups usually consist of academics with expert knowledge in the industry, and representatives of interested parties. The accommodation of conflicting interests is usually accomplished through deliberation before the advisory board or study group. When they produce a final advisory recommendation, therefore, the agency can be more or less certain that the accommodation of interests has already been accomplished and the agency is ready to draft a Bill based on that recommendation. By carefully selecting the members of these groups, an administrative agency can make sure that the recommendations of these groups do not deviate from the basic policy of the agency.

Quite often, bureaucrats must consult with bureaucrats from other departments of the executive, which may have conflicting interests in the regulated industry. Sometimes, intergovernmental conflicts of interest can prevent an agency from introducing necessary legislation.

Since Cabinet Bills are drafted by government bureaucrats, they are generally drafted to give broad discretion to the bureaucrats and to allow them to make the specific shape of the government policy as flexible as it can be.

Moreover, as a result of the dominance of Cabinet Bills, legislators generally lack the drafting skills necessary to introduce a Bill. As was noted, unlike the in the United States Congress, few legislators are lawyers. Moreover, they do not have sufficient personal staff to prepare a Bill. They also cannot rely on the expertise of the Cabinet Legal Bureau to check the text of the Bill or to cross check with conflicting provisions in other statutes. This lack of skill and understaffing has forced legislators to depend more heavily on government bureaucrats.

LEGISLATORS OR BUREAUCRATS?

What is the relationship between bureaucrats and lagislators or politicians in general? Are these bureaucrats making policy and the politicians simply following their decisions?

[38] FJ Schwartz, *Advice and Consent: The Politics of Consultation in Japan* (Cambridge, Cambridge University Press, 1998).

Of course, in some situations, politicians, such as ministers, propose a policy change and let bureaucrats draft legislation. Yet, it is rare for a minister to propose a policy change without the advance support of the bureaucrats.

When bureaucrats propose a policy change and draft a Bill, they have to persuade the politicians of the ruling party to enact the Bill. The LDP has groups of politicians who have special interests in particular fields of administration. They are generally called *zoku-giinn* (politicians affiliated with particular interest groups) and often they belong to a committee inside the LDP on specific fields of interest. The LDP used to have a policy of requiring explanation by bureaucrats of new legislation before the relevant committee and requiring committee approval. Normally, therefore, bureaucrats explained a policy before these LDP committees and attempted to receive approval. If the policy or Bill was approved by the committee, then it would likely be approved by the LDP. Often, politicians evaluated the Bill based on the possible benefits to them and possible harm to their constituents. As a result of consultation, bureaucrats were often forced to amend a Bill or promise some benefits to politicians in return for their support.

Since Cabinet Bills were submitted only after approval by the relevant committee of the ruling party, they were destined to be supported by the members of the ruling party. Since the party's decision is generally binding on members of the party, it is rare to see divergent votes in the Diet. Most of the time, committee approval was thus sufficient to assure the passage of a Bill.

As a result, there has been controversy over who has stronger power in Japan, politicians or bureaucrats. Some argued that it is the bureaucrats who are actually making policy and the politicians who are merely serving as a check on them.[39] Others argued that these bureaucrats are in reality working in the interests of the ruling party and ultimately it is the politicians who control the bureaucrats.[40]

[39] TJ Pempel, 'The Bureaucratization of Policymaking in Postwar Japan' (1974) 18 *American Journal of Political Science* 647; C Johnson, *MITI and the Japanese Miracle: The Growth of Industrial Policy, 1925–1975* (Stanford, Stanford University Press, 1982).

[40] JM Ramseyer and F McCall Rosenbluth, *Japan's Political Marketplace* (Cambridge, Harvard University Press, 1993). See also, Yoshiro Miwa and JM Ramseyer, 'The Legislative Dynamic: Evidence from the Deregulation of Financial Services in Japan' in DH Foote (ed), *Law in Japan: A Turning Point* (Seattle, University of Washington Press, 2007) 153.

It is hard to say exactly which group has more authority in policy making. The relationship between bureaucrats and politicians is interactive and, moreover, depends on the historical context. When bureaucrats are criticised by the public for misbehaviour, for instance, politicians can assert stronger authority. When the ruling party is facing public criticism, on the other hand, bureaucrats can assert stronger power. One thing is certain; bureaucrats in Japan definitely have more power than bureaucrats in many other countries of the world.

The relationship between bureaucrats and politicians radically changed under the DPJ Government. Now instead of relying on initiatives of bureaucrats, the government insists on the initiatives of politicians. It is too early to tell whether this change of philosophy is actually bringing about the change in practices. Yet, the truth may still remain that bureaucrats in Japan maintain very strong power over legislative process.

CONCLUSION

Aspiring to establish representative democracy, the Constitution proclaimed the Diet to be the highest organ of the state and its sole legislative organ. Consisting of members directly elected by the people, the Diet is supposed to play the most important policy-making role in the government.

Yet, the reality is quite different. Most of the Bills introduced are Cabinet Bills, drafted by bureaucrats in the executive. The Diet merely gives approval to them. It is rare to find any heated discussion over the content of the legislation or any negotiation in the Diet, since Cabinet Bills are introduced into the Diet after approval of the ruling party and they are most likely to be passed by the majority in the Diet.

Moreover, since most of the Bills are Cabinet Bills drafted by government bureaucrats, these Bills are designed to give broad discretion to the bureaucrats. The executive departments have quite a wide discretion as a result of this broad delegation of power. The House has the power to investigate government affairs but it has been reluctant to exercise this power. Legislative control over the executive is thus quite insufficient.

This is a far cry from the status of the Diet as being the highest and sole legislative organ of the state.

FURTHER READING

GD Allinson and Yasunori Sone (eds), *Political Dynamics in Contemporary Japan* (Ithaca, Cornell University Press, 1993).

LD Hayes, *Introduction to Japanese Politics* 5th edn (Armonk, M.E. Sharpe, 2009) 47–60.

Takeshi Ishida and ES Krauss (eds), *Democracy in Japan* (Pittsburgh, University of Pittsburgh Press, 1989).

Purnendra Jain and Takeshi Inoguchi, *Japanese Politics Today: Beyond Karaoke Democracy?* (New York, St Martin's Press, 1997).

B Richardson, *Japanese Democracy: Power, Coordination, and Performance* (New Haven, Yale University Press, 1997) 127–51.

JAA Stockwin, *Governing Japan* 4th edn (Oxford, Blackwell Publishers, 2008) 156–78.

4

The Cabinet and the Executive Power

Introduction – PART I: THE STATUS OF THE CABINET AND THE PRIME MINISTER – The Cabinet – The Prime Minister and the Cabinet – PART II: THE POWERS OF THE CABINET – Executive Power – The Other Powers of the Cabinet – Emergency Powers – PART III: THE RELATIONSHIP BETWEEN THE CABINET AND THE DIET – The Parliamentary System – Dissolution of the House of Representatives – PART IV: THE PRIME MINISTER, THE CABINET AND BUREAUCRATS – The People Cannot Choose the Prime Minister – Weak Leadership Role of the Japanese Prime Minister – Executive Departments and Administrative Agencies – The Executive and Economic Policy – Strong Power of the Bureaucrats – Past Reforms and Future Reform Agenda – PART V: LEGAL CONTROL OF THE EXECUTIVE – Diet Control of the Executive – Due Process and Fair Procedure – Freedom of Information – Judicial Control over the Executive – Conclusion

INTRODUCTION

UNDER THE JAPANESE Constitution, it is the Cabinet that has been given the power to execute legislation passed by the Diet. The Diet is supposed to choose the Prime Minister and the Prime Minister is supposed to choose other ministers to form the Cabinet. The executive, consisting of the Cabinet Office and 11 ministries, under the supervision of the Cabinet, enforces the law passed by the Diet. The Cabinet is supposed to be jointly responsible to the Diet. The goal of responsible government will be then achieved.

Yet, in Japan, many people criticise the absence of an opportunity for the public to choose the Prime Minister; citizens have also criticised the Prime Ministers for their failure to play leadership roles. Moreover, it has been pointed out that the bureaucrats in the executive departments have strong policy-making power and politicians are not effectively controlling them. Is this true? What are the reasons for this criticism? What reforms are needed?

In this chapter, we will examine the status of the Cabinet and the Prime Minister, the power of the Cabinet and the relationship between the Cabinet and the Diet. We will also examine the interface between the politicians and bureaucrats inside the executive departments; we will explore past reforms and the future reform agenda.

PART I: THE STATUS OF THE CABINET AND THE PRIME MINISTER

THE CABINET

Chapter V: The Cabinet of the Japanese Constitution is devoted to the Cabinet and executive power. According to this chapter, executive power shall be vested in the Cabinet (article 65). The Cabinet is a collegial body consisting of the Prime Minister, who shall be its head, and other Ministers of State, as provided for by law (article 66, section 1). Unlike in the United States, where executive power is given to the President, Japan has adopted the system of giving executive power to the collegiate body.

The Prime Minister shall be designated from among the members of the Diet by a resolution of the Diet. This designation shall precede all other business (article 67, section 1). If the House of Representatives and the House of Councillors disagree and if no agreement can be reached even through a joint committee of both Houses, provided for by law, or the House of Councillors fails to make designation within ten days, exclusive of the period of recess, after the House of Representatives has made designation, the decision of the House of Representatives shall be the decision of the Diet (article 67, section 2). The Emperor then appoints the Prime Minister (article 6, section 1).

The Prime Minister shall appoint the Ministers of State (article 68). The Prime Minister can appoint non-members of the Diet as Ministers of State. However, a majority of their number must be chosen from among the members of the Diet (article 68).[1] The Prime Minister and other Ministers of State must be civilians (article 66, section 2).[2] The Prime Minister may remove the Ministers of State as he or she chooses (article 68).

The Cabinet system was developed in the United Kingdom to assist the Sovereign in exercising executive power. Originally, the Sovereign selected the Prime Minister on his or her discretion. The Cabinet was responsible to the Sovereign and exercised power based on the Sovereign's trust. Gradually, the Sovereign lost political power to the Cabinet. The convention of appointing the leader of the ruling party in the legislature as Prime Minister developed and the Cabinet came to exercise its power based on the trust of the legislature. The Cabinet was thus responsible to the legislature. This constitutional system is known as the 'Westminster model'.

The Meiji Constitution presumably intended to introduce this Cabinet system. Yet, under the Meiji Constitution, the Emperor was supposed to be assisted by individual Ministers of State (article 55) and there was no provision for the Cabinet. As a result, even though the Cabinet was created, its status was based on an executive order and the Prime Minister was not given any superior power over other ministers of state (he was regarded as *primus inter pares*, or 'first among equals'). Moreover, the Emperor had sovereign prerogatives, which could be exercised without advice from the ministers.

The Japanese Constitution intended to follow this tradition but decided to adopt the modern Westminster model. Unlike in the United Kingdom and other countries which have followed its tradition, however, the Japanese Constitution specifically provides for the Cabinet and also recognizes the role of the Diet to provide for the organization of the Cabinet. The Diet thus enacted the Cabinet Act to regulate the organization and activities of the Cabinet. The number of Ministers is

[1] In practice, the Prime Minister occasionally appoints one or two non-members of the Diet. Most Cabinet members are thus Diet members.

[2] This clause was inserted in the Constitution based on a request from the Far Eastern Commission, which was concerned with the possibility of remilitarization of Japan after the Ashida amendment. See below, ch 8, n 8. It has been construed to preclude current or prior professional military officers from the minister of state. Yet after the Self-Defence Force (SDF) was established, it has also been construed to exclude the current SDF officers from becoming ministers of state.

limited to 14 by the Cabinet Act but can be expanded to 17 in exceptional cases (Cabinet Act; article 3).

When there is a vacancy in the post of Prime Minister, the Cabinet shall resign en masse (article 70), but the Cabinet is supposed to continue its functions until the time when a new Prime Minister is appointed (article 71). The Constitution does not specify, however, who is supposed to exercise executive power when the Prime Minister dies suddenly or when he or she falls ill and is unable to exercise his or her power. The Cabinet Act provides that the Prime Minister can designate which Minister of State will act as Prime Minister in a case where the Prime Minister cannot perform his or her duties due to accidents or illness. This Minister is generally called as the deputy Prime Minister (article 9).The appointment is not mandatory, however, and it used to be quite common not to appoint such a deputy Prime Minister. As a result, there is a critical lacuna in the Constitution.[3]

In order to secure the smooth functioning of the Cabinet, the Constitution provides that the Ministers of State, during their tenure of office, shall not be subject to legal action without the consent of the Prime Minister. However, the right to take that action is not thereby impaired (article 75). It has been assumed that this provision only grants legal immunity from criminal prosecution during the ministers' terms of office. The Prime Minister should enjoy the same privilege during his or her term.

THE PRIME MINISTER AND THE CABINET

The Cabinet is a collegiate body. Therefore, the Cabinet is supposed to exercise its power through Cabinet meetings (Cabinet Act, article 4, section 1), and it has been assumed that the decision of the Cabinet

[3] In 2000, Keizou Obuchi the Prime Minister, collapsed from a stroke, lost consciousness and died 43 days later. Chief Cabinet Secretary Mikio Aoki announced that he had been appointed as acting Prime Minister and the Cabinet decided to resign en masse in order to choose a new Prime Minister. There were, however, questions as to how the Prime Minister, who could barely speak, could make such an appointment. It had been customary since then to designate the Cabinet Secretary Minister as the minister of state who is supposed to act as Prime Minister when the Prime Minister is unexpectedly incapacitated. Yukio Hatoyama, the DPJ Prime Minister, appointed Naoto Kan, Minister of State for National Policy, and later Finance Minister, as a deputy Prime Minister.

meeting has to be unanimous because the Cabinet is responsible to the Diet collectively. All the Cabinet ministers must personally sign the Cabinet decision in support of it. If some members disagree, the Cabinet cannot make a decision unless those ministers are dismissed and replaced with someone who supports the decision.[4]

Since the Cabinet is jointly responsible to the Diet, each member of the Cabinet should not express a different opinion from the official position of the Cabinet. The responsibility of the Cabinet as a whole does not prevent the Diet from passing a resolution calling for the resignation of a particular Cabinet member.

According to article 72, the Prime Minister, 'representing the Cabinet', submits Bills, reports on general national affairs and foreign relations to the Diet and exercises control and supervision over various administrative branches. Does the Prime Minister exercise this 'control and supervision over various administrative agencies' representing the Cabinet? Could he or she exercise this power without a Cabinet decision?

This issue was the focus of the *Lockheed Case*.[5] In this case, Kakuei Tanaka, the former Prime Minister, was prosecuted for receiving a bribe from the Marubeni Corporation, which represented the Lockheed Corporation, in exchange for ensuring the All Nippon Airways (ANA) Company purchased aircraft from it. The most significant issue centred on whether Tanaka had the power to direct ANA to purchase aircraft from a particular company or whether he had the power to direct the Transportation Minister to force ANA to purchase aircraft from a particular company. There was of course no specific Cabinet decision for either action. The majority of the Supreme Court held that the Prime Minister can at least advise and instruct the Transportation Minister to advise ANA to purchase aircraft from the Lockheed Corporation without a Cabinet decision, although he or she needs the Cabinet decision to control and supervise the administrative agency. The minority argued, however, that the Prime Minister can control and supervise the Transportation Minister without a Cabinet decision. Another minority of the Supreme Court insisted, however, that the Prime Minister could not act without a Cabinet decision but concluded that he could control the department by means of general Cabinet decisions. As a result

[4] See below, n 14.

[5] Supreme Court, grand bench, 22 February 1995, 49 *Minshu* 1. For the Lockheed bribery scandal, see PJ Herzog, *Japan's Pseudo-Democracy* (Sandgate, Japan Library, 1993) 158–73.

of this decision, it became clear that a Prime Minister's control and supervision must be based on a Cabinet decision, even though he or she can informally advise and instruct an agency without a Cabinet decision.

PART II: THE POWERS OF THE CABINET

EXECUTIVE POWER

The Constitution vests 'executive power' in the Cabinet. However, it does not specify what executive power means and what the implication of the grant of executive power to the Cabinet is.

The 'executive power,' as defined in article 65, has been interpreted by many academics to mean all governmental power except for legislative and judicial power or all governmental power to enforce legislation except for judicial power.[6] This residual theory perhaps fits with the historical development of the constitutional monarchy, where the legislature and the judiciary came to assert independence from the Sovereign. The Sovereign thus came to exercise all governmental power except for legislative and judicial power. Yet, this theory does not fit with the United States model, where executive power is given to the President while legislative power is given to Congress, and judicial power is vested in the courts. All these powers of the federal government are construed as limited in contrast to the state plenary power. Since, under the Japanese Constitution, the Emperor does not have any political power and three powers are distinguished and vested with three different branches separately, it makes more sense to also view the executive power as limited just as legislative and judicial power. The residual theory does not thus fit with this constitutional design. It could be argued, therefore, that like in the United States, executive power should be construed as limited to the power to execute the law.[7] Under this interpretation, even though the Japanese Constitution has adopted the Westminster model, the Japanese model is different from the UK model, since the Emperor

[6] Kiyomiya, 300–01; Ashibe, 307; Ito, 513.

[7] Nonaka II, 189–90 (Takahashi). Some argue that the executive power is the power to establish fundamental policies of the government and to supervize the executive agencies and that it is better characterized as the 'power to govern' as distinguished from mere execution of law. Sato, 211–13.

does not have any political powers and the Cabinet is not exercising the political power of the Emperor through advice and approval.

Although executive power is vested in the Cabinet, it has been construed that the Cabinet does not have to exercise all executive power by itself. In actual administration, executive power is exercised by each department of the executive and the Cabinet merely supervises these departments and coordinates their exercise of power.

What about the status of independent administrative agencies? Independent administrative agencies are often used in the United States as agencies equipped with quasi-legislative rulemaking power and quasi-judicial adjudicative power, and act independently from the President. In Japan, such administrative agencies were introduced during occupation. Although many of them were abolished or transformed into some sort of consultative body after the end of occupation, there still remain some important independent administrative agencies, such as the National Personnel Authority, the Fair Trade Commission and the National Public Safety Commission. It has been assumed that these independent administrative agencies are justified in the fields where there is a strong demand for political neutrality so long as there are sufficient controls by the Diet.[8]

THE OTHER POWERS OF THE CABINET

The Constitution vested some additional powers in the Cabinet. According to article 73, the Cabinet, in addition to other general administrative functions, shall perform the following functions:

1. Administer the law faithfully; conduct affairs of state;
2. Manage foreign affairs;
3. Conclude treaties. However, it shall obtain prior or, depending on circumstances, subsequent approval of the Diet;
4. Administer the civil service, in accordance with standards established by law;
5. Prepare the budget, and present it to the Diet;
6. Enact cabinet orders in order to execute the provisions of this Constitution and of the law. However, it cannot include penal provisions in such cabinet orders unless authorized by such law;

[8] Ashibe, 308; Sato, 217.

7. Decide on general amnesty, special amnesty, commutation of punishment, reprieve, and restoration of rights.

It is not clear whether these powers are among the executive powers vested in the Cabinet by article 65 or powers somehow different from executive power and specifically vested by article 73.

The power to administer the law faithfully naturally occupies the central part of the executive power. Yet, the meaning of the power to 'conduct affairs of state' is rather ambiguous. Traditionally, little emphasis had been placed on this power, for it has been regarded simply as the power to coordinate executive departments in the government. Many take the view that the Diet should be the central organ of the government and the Cabinet is simply an organ to enforce statutes passed by the Diet. As a result, however, the Cabinet has not played a significant role in the political process. Critics thus came to argue that the Cabinet should be given far stronger powers. They came to rely on the power to conduct affairs of state as the power to play a leadership role in the political process.[9] They argue that the Prime Minister, together with the Cabinet, should propose policies to be enforced during an election and should attempt to enforce those policies by introducing necessary legislation when it wins an election.

EMERGENCY POWERS

Some countries allow the President or Prime Minister to suspend the constitutional system and act without statutory authorization in times of emergency. There is no provision on emergencies in the Constitution, except for a provision on the emergency session of the House of Councillors when the House of Representatives is dissolved (article 54, section 2). As a result, there has been some dispute as to whether the Cabinet has emergency powers. Some argue that the Cabinet should be allowed to exercise emergency powers since 'emergency knows no law'. Yet, many academics tend to believe that the Cabinet cannot suspend the constitutional system and act without statutory authorization since such a power is not mentioned in the Constitution.[10]

[9] Sato, 211.

[10] Shugiin (House of Representatives), Anzenhoshou oyobi Kokusaikyouryoku tou ni kansuru chousa shouiinnkai (Research Subcommittee on National Security

This issue is quite significant since the government could not enact emergency legislation in order to allow necessary action even after the Self-Defence Force (SDF) was established. The SDF Act allows the SDF to engage in defence actions (article 76 and 88). Yet, in order to engage in defence actions, the SDF needs the power to ignore all obligations imposed by other statutes, to order the evacuation of the public, to restrict their freedom and order cooperation. Yet, no such power had been given in the past due to opposition to enactment of such emergency legislation (the SDF vehicles were not allowed to drive on other than the public roads even during the time of emergency).

The 9/11 terrorist attacks in the United States, together with tension with North Korea, have finally made it possible for the government to enact two pieces of emergency legislation. The Diet enacted the Armed Attack Act (Act Concerning the Peace and Independence of Our Country and Security of the Country as well as Citizens in Time of Situation of Armed Attack) in 2003, together with necessary amendments to the SDF Act. This enables the SDF to engage in defence activities and to prepare for attack by giving authority to the SDF to ignore a variety of regulatory statutes when engaging in such activities (such as SDF Act, article 92-2). Moreover, in 2004, the Diet enacted the Citizen Protection Act (Act Concerning the Protection of Citizens in the Situation of Armed Attack) in order to enable the government to order the mandatory evacuation of people who might suffer harm as a result of an attack, to order property owners to allow the passage of the SDF and to mandate local governments as well as some important private companies such as television companies, gas and utilities companies, transportation companies and hospitals to cooperate with the government in times of attack.

As a result of this legislation, the government is now authorized by statute to engage in defensive activities in times of armed attack or in anticipation of armed attack. Yet, there is no statute authorizing the government to suspend or restrict the civil rights and liberties of the citizenry during emergencies. Therefore, this issue will become significant when there is a necessity for taking such measures and when there is no time for the Diet to enact legislation.

and International Cooperation), 'Kinkyuujitai to Kenpou ni kansuru Kisoteki Siryou' ('Basic Materials for Emergency and the Constitution') (25 March 2004): www.shugiin.go.jp.

PART III: THE RELATIONSHIP BETWEEN THE CABINET AND THE DIET

THE PARLIAMENTARY SYSTEM

As stated above, the Cabinet system or the parliamentary system was developed in the United Kingdom. The Cabinet was created by the Sovereign to give advice to him or her. It was responsible only to the Sovereign. Gradually, however, the Sovereign came to select the Prime Minister from the ruling party in Parliament. The Cabinet came to be responsible to both the Sovereign and to Parliament. Eventually, the Sovereign gradually lost almost all political powers and the Cabinet came to be held responsible to the majority in the Parliament. In the modern British system, the House of Commons has the power to pass a no-confidence resolution against the Cabinet and the Cabinet has in return the power to dissolve the House of Commons.

Similar systems came to be adopted in other countries as well. In France, however, the Cabinet lost virtually all power to dissolve the legislature since such power was regarded as undemocratic. As a result, the legislature had superior power over the Cabinet during the Third and Fourth Republics. The government was thus placed in inferior status to the legislature.

Although it is clear that the Japanese Constitution adopted the parliamentary system, there are some doubts as to whether the Japanese system is closer to the British Westminster model or to the traditional French model. This issue came to be discussed in relation to the power of dissolution of the House of Representatives.

DISSOLUTION OF THE HOUSE OF REPRESENTATIVES

The Cabinet, in the exercise of executive power, shall be collectively responsible to the Diet (article 66, section 3). The Constitution gives the House of Representatives the power to pass a no-confidence resolution, to force the Cabinet to resign en masse or to call for a general election. Thus, if the House of Representatives passes a no-confidence resolution, or rejects a confidence resolution, the Cabinet shall resign en masse, unless the House of Representatives is dissolved within ten days (article 69). If the Prime Minister decides to resign, then the Diet will select a new Prime Minister. Until the new Prime Minister is appointed, the Cabinet will continue to function (article 71). If the Prime Minister decides to dissolve the House of the Representatives, the Emperor then announces its dissolution based on the advice and approval of the Cabinet (article 7, item 3). A general election is supposed to be conducted within 40 days from the date of dissolution, and the Diet must be convoked within 30 days from the date of the election (article 54). On the first convocation of the Diet after a general election of members of the House of Representatives, the Cabinet shall resign en masse (article 70).

The Constitution does not have any provision on when the House of Representatives can be dissolved except as provided in article 69. It is thus unclear whether the Prime Minister can dissolve the House of Representatives without a no-confidence resolution against the Cabinet. But Prime Ministers in the past have dissolved the House of Representatives even without a no-confidence resolution.[11] The justification for such dissolution remains ambiguous.

Prime Ministers have resorted to article 7 as a basis for dissolution. Some indeed argue that article 7 could be a textual source for the Emperor to dissolve the House of Representatives and the Cabinet could decide the dissolution by way of its power to give advice and approval to the Emperor.[12] Yet, the Constitution denies the Emperor any power related to the government (article 4, section 1). Giving the power to make a decision on dissolution of the House of Representatives to the Emperor under article 7 would violate this basic principle. Therefore, article 7 must be read merely to authorize the Emperor to announce the dissolution rather than to make a decision on dissolution. The power of giving advice and approval of the Cabinet to the Emperor thus merely enables the Cabinet to give advice and consent on the procedure for announcing the dissolution (the Emperor signs the imperial document

[11] Votes of no-confidence were passed only four times out of 21 dissolutions in the postwar period. Other dissolutions were all based on discretionary decisions of the Prime Minister. The most recent no-confidence vote was passed in 1993 against the Kiichi Miyazawa Cabinet, which failed to pass a political reform Bill despite its avowed commitment to it. Some members of the LDP voted for the no-confidence motion, thus triggering a general election.

[12] Nonaka II, 207 (Takahashi).

calling for the dissolution of the House and the House will be dissolved when this document is read by the chairperson in the House). Article 7 should not therefore be construed to authorize the Prime Minister to dissolve the House of Representatives.

Thus, in order to justify the dissolution by the Prime Minister without a no-confidence resolution, authority must be sought elsewhere. Some therefore argue that because of the necessity of balance of power between Parliament and the Cabinet, the Cabinet must be allowed to exercise the power to dissolve the House. It is doubtful, however, that there must be such a balance of power between the Diet and the Cabinet and that dissolution serves to preserve such a balance. Therefore, that authority must be inferred from the 'structure of the Constitution', ie, from fact that the Japanese Constitution is based on the Westminster model and the power to dissolve the House is necessary to hold the Cabinet responsible based on the public trust.[13] Then, one can argue that the Cabinet has a power to dissolve the House even when the no-confidence resolution was not passed according to article 69, while giving the Emperor merely a power to announce the dissolution already decided by the Cabinet.

Under either interpretation, however, the power to dissolve the House of Representatives is believed to belong to the personal decision of the Prime Minister, although technically it belongs to the Cabinet.

Even if the Cabinet is justified in dissolving the House of Representatives without a no-confidence resolution, most would agree that the Cabinet needs some justification for dissolution. The Cabinet might be justified in dissolving the House of Representatives, for instance, when there is a very important issue for the Cabinet to consult public opinion, when a very important Bill introduced by the Cabinet is rejected by the Diet, when there is a significant reorganization of a coalition of parties, when the Cabinet wants to change its fundamental policy or when the end of the term is approaching. Dissolution without such justification is deemed to be illicit.[14]

[13] Sato, 170–71.

[14] Koizumi, the Prime Minister dissolved the House of Representatives when the Bill to privatize the postal service, a Bill he strongly pushed, was rejected by the House of Councillors in August 2005. See above ch 3, p 81. He had to dismiss Yoshinobu Shimamura, the Agriculture, Forestry and Fisheries Minister, who refused to sign the Cabinet decision, to dissolve the House. There was a dispute as to the constitutionality of this dissolution.

However, it is doubtful whether the Supreme Court can review the constitutionality of dissolution of the House. In the *Tomabechi Case*,[15] a former member of the House of Representatives challenged the constitutionality of the 1952 dissolution of the House and sought payment of remuneration for Diet members. The Supreme Court held that the dissolution of the House raised a highly political question, which directly involves democratic governance, and the issue should be placed beyond the reach of judicial courts. He was challenging the dissolution because it was made according to article 7 without a no-confidence resolution as stipulated in article 69 and also there was allegedly no Cabinet decision to give advice and approval on the dissolution to the Emperor. As a result, even if the dissolution of the House was illicit, there would be no legal recourse.

PART IV: THE PRIME MINISTER, THE CABINET AND BUREAUCRATS

THE PEOPLE CANNOT CHOOSE THE PRIME MINISTER

Under the Japanese Constitution, the Diet is supposed to select the Prime Minister. As a result, the people do not have a say in the selection of the Prime Minister.

Theoretically speaking, the public votes for a political party expecting that the leader of that political party will become the Prime Minister. In the UK, for instance, where there are two prominent parties that compete with each other, voters can cast votes for the Conservative Party or the Labour Party expecting the party leader to become the Prime Minister if their party wins the majority of seats in Parliament. In Japan, the Liberal Democratic Party (LDP), which practically ruled the country from 1955 to 2009, consists of various 'factions' and the Prime Minister used to be chosen in closed-door talks among leaders of these factions. Factions are groups of LDP members headed by particular leaders and are committed to different ideologies. Affiliation with powerful factions helped LDP members to be appointed as executive members of the

[15] Supreme Court, grand bench, 8 June 1960, 14 *Minshu*, 1206. See below, ch 5, n 50.

party, as well as ministers of state, and helped them to receive financial help and support in elections. The faction leaders were also candidates for the position of president of the LDP and Prime Minister. Although there has been a call to abolish factions, factions remain an enduring characteristic of the LDP. As a result, even voters who had voted for the LDP did not know who would be chosen as Prime Minister.[16]

There have been some efforts to vest in the people the right to select the Prime Minister.[17] The most drastic proposal is to amend the Constitution and grant the public the right to vote for Prime Minister. Under this proposal, it is probable that the Prime Minister will become much more like a President under the US Constitution. Another possibility is to amend the Constitution to mandate political parties to select their candidates for Prime Minister at the time of a general election. Yet another possibility is the creation of a mechanism that allows the public to choose the candidate for Prime Minister while leaving the final decision to the Diet.

These proposals have been opposed, however, because they would give a very strong political mandate to the Prime Minister, even allowing him or her to act as a dictator.

WEAK LEADERSHIP ROLE OF THE JAPANESE PRIME MINISTER

In the past, Japanese Prime Ministers have not played strong leadership roles. Since the Prime Minister under the LDP Government used to be chosen in closed-door talks among leaders of various factions, many of the leaders preferred the person to play a coordinating role among these factions. It was difficult for a person of strong character to become the leader of a faction in the first place. It is likely that many leaders must

[16] Recently, the LDP has conducted elections by party members to choose their president. However, the fact remains that the public is excluded from the selection. In the general election of 2005, Koizumi, the Prime Minister, won a landslide victory on the issue of privatization of the postal service. Yet, since he had stepped down, Prime Ministers Shinzo Abe, Yasuo Fukuda and Tarou Aso had been chosen as Prime Ministers without public election. In 2009, however, the DPJ won a landslide victory in the general election and the DPJ leader, Yukio Hatoyama, was appointed as the new Prime Minister. Yet, after Hatoyama stepped down in 2010, Naoto Kan was elected by the DPJ Diet members as his successor and became the Prime Minister.

[17] The Advisory Council on Public Selection of the Prime Minister, *Final Report* (7 August 2002): www.kantei.go.jp/jp/singi/kousen/kettei/020807houkoku.html.

have believed that if they chose a person of strong character, that person might acquire strong popular support and could prevent other leaders from becoming the next Prime Minister. Moreover, Japanese Prime Ministers did not remain in office for a long time.[18] Since the leader of the LDP did not have strong leadership power and was always threatened by other faction leaders who aspired to become the next Prime Minister, a Prime Minister in Japan was more likely to be forced to step down for losing an election or because of a scandal. Further, most Prime Ministers usually did not have sufficient time to play leadership roles.

Although the Prime Minister has the power to appoint ministers of state, in reality, these appointments used to be based on recommendations from leaders of various factions under the LDP Government. The most important consideration for appointment of ministers of state was to keep the proper balance among the various factions. Seniority was another important consideration. The Prime Minister did not have much of a choice when deciding on this appointment. Even though he had the power to dismiss a minister of state, he could not do so without regard to maintaining a good relationship with the leader of the faction to which the minister of state belongs. Since the decision of the Cabinet meeting was supposed to be made by unanimous vote, sometimes opposition from some ministers had prevented the Cabinet from supporting the proposal the Prime Minister was contemplating.

We have to wait and see whether the DPJ Prime Ministers will, or will not be different.

EXECUTIVE DEPARTMENTS AND ADMINISTRATIVE AGENCIES

The executive branch is currently comprised of the Cabinet office and 11 ministries: the Ministry of Internal Affairs and Communication; the Ministry of Justice; the Ministry of Foreign Affairs; the Ministry of Finance; the Ministry of Education, Culture, Sport, Science and Technology (MEXT); the Ministry of Health, Labour and Welfare; the Ministry of Agriculture, Forestry and Fisheries; the Ministry of Economy, Trade and Industry (METI); the Ministry of Land, Infrastructure, Transport and Tourism; the Ministry of the Environment and the

[18] The average length of office for one Prime Minister in the postwar period is 796 days. The shortest is 54 for Higashikuninomiya, Prime Minister in 1945. The average length of office for one Cabinet is 272 days: www.verde01.com/index.html.

Ministry of Defence. The National Police Agency is supervised by the National Public Safety Commission established in the Cabinet Office and the SDF is supervised by the Ministry of Defence. The Imperial House Agency is also placed in the Cabinet Office.

There are some independent administrative agencies, although they are established in some of the departments. The Public Personnel Authority, established directly under the Cabinet, is an independent agency which supervises the personnel decisions concerning national public workers. The National Public Safety Commission, established under the authority of the Prime Minister as an outside office of Cabinet Office, supervises the national police force. The Fair Trade Commission, also acting under the authority of the Prime Minister as an outside office of the Cabinet Office, enforces the Anti-trust Act (Act Concerning Prohibition of Private Monopolization and Assurance of Fair Trade). Although these agencies are carrying out some important functions, the executive departments play a far more important role in Japan.

At one time there were public corporations which provided necessary services to the public, eg, the National Railroad, Japan Tobacco Corporation and Japan Telephone and Telegraph, but all were later privatised during the 1980s in response to an increased call for privatization. The Postal Service also used to be a public corporation but it was also privatised in 2007 (its status will be reconsidered under the DPJ Government). These are called 'special companies', as distinguished from regular private companies. However, there are also many 'independent administrative corporations', which provide public services for the government. Almost all of the workers for these corporations are treated as national public workers. These independent administrative corporations are often criticised for accepting former executive bureaucrats of the central government after early retirement as their executives and paying handsome retirement benefits for meaningless service. The reduction in the number of such corporations and further privatization has been a focus of debate for some time.

THE EXECUTIVE AND ECONOMIC POLICY

Some 300,000 classified national public workers are working in the central government. Of these, 15,000 of them are Class I national public workers, occupying the supervisory positions in each department. They have to pass a national examination and must be hired by each department. The examination is highly competitive and most of those who have passed are graduates of prestigious universities, such as the University of Tokyo or the University of Kyoto. They are literally the best and brightest; they make policy decisions for the government, enforce the statutes passed by the Diet and draft the Bills to be submitted to the Diet.

There is a dispute as to precisely what role the bureaucrats played in economic development after the Pacific War. Japan managed to achieve a magnificent economic recovery following the devastation of the Pacific War and went on to become one of the leading economies of the world. In particular, after Hayato Ikeda, the Prime Minister, announced his policy of doubling the incomes of Japanese households in 1960, government agencies established economic development policies in an attempt to promote economic development. Some argue that the Ministry of International Trade and Industry (MITI), predecessor of the current Ministry of Economy, Trade and Industry (METI), played a pivotal role in economic development;[19] others, however, say that the MITI was not always successful and that other factors, such as the stable political policies of the LDP and some peculiarities of Japanese companies and employment practices, also played a significant role.[20]

Whatever role the government bureaucrats have played, such a role was made possible by the existence of various statutes requiring permits and approval from the government to engage in various business activities and by vesting agencies with very broad regulatory powers. Moreover, if there is any need for additional power, it is these bureaucrats who are supposed to draft legislation. It is no wonder that most of the statutes grant very broad authority to the agencies and allow them to implement the statutes by orders.

Furthermore, the agency bureaucrats often use informal 'administrative guidance' to control the behaviour of the public and to regulate industries. Administrative guidance is considered advice from the agency and has no legally binding power. It may be issued by letter or notice or by oral communication. It advises the public to act in a certain way or to avoid certain conduct. It can be issued without explicit statutory authorization. For instance, many municipalities have development guidelines, advising

[19] C Johnson, *MITI and the Japanese Miracle: The Growth of Industrial Policy, 1925–1975* (Stanford, Stanford University Press, 1982).

[20] DI Okimoto, *Between MITI and the Market: Japanese Industrial Policy for High Technology* (Stanford, Stanford University Press, 1989).

developers to meet certain demands beyond statutory requirements, like construction of a park or cooperation with the establishment of school, when the developer plans for a large-scale housing development. If developers are unwilling to obey these guidelines, municipal governments can refuse acceptance of the application for development permit or, in some cases, refuse to supply water.[21]

Industries and private businesses are generally willing to comply with administrative guidance. In order to cooperate with the agencies, major industries have formed industrial associations. Most companies also accepted former executive bureaucrats as their executives after early retirement in order to maintain good relationships with the government. The bureaucrats can thus control industries without resorting to legal powers. Such a close relationship between government and regulated industries has made it possible to achieve coordinated effort for economic development.

STRONG POWER OF THE BUREAUCRATS

As noted above, there is a very strong bureaucratic system in Japan. Although bureaucrats are supposed to work for a particular minister of state, who is in charge of a department, political control over bureaucrats is often not strong enough; there are several reasons for this.

First, the number of politicians involved in the supervision of bureaucrats is quite small. Although the Prime Minister can appoint several senior vice-ministers as well as junior vice-ministers to each department,[22] the total number of politicians who are supposed to supervise bureaucrats is still limited. Secondly, under the LDP Government, the appointment of ministers was generally made based on seniority and with regard

[21] The Court has held, however, that the refusal of the municipality to supply water as a sanction against the refusal to obey the development guideline is illegal, since the municipally is required to conclude water supply contracts with residents: Supreme Court, 2nd petty bench, 8 November 1989, 1382 *Hanreijihou* 16. The Court also held that the de facto imposition of the burden to cooperate with the education of children in the development project over the explicit rejection by the developer is illegal: Supreme Court, 1st petty bench, 18 February 1993, 47 *Minshu* 574. See further below, n 27.

[22] Under the 2009 LDP Aso Cabinet, 23 senior-vice-ministers and 27 vice-ministers were appointed from the Diet. Under the DPJ Hatoyama Cabinet, 25 senior-vice-ministers and 22 vice-ministers were appointed.

to keeping a balance among various factions inside the LDP. As a result, the chosen minister often did not have sufficient knowledge and experience in the particular field of the department he or she was supposed to supervise. Thirdly, the Cabinet changes quite often in Japan and most ministers therefore do not stay for long, making it difficult for them to effectively control bureaucrats.

In the past, therefore, when the minister was questioned during committee sessions of the Diet as to the actual administration of the department, he or she usually asked the senior bureaucrats participating in the Diet sessions as government committee members to answer the questions. Even when this practice was abolished in 2001, forcing the ministers to answer questions personally, most of the ministers' answers were prepared by bureaucrats and the ministers simply read them in the session.

Moreover, the entire agenda of the Cabinet meeting used to be decided in a meeting of administrative vice-ministers, the top bureaucrats of all departments. An item opposed by any member would not be put on the official agenda of the Cabinet meeting. It was probable that any such item would not be discussed in the first place, since only items which are supported by all relevant agencies can be picked up.

PAST REFORMS AND THE FUTURE REFORM AGENDA

There have been some efforts to change the dominance of bureaucrats and weak political control as well as the weak leadership role of the Prime Minister. In particular during the period of administrative reform in the 1990s, there were attempts to give the Prime Minister stronger powers and to elevate the status and power of the Cabinet over the administrative agencies.

The Council for Administrative Reform thus issued its final report in 1997,[23] proposing the strengthening of the power of both the Cabinet and the Prime Minister. The report was written on the assumption that the Cabinet is supposed to perform more of a political function in order to conduct affairs of state and that the Cabinet is the body that carries out the policy decisions of the Prime Minister. In order to strengthen

[23] Administrative Reform Council, *Final Report* (3 December 1997): www.kantei.go.jp/jp/gyokaku/report-final/index.html.

the power of the Cabinet, the report proposed the adoption of majority vote rather than a unanimous Cabinet decision, a measure to allow the minister to talk about issues not included on the agenda approved by the meeting of administrative vice-ministers, and reducing the number of ministers. In order to strengthen the power of the Prime Minister, the report proposed an explicit statutory provision allowing the Prime Minister to propose fundamental policy issues at Cabinet meetings, a more flexible power for the Prime Minister to supervise administrative departments and the creation of an administrative department to enable the Prime Minister to play a more active role in policy making. As a result of this report, the Cabinet Act was amended to reflect many of its proposals.[24]

As a result of these changes, the power of the Cabinet as well as of the Prime Minister has definitely been strengthened on the face of the law. Yet, it is doubtful whether these changes brought significant alteration in the actual relationship between politicians and bureaucrats.

During the 2009 House of Representatives election, the Democratic Party of Japan (DPJ) strongly argued for the necessity of political control over bureaucrats. After winning the election, the DPJ abolished the meeting of administrative vice-ministers, prohibited bureaucrats from explaining policy issues to the media, stopped relying on the briefing of bureaucrats before official interviews with ministers and stopped relying on bureaucrats explaining the details of the administration in the Diet. The DPJ Government is also planning to increase the number of politicians working in the executive supervising bureaucrats and even to ban bureaucrats from explaining administrative details in the Diet. The DPJ Government also plans to prohibit bureaucrats from becoming executives of independent administrative corporations and other public organizations after retirement, cut government spending to these independent administrative corporations that accept bureaucrats as their executives and to cut down the number of these independent administrative corporations. It will be very interesting to see whether these changes fundamentally alter the dominance of bureaucrats in Japanese government.

[24] Kazuyuki Takahashi, 'Ongoing Changes in the Infrastructure of a Constitutional System: From "Bureaucracy" to Democracy' in DH Foote (ed), *Law in Japan: A Turning Point* (Seattle, University of Washington Press, 2007) 237, 242–47. The provision on voting in Cabinet meetings was not inserted, since unanimous voting is merely customary and it is still believed that Cabinet decisions must be unanimous.

PART V: LEGAL CONTROL OF THE EXECUTIVE

DIET CONTROL OF THE EXECUTIVE

The Japanese Constitution presupposes that the Diet must supervise the executive departments. The Diet can pass statutes to control the executive departments. Each House also has the power to investigate the affairs of state. Yet, as stated in chapter three, in actual practice, these legislative controls of the executive are quite ineffective in Japan.

First of all, most Bills are drafted by bureaucrats and submitted to the Diet and most of these Bills are meant to give very broad legislative power to the executive department. As stated above, even though there are limits to the delegation of legislative power, the Supreme Court has been very reluctant to strike down this broad legislative delegation. Because of the parliamentary system, the Cabinet and the majority of the Diet belong to the same political party. It is no wonder that the Diet has no incentive to interfere with the Cabinet and the executive. Secondly, although each House has the power to investigate executive affairs, the majority of the Diet is reluctant to investigate any maladministration or misconduct of the executive department, since the Cabinet is supported by the majority party in the Diet.

As a result, in order to increase legislative control over the executive, some reforms, such as re-invigoration of the non-delegation doctrine and revision to allow one-third of the members of the House to summon witnesses to testify, must be introduced.

DUE PROCESS AND FAIR PROCEDURE

Unlike in the UK or the United States, where natural justice or due process requires procedural justice, many civil law countries had no tradition of demanding fair procedure before administrative agencies. Under the Meiji Constitution, therefore, there was no constitutional guarantee of fair procedure as to administrative process.

Under the Japanese Constitution, however, article 31 provides that '[n]o person shall be deprived of life or liberty, nor shall any other criminal penalty be imposed, except according to procedure established by law' and is construed as protecting due process. It has been argued that article 31 should also be applied to administrative procedure. Yet, the Supreme Court has been rather ambiguous about the reach of article 31 and has been reluctant to demand fair procedure beyond the procedure required by statute.

In the *Narita International Airport Act Case*,[25] for instance, the Supreme Court was faced with the question of whether article 31 requires administrative agencies to provide for the opportunity for a hearing before issuing an order prohibiting the use of property for public gatherings. Some local residents strongly opposed the construction of Narita International Airport and radical student groups came to support their opposition. The opposing farmers and radical members built a 'fortress' on the property owned by these farmers inside the controlled area to prevent the operation of the airport. The Diet passed the Emergency Measures Act Concerning the Security of the New Tokyo International Airport. This allowed the Transportation Minister to issue an order prohibiting the use of property inside the controlled area as a gathering place for members of groups engaging in violent mass destruction activities. The opposing farmers challenged the order as a violation of article 31, among other things, since they were not afforded any opportunity for a hearing before the order. Although article 31 is mainly focused on criminal proceedings, the Supreme Court held that administrative procedure is not wholly exempt from its application for the simple reason that the procedure is not criminal in nature. Yet, even when article 31 is to be applied, the Supreme Court stated that the necessity of an advance hearing should be decided by balancing the content and nature of the interests involved, and the degree of restriction, against the nature and degree of public interest and the necessity for urgency. It concluded that it was not a violation of the 'basic philosophy' of article 31 for the Transportation Minister to issue the order without affording an opportunity for a hearing.

In the past, the government was unwilling to enact a comprehensive administrative procedure act to demand uniform fair procedure. Some regulatory statutes demanded some kind of procedure, yet most of them did not require any specific procedure. As a result, procedural rights were not well protected in Japan.

[25] Supreme Court, grand bench, 1 July 1992, 46 *Minshu* 437.

Trade conflict during the 1980s brought a fierce cry for transparency and fair procedure in the face of regulation from foreign countries, especially the United States. The government finally decided to enact the Administrative Procedure Act in 1993.[26] There are many loopholes, however, in this Act, which has many exclusions (article 3) and exceptions and as a result its applicability is severely limited. Moreover, it basically requires a trial-type hearing only in the case of adverse legal action by the administrative agencies, such as revocation of licences (article 13, section 1, item 1). It also requires an informal procedure before decision on applications, such as the rejection of an application (article 13, section 1, item 2). All other procedures are totally immune from any procedural requirements. It is, therefore, quite questionable whether this Act drastically alters procedural protection before the administrative agencies.[27]

FREEDOM OF INFORMATION

Traditionally, the administrative agencies did not have any obligation to disclose their documents. The management of governmental documents used to be regarded as a matter of internal management to be decided at the discretion of the agencies. As a result, citizens did not have any legal recourse to force the agencies to disclose documents. With the rising call for transparency in the government process, however, the government ultimately decided to enact the Information Disclosure Act (Act Concerning Disclosure of Public Information Held by the Administrative Agencies) in 1999.[28]

[26] Katsuya Uga, 'Development of the Concept of Transparency and Accountability in Japanese Administrative Law' in DH Foote (ed), *Law in Japan: A Turning Point* (Seattle, University of Washington Press, 2007) 276, 277–88.

[27] Uga, *ibid*, 288–91; K Duck, 'Comment: Now That the Fog has Lifted: The Impact of Japan's Administrative Procedures Law on the Regulation of Industry and Market Governance' (1996) 19 *Fordham International Law Journal* 1686. It must be noted that the Administrative Procedure Act does not require any procedure before rule making, but the government decided to introduce the public comment system before adoption of a rule. See Uga, *ibid*, 291–93. The Administrative Procedure Act also requires agencies to hand down a written document regarding administrative guidance when requested (art 35) and prohibits agencies from forcing the acceptance of guidance if it is refused (art 33).

[28] Uga, *ibid*, 293–98; D Boling, 'Access to Government-held Information in Japan: Citizens' "Right to Know" Bows to the Bureaucracy' (1998) 34 *Stanford Journal of International Law* 1.

Under the Act, anyone can request the administrative agencies of the government to disclose the public documents used in the agencies (article 3). On receiving a request, the agencies must decide whether to disclose or to refuse disclosure. The agencies cannot refuse disclosure unless some of the information contained in a requested document falls within narrowly defined exceptions, such as information infringing personal privacy, national security, or public safety, or information which will make it difficult to make a decision or to execute duties (article 5). If the agencies refuse the request, the claimant can file an objection to the decision and the agency head is required to submit the case to the Freedom of Information and Privacy Protection Commission established inside the Cabinet Office (article 18). The Commission consists of full-time commissioners and part-time commissioners who are appointed among lawyers, academics and professionals. The Commission reviews the objection and issues a report. The agencies are supposed to accept the report and decide whether to disclose the documents, although this requirement is not legally binding.

As a result of this Act, a large number of requests have been filed in the administrative agencies and a significant number of objections filed with the Commission. The Commission has been quite active in vindicating the rights of individuals. Even the courts have showed their willingness to enforce this Act rather strictly. While there are still limits to the freedom of information, this Act has proven to be an effective tool for controlling the executive departments.[29]

JUDICIAL CONTROL OVER THE EXECUTIVE

Judicial control over the executive is generally quite ineffective in Japan. Unlike the Meiji Constitution, the Japanese Constitution vests the power to adjudicate on matters of the administrative agencies in the judicial courts (article 76, section 1). The Constitution prohibits the establishment of special courts, such as administrative courts, or to give final adjudicative power to administrative agencies (article 76, section 2). The judicial courts are expected to legally control the executive.

However, the Diet passed the Administrative Case Litigation Act in 1962 to provide for special procedures for attacking the conduct of

[29] Uga, *ibid*, 298–300.

administrative agencies. After the Pacific War, administrative cases were heard as civil cases under the Code of Civil Procedure. The courts had a power to order interim remedies against the defendants even before the courts gave final judgments. During the occupation, however, when the SCAP attempted to expel Rikizou Hirano, the Agriculture Minister of the socialist Katayama coalition Cabinet from the government for his past ultra-militant behaviour, Hirano filed a civil suit asking the court to preserve his status until the final court judgment. The court order, which was favourable to Hirano, upset the SCAP, and in 1948 the SCAP forced the Diet to pass the Act Concerning Special Treatment of Administrative Cases to limit the provisional remedies of the court in administrative cases. The 1962 Administrative Case Litigation Act is the successor to the 1948 legislation.

According to the Administrative Case Litigation Act, the basic cause of action against administrative agencies used to be a suit seeking judicial revocation of an order of the relevant agency (article 3, section 2). This means that citizens were not allowed to seek judicial review in advance of actual application. No pre-enforcement suits were thus allowed. Moreover, it was only an 'order' that was subject to judicial review. The courts could not review the legality of a plan or administrative guidance, since they do not have any legal effect. Furthermore, the only remedy available used to be judicial revocation of an order. The agencies were free to make the same order for different reasons. The courts could not order the agencies to act in a certain way. At one time there was an argument that judicial injunction or mandamus against the executive is against the constitutional separation of powers principle. Moreover, in order to file a suit for judicial revocation, the plaintiff had to show standing (article 9), ie, that the plaintiff had a sufficient legal right or interest to challenge the administrative action. The courts often denied standing when it could not find a specific statute which granted individual legal rights or interests.[30]

There was also no provisional remedy available. Even when a citizen filed a suit, the administrative agency could continue its conduct (article 25, section 1). The courts were authorized to suspend the conduct of the agency under special circumstances (article 25, section 2). Yet, the court order had to be revoked when the Prime Minister objected to a suspension order, invoking the public interest (article 27). Moreover,

[30] See below, ch 5, pp 136–37.

even when the court found an administrative order illegal, it could refuse to invalidate it, if it found the public interest outweighed the interest requiring invalidation (article 31). This mechanism made it difficult for the court to hold the administrative action to be illegal.

As a result, the number of administrative cases was limited to almost 3000 to 4000 cases a year[31] and the government won in almost 85–90 per cent of cases.[32] It was simply too difficult for a citizen to challenge the administrative agencies. Frustrated with ineffective judicial control, many citizens came to demand the revision of the Administrative Case Litigation Act. The Diet finally decided to revise it in 2004 as a part of judicial reform in order to facilitate administrative litigation. The amendment thus made clear that the standing requirement could be met after considering all the relevant statutory provisions (article 9, section 2). It also added provisions on injunction suits and suits seeking to mandate the agencies to act in certain way (article 3, sections 6 and 7, articles 37-2, 37-3 and 37-4).

When the administrative agencies infringe the rights and legal interests of an individual, that individual can seek damages against the government according to the Government Liability Act. This Act was enacted to conform with article 17 of the Constitution. This was a radical change from the Meiji Constitution, according to which the government did not have any legal obligation to pay damages for illegal exercise of power.

In order to seek damages, the injured individual must prove that government officials illegally infringed his or her rights or legal interests, that the infringement was intentional or the result of negligence, that there was damage and that the damage was caused by the illegal exercise of power (article 1). The injured individual can also seek damages if he or she suffered injury as a result of some faulty structure or mismanagement of a public facility (article 2). However, the court will dismiss the claim if the plaintiff cannot prove any infringement of rights or legal interests. Moreover, the courts tend to require proof of egregious breach of duties in order to find a public official negligent. Finally, the only available remedy is a damages award. As the courts are more willing to award

[31] Supreme Court, Judicial Statistics (2007): www.courts.go.jp/sihotokei/nenpo/pdf/B19DMIN1-2.PDF.

[32] Japan Federation of Bar Associations, 'Shihou no gyousei nitaisuru check kinou shitsumon koumoku nitaisuru kaitou' ('A Reply to Questionnaire on the Checking Function over the Executive by the Judiciary') (26 December 2000): www.kantei.go.jp/jp/sihouseido/dai42/pdfs/42nitibenren.pdf.

damages than to invalidate the actions of the administrative agencies, the damage suit is still therefore an ineffective control over the executive.[33]

CONCLUSION

It is the Cabinet which is granted the executive power under the Constitution and the Prime Minister is supposed to lead the Cabinet in executing the statutes passed by the Diet. Yet, in reality, the Japanese Prime Minister has not played much of a leadership role in the past and Cabinets have not been expected to fulfil the leading role in politics. As Japan is heading towards an era in which there is no clear blueprint for the future and there are no clear-cut goals to achieve, someone must play a role in proposing such goals and must take on a leadership role. Although many used to expect the Diet to play the most important role in coordinating and adjusting various interests to achieve consensus, it is doubtful whether the Diet is a body suited to such a task. It is the Prime Minister and the Cabinet that should play more of a leadership role in formulating government policy and in attempting to implement it though the Diet.

Moreover, legislative, political and judicial controls over the agency bureaucrats are all insufficient. Bureaucrats dominate the legislative process and the Cabinet and ministers seem to lack political power. Although they cannot ignore the interests of the ruling party, and most often they cooperate with the ruling party in implementing policies supported by Cabinet, they tend to have independent interests and are not totally subordinated to political control. Provided with broad powers and the ability to hand down informal administrative guidance, they are able to exercise very broad discretion.

There is thus a critical need to strengthen political control of the executive, legislative control by the Diet and judicial control. The attempt to increase the leadership role of the Prime Minister and to strengthen

[33] Moreover, many of the civil prosecutors defending the suit against the government were judges, who were seconded to the Ministry of Justice. The Supreme Court sends roughly 50 judges to prosecutors' offices including 16 to 17 judges as civil prosecutors every year. The Justice Committee of the House of Representatives (14 October 2005) (statement of parliament secretary Takashi Mitsuhashi of the Ministry of Justice): www.shugiin.go.jp/index.nsf/html/index_kaigiroku.htm. They will return to the courts as judges and hear the cases against the government.

political control by the Cabinet is surely a step towards that goal. Yet, there is definitely a need for further reform.

FURTHER READING

B Richardson, *Japanese Democracy: Power, Coordination, and Performance* (New Haven, Yale University Press, 1997) 95–126.

JM Schlesinger, *Shadow Shoguns: The Rise and Fall of Japan's Postwar Political Machine* (Stanford, Stanford University Press, 1997).

JAA Stockwin, *Governing Japan* 4th edn (Oxford, Blackwell, 2008) 48–155.

Karel van Wolferen, *The Enigma of Japanese Power* (London, Macmillan, 1989).

5

The Courts and the Judicial Power

Introduction – PART I: THE COURTS – The Courts and Judicial Power – Structure of the Courts – Judges – Independence of the Judges and the Judiciary – Judicial Process – Judicial Reform – PART II: JUSTICIABILITY – The Constitution and the Justiciability Requirement – Specific Requirements – PART III: THE POWER OF JUDICIAL REVIEW – The Nature of the Power of Judicial Review – Process of Constitutional Litigation – Judicial Review and Democracy – Conclusion

INTRODUCTION

THE JAPANESE CONSTITUTION vested the 'whole judicial power' in 'a Supreme Court and in such inferior courts as are established by law' (article 76, section 1). The judiciary, headed by the Supreme Court, is thus expected to adjudicate cases and controversies in accordance with law. Moreover, the Constitution gave to the judiciary the power to review the constitutionality of a statute and other actions of the government by providing that '[t]he Supreme Court is the court of last resort with power to determine the constitutionality of any law, order, regulation or official act' (article 81). The judiciary is thus expected to control the Diet and prevent the government from encroaching on the Constitution.

This chapter considers the structure of the judiciary, judges, judicial process, the power of the judiciary, the power of judicial review and the process of constitutional litigation. We will see that the judiciary has played a very small role in adjudicating legal disputes and especially adopted the very conservative jurisprudence of upholding almost all governmental restrictions on individual rights. We will examine the reasons for such a passive role and the recent judicial reforms to see to what extent they could change the attitude of the courts.

PART I: THE COURTS

THE COURTS AND JUDICIAL POWER

The Japanese Constitution provides in Chapter VI: The Judiciary that '[t]he whole judicial power is vested in a Supreme Court and in such inferior courts as are established by law' (article 76, section 1) and that '[n]o extraordinary tribunal shall be established, nor shall any organ or agency of the Executive be given final judicial power' (article 76, section 2).

The Meiji Government established the modern judicial system after the Meiji Restoration. Under the Meiji Constitution, the courts were supposed to exercise 'judicial power' in the name of the Emperor (article 57). Although the judicial independence was supposed to be guaranteed, the Ministry of Justice had a supervisory power over the courts. Moreover, the people could not file suits in the judicial courts attacking the government exercise of power. The judicial power as defined in the Meiji Constitution was thought to include only determination of civil and criminal cases but not administrative cases. In order to challenge the governmental exercise of power, a citizen had to file a suit in the Administrative Court, which was believed to be an administrative organ and not a judicial court. There was only one Administrative Court and the citizen could file a suit based only on listed causes. Furthermore, a citizen was obliged to exhaust administrative remedies before filing a suit. As citizens could not seek damages against the governmental exercise of power in the judicial courts either, judicial control over administrative power was utterly ineffective. Furthermore, the courts were believed to have no power of judicial review.

The current Japanese Constitution radically altered this system. Now 'judicial power' as defined in article 76, section 1, of the Constitution includes determination of civil, criminal and administrative cases and a citizen can file a suit in the judicial courts attacking governmental exercise of power. The Constitution explicitly prohibits in article 76, section 2, the establishment of extraordinary tribunals, such as the

Administrative Court, and also prohibits giving final judicial power to an organ or agency of the executive. It also specifically vested the power of judicial review with the courts (article 81).

The Japanese Constitution also makes clear that citizens have a right of access to the courts (article 32). It also removes the immunity of the government. Article 17 stipulates that, '[e]very person may sue for redress as provided by law from the State or a public entity, in case he has suffered damage through illegal act of any public official'.

It must be noted that Japan is not a federal state. There are no state or provincial courts in Japan; all the courts in Japan are parts of the central governmental organization.

STRUCTURE OF THE COURTS

The 1947 Judiciary Act established the Supreme Court, High Court, District Court, Family Court and Summary Court.[1]

The District Court is the lowest court of general jurisdiction (Judiciary Act, articles 24 and 25). There are 50 District Courts. Each of the 47 prefectures has one District Court, except for Hokkaido, which has four District Courts because of its large geographical area. The District Court hears all civil, administrative and criminal cases as the first instance court except for (1) small claims civil cases worth up to 1.4 million yen, which are heard in the Summary Court; (2) criminal cases involving petty crimes punishable only by fine, which are heard in the Summary Court; (3) domestic matters and juvenile cases, which are heard in the Family Court and (4) administrative cases that belong to the Tokyo High Court, such as a suit against the adjudication of Fair Trade Commission. District Court cases are heard either by single judge or by a panel of three judges.

If the parties are dissatisfied with the judgment of the District Court, they can appeal to the High Court (Judiciary Act, article 16). There are eight High Courts[2] and the parties must file an appeal to the High Court that has jurisdiction over the District Court involved. High

[1] PR Luney, 'The Judiciary: Its Organization and Status in the Parliamentary System' in PR Luney and Kazuyuki Takahashi (eds), *Japanese Constitutional Law* (Tokyo, University of Tokyo Press, 1993) 123.

[2] The Tokyo High Court has a branch called the Intellectual Property High Court. Shigenori Matsui, 'The Intellectual Property High Court of Japan' in A Harding and P Nicholson (eds), *New Courts in Asia* (Abingdon, Routledge, 2010) 83.

Court appeals are heard by a panel of either three or five judges *do novo* (Judiciary Act, article 18). The High Court thus finds facts and applies the law independently from the District Court.[3]

If the parties are dissatisfied with the judgment of the High Court, they can file a further appeal in the Supreme Court (Judiciary Act, article 7). The Supreme Court deals with questions of pure law and a party can file an appeal only when there are legal grounds permitted under the statutes. In criminal cases, a party can appeal to the Supreme Court if there is a violation of the Constitution, or when the judgment below is contrary to the precedents of the Supreme Court (Code of Criminal Procedure, article 405). The Supreme Court can also review the lower court judgment if it believes that significant legal issues are implicated (Code of Criminal Procedure, article 406). In civil cases, a party can only file an appeal if there is a violation of the Constitution (Code of Civil Procedure, article 312, section 1). The Supreme Court has discretion to accept other appeals where a party presents a petition (Code of Civil Procedure, article 318, section 1).

The Supreme Court normally sits as one of three petty benches, each consisting of five Justices. It is only when trying cases involving potential constitutional invalidity of a statute, order or regulation that the Supreme Court must sit as a grand bench consisting with all 15 Justices (Judiciary Act, article 10). The configuration of the Court during treatment of other cases is left to the discretion of the Supreme Court.

The Family Court deals with domestic disputes and juvenile cases including protection of juvenile delinquents (Judiciary Act, article 31-3). There are 50 Family Courts alongside the District Courts. The Supreme Court has held that Family Courts are not 'extraordinary' tribunals banned under article 76, section 2 of the Constitution, since they are lower courts subject to the jurisdiction of the Supreme Court.[4]

Judicial administration is handled by the Supreme Court via its General Secretariat. Its officials are all appointed by the Court and the high-ranking positions are occupied by judges. In addition, the Supreme Court maintains the Judicial Research and Training Institute, which is designed to provide practical training to those who pass the Bar examination and want to become lawyers, and to provide ongoing training for judges.

[3] See below, p 130.

[4] Supreme Court, grand bench, 30 May 1956, 10 *Keishu* 756.

JUDGES

The Supreme Court consists of the Chief Justice, who is to be designated by the Cabinet and appointed by the Emperor, and 14 Associate Justices to be appointed by the Cabinet (article 79, section 1). A Supreme Court Justice has to be over the age of 40 and have an intellectual grasp of the law (Judiciary Act, article 41) but there is no requirement that Supreme Court Justices must be lawyers. However, at least ten out of 15 must have experience for certain number of years as judges, prosecutors, attorneys or university law professors. The appointment is not lifelong; Justices are supposed to retire at the age set by statute (article 79, section 5) which is currently 70 years (Judiciary Act, article 50).

The appointment of the Justices of the Supreme Court shall be reviewed by the people at the first general election of members of the House of Representatives following their appointment, and shall be reviewed again at the first general election of members of the House of Representatives after a lapse of ten years and in the same manner thereafter (article 79, section 2). When the majority of the voters favours the dismissal of a Justice, he or she shall be dismissed (article 79, section 3).[5]

Supreme Court Justices are appointed at the discretion of the Cabinet. Although the earliest appointments of Justices were based on recommendations of an advisory board, no permanent advisory board was established thereafter. The Prime Minister has unbridled discretion to make appointments.

Over time, however, certain customs have developed around appointments. First, it is now the custom for the Chief Justice of the Supreme Court to recommend a candidate to the Prime Minister when one of the Justices is about to retire or when there are vacancies. Prime Ministers have historically respected these recommendations.

Secondly, it is customary to appoint six judges, four private attorneys, and five others, including two prosecutors, two government bureaucrats and one academic. Therefore, if a Justice who was appointed in the

[5] Under the current system, those voters who want to dismiss a Justice must mark 'x' on the name of that Justice. This system was challenged as infringing the freedom of conscience protected under art 19, since it treats voters who are not sure whether to dismiss a Justice in the same way as those who do not wish to dismiss a Justice. Nevertheless, the Supreme Court construed art 79 as authorizing dismissal and upheld the system: Supreme Court, grand bench, 20 February 1952, 6 *Minshu* 122.

'judges' category is about to retire, the Chief Justice will recommend a candidate who is a judge and the Prime Minister is likely to appoint that candidate to the Supreme Court. As a result, eight out of 15 Justices are always appointed from among former judges or former prosecutors, thus ensuring they constitute the majority.

Thirdly, although the Cabinet can select young Justices just over the age of 40, it has been the custom to appoint Supreme Court Justices roughly at the age of 64 or 65. Since the lower court judges must retire at the age of 65, this means that the position of the Supreme Court Justice has become the final honorary position for judges after retirement. Most of the Justices who are appointed from among the ranks of judges have had experience as chief judges of a major High Court such as the Tokyo High Court or the Osaka High Court.[6] This pattern is also evident with respect to other appointees. For instance, Justices who are appointed from attorneys are generally former presidents of major Bar associations. Justices who are former prosecutors are likely also to be high-ranking prosecutors in the Prosecutors' Office.

As a result of the customary age requirements, most of the Justices can stay on the bench for only five to six years. They would not serve the Court long enough to develop independent constitutional jurisprudence. Moreover, as a result, the popular vote system has not functioned as was expected. Most of the Justices face popular votes shortly after appointment and citizens usually do not have sufficient information as to the experience of Justices in order to properly evaluate them. Further, many will have to retire before the next popular vote. The citizens also showed little interest in this popular vote system. Usually, Justices receive roughly five to ten per cent dismissal votes regardless of their personal career or judgments in which they participated. No Justice has ever been dismissed based on this system.[7]

The judges of the inferior courts shall be appointed by the Cabinet from a list of persons nominated by the Supreme Court (article 80). All such judges shall hold office for a term of ten years with privilege of

[6] Moreover, many have had long experience in the General Secretariat as administrators, not as judges.

[7] In order to assist Supreme Court Justices, 37 law clerks are working in the Supreme Court. Unlike in the United States, these law clerks are all veteran judges who have more than 10 years' experience as judges and they are not assigned to individual Justices. They review the petitions to the Supreme Court, prepare research memos to the Supreme Court Justices and write drafts to the Supreme Court. Many point out the strong influence of these law clerks on the decisions of the Supreme Court.

reappointment, provided that they shall be retired on the attainment of the age as fixed by law. Currently, the retirement age is 65 years for lower court judges, except for Summary Court judges, who must retire at the age of 70 (Judiciary Act, article 50).

In order to become judges, candidates have to graduate from law schools, pass the national Bar examination and receive practical training at the Research and Practice Institute of the Supreme Court for one year.[8] Once a person has successfully completed all the programmes of the Institute and has passed the final examination, he or she can become a judge, prosecutor or attorney. Before the legal education reform of 2004, it was necessary to pass the national Bar examination and receive two years (later one and a half year's) practical training at the Research and Practice Training Institute. The number of persons who could pass the Bar examination was limited in the past to 500 and the passing rate of the Bar examination was less than three per cent. This system has contributed to the small number of lawyers in Japan.

Unlike in the United States, where judges are appointed from among practising attorneys, most Japanese judges are appointed soon after completion of their training and serve in the courts until retirement age. Therefore, Japanese judges are career judges. In the first ten years, they are appointed as assistant judges and cannot try cases alone (after five years most will be allowed to try case alone as an exception). After the completion of their first ten-year term, they will be reappointed as full judges for another ten-year term and thereafter can try cases alone.

Since the Cabinet appoints judges based on a list prepared by the Supreme Court, if one is not on the list, there is no possibility of appointment or reappointment. There are no stated Supreme Court criteria for putting names on the list and the Supreme Court has viewed its power to put names of candidates for appointment and reappointment as wholly discretionary. Many argue that the Court should reappoint lower court judges unless there are questions as to their capacity or suitability.[9]

In order to restrict arbitrary choice, the Supreme Court has agreed in 2003 to establish an advisory board composed of 11 members: five representatives from among the judges, prosecutors and attorneys; and six representatives from among the legal academics. The Supreme Court also agreed to respect the recommendations of the advisory board

[8] Exception is the Summary Court judges, who do not to have to have a qualification as a lawyer to be appointed (Judiciary Act, arts 44 and 45).

[9] Kiyomiya, 356; Sato, 315.

for appointment of lower court judges. Following its establishment, every year the advisory board has recommended not reappointing several judges. Most of the judges who were denied recommendation subsequently withdrew their applications.[10]

INDEPENDENCE OF THE JUDGES AND THE JUDICIARY

Judicial independence is constitutionally guaranteed. According to article 76, section 3 of the Constitution, 'all judges shall be independent in the exercise of their conscience and shall be bound only by this Constitution and the laws'. Moreover, judges shall not be removed except by public impeachment unless judicially declared mentally or physically incompetent to perform official duties. No disciplinary action against judges shall be administered by any executive organ or agency (article 78). Judges may be dismissed for gross breach of professional duty or for misconduct which impairs the trust of the public. Dismissal is based on conviction by the Judge Impeachment Court established by the Diet in accordance with article 64 of the Constitution. The procedure is provided for in the Judge Impeachment Act. So far, six judges have been impeached under this legislation. It must be noted that a judge can also be removed if he or she suffers an irreparable disability resulting in inability to perform his or her duty. Removal on these grounds is based on the judgment of the court under the Judge Discipline Act. Judges may also be disciplined for misconduct by reprimands or fines, as determined by the judgment of the court. Finally, the judges of the inferior courts shall receive, at regular, stated intervals, adequate compensation which shall not be decreased during their terms of office (article 80).[11]

[10] In December 2009, the advisory board recommended that 3 out of 189 candidates should not be reappointed as judges: www.courts.go.jp/saikosai/about/iinkai/kakyusaibansyo/pdf/iinkai_40th.pdf. Similarly, the advisory board recommended that 1 out of 100 candidates for new appointment as assistant judges should not be appointed: www.courts.go.jp/saikosai/about/iinkai/kakyusaibansyo/pdf/iinkai_41th.pdf. Judge Kaoru Inoue, who had publicly criticized judges saying they were 'talking too much' and had himself written very short opinions, was denied recommendation for reappointment by the advisory board in 2005. He ultimately withdrew his application for reappointment.

[11] The Supreme Court decided in 2002 that pay cuts for all judges together with all other public servants were constitutional.

The independence of the judiciary is also protected in addition to the independence of individual judges. The Supreme Court is vested with rule-making power under which it determines the rules of procedure and of practice, and of matters relating to attorneys, the internal discipline of the courts and the administration of judicial affairs (article 77). Public prosecutors shall be subject to the rule-making power of the Supreme Court. The Supreme Court may delegate the power to make rules for inferior courts to such courts.[12]

However, there are some questions as to whether Japanese judges and judiciary are truly independent. For instance, there is always the possibility that the government will attempt to interfere with the courts. The Judiciary Committee of the House of Councillors investigated a case in which a mother killed her three children and tried to kill herself out of despair over the failure of her husband to work. When a lower court judge convicted her and sentenced her to three years' imprisonment but suspended the enforcement of the sentence, the Judiciary Committee called the defendant, defendant's husband and prosecutor to the committee, and criticized the sentence as being too lenient. The Supreme Court fiercely protested that such a move was an infringement of the independence of the judiciary.[13] Moreover, in the late 1960s and early 1970s, there was fierce criticism from the conservative politicians against the judiciary, especially against judges who belonged to Young Lawyers' Guild, a leftist group committed to democracy and peace. These conservative politicians were upset by the *All Postal Workers, Tokyo Central Post Office Case*,[14] which strictly restricted the power of the government to punish public workers for illegal strikes, and decisions of the lower court refusing detention of students involved in student movements. In response, as will be examined below, the Supreme Court

[12] Independence of the judiciary is also protected in financial aspect. Even though the Cabinet has a power to submit the budget to the Diet, the Cabinet is required to submit the budget for the courts separately (Judiciary Act, art 83) and the Chief Justice of the Supreme Court will submit to the Cabinet the budget request, including the salary for the judges (Government Finance Act, art 17). When the Cabinet submits the budget for the judiciary lower than requested by the Supreme Court, the Cabinet must submit the budget together with the request from the Supreme Court. It must also indicate the possible source of money to allow the Diet to increase the budget as requested (Government Finance Act, art 19).

[13] See above, ch 3, n 31 (*Urawa Case*).

[14] Supreme Court, grand bench, 26 October, 1966, 20 *Keishu* 901. See below, ch 7, n 115.

came to condemn the affiliation of judges with any political groups and started to introduce various mechanisms to control lower court judges. Tight control mechanisms over judges may be viewed as a response to political pressure.

Furthermore, judges are subject to supervision and control within the judiciary. Lower court judges are assigned to particular courts after appointment by the Supreme Court. They are then usually rotated to different courts after three years. Lower court judges are promoted to higher positions via this rotation mechanism. Consideration for reappointment is mandatory after ten years and for reappointment the Supreme Court must put a lower court judge's name on the list for reappointment. Naturally, lower court judges must consider the prospect of evaluation by the Supreme Court.

Indeed, the Supreme Court has been quite insistent on judges keeping a distance from politics. Active political activity on the part of judges is prohibited by the Judiciary Act (article 52, item 1) but there is no ban on affiliation with political groups. Yet, the Supreme Court takes a dim view of participation of judges in politics especially after the criticisms from conservative politicians in the late 1960s and early 1970s.

In 1969, the Supreme Court condemned the Young Lawyers' Guild as a political association and urged judges not to affiliate with that association. Moreover, the Supreme Court refused to put forward the name of judge Yasuaki Miyamoto for reappointment in 1971 and many speculated that his affiliation with the Young Lawyers' Guild must have been the reason for the refusal.

When judge Shigeo Fukushima was hearing the *Naganuma Case*,[15] a suit against the anti-missile base of the SDF, the head of the District Court, Kenta Hiraga, gave him 'friendly advice' to avoid constitutional ruling in 1969. Judge Fukushima was a member of the Young Lawyers' Guild. When he revealed this advice to the public, many criticized the advice as an infringement of the independence of a judge. Hiraga was warned by the Supreme Court for his inappropriate conduct. However, the Impeachment Court of the Diet picked up this incident and decided not to prosecute Hiraga while suspending a prosecution against Fukushima for revealing Hiraga's advice. The Supreme Court later transferred Hiraga and reprimanded Fukushima. Yet, Hiraga ended up serving on the High Court, hardly an adverse action against him, and Fukushima,

[15] See below, n 29 and ch 8, n 25.

who declared the SDF unconstitutional in the *Naganuma Case*, served in the Family Court for 12 years before quitting.

The Supreme Court also upheld the disciplinary action against assistant judge Kazushi Teranishi,[16] who wrote an opinion letter to the newspaper against the pending wiretapping legislation, pointing out that search warrants are routinely granted by judges without scrutiny, and participated in the citizen rally against the legislation as a participant when the head of the District Court did not allow him to participate as a panellist. The Supreme Court rejected the argument of infringement of his freedom of expression, since the ban on active political activity is essential to secure the political neutrality as well as appearance of political neutrality for judges, and participation in the political rally undermined the public trust in judges.

Although these episodes might be viewed as attempts by the Supreme Court to maintain judicial integrity and political neutrality,[17] it is questionable whether the independence of each judge is sufficiently protected inside the judiciary.[18]

JUDICIAL PROCESS

The judicial process in Japan is regulated by the Code of Civil Procedure and the Code of Criminal Procedure. A suit against the exercise of government power is regulated by the Administrative Case Litigation Act.

A civil suit seeking damages of less than 1.4 million yen must be filed in the Summary Court. A civil suit seeking a damages award of more than 1.4 million yen, or a suit seeking other remedies, such as injunctions, must be filed in the District Court. Once a suit is filed with the court, the court sends the copy of the complaint to the defendant and summons

[16] Supreme Court, grand bench, 1 December 1998, 52 *Minshu* 1761. See below, ch 7, n 63.

[17] JO Haley, *The Spirit of Japanese Law* (Athens, University of Georgia Press, 1998); JO Haley, 'The Japanese Judiciary: Maintaining Integrity, Autonomy, and the Public Trust' in DH Foote (ed), *Law in Japan: A Turning Point* (Seattle, University of Washington Press, 2007) 99. See also, FK Upham, 'Political Lackeys or Faithful Public Servants? Two Views of the Japanese Judiciary' (2005) 30 *Law & Social Inquiry* 421.

[18] Setsuo Miyazawa, 'Administrative Control of Japanese Judges' in PSC Lewis (ed), *Law and Technology in the Pacific Community* (Boulder, Westview, 1994) 263; JM Ramseyer and F McCall Rosenbluth, *Japan's Political Marketplace* (Cambridge, Harvard University Press, 1993) 142–81.

him or her to court. The judge will meet the parties together with lawyers to narrow the issues and decide on the evidence or witnesses to be examined during trial. The court will then hold trial(s) to examine evidence and witnesses. There are no civil juries. The judge has discretion as to the evidentiary value of all evidence.

Roughly the same kind of procedure is followed in suits against administrative agencies. Generally, a suit seeking judicial revocation of an administrative order is to be filed in a District Court. There are some differences between ordinary civil suits and administrative suits. There is a very short time limitation for filing a suit (a suit must be filed within six months of learning about the order) (Administrative Case Litigation Act, article 14). Generally, provisional remedies are not allowed in administrative suits (Administrative Case Litigation Act, article 25). Moreover, strictly speaking, an administrative suit is not totally adversarial, since the courts can review the evidence *ex officio*, that is to say, by its own authority (Administrative Case Litigation Act, article 24).

With respect to some administrative decisions, a special procedure is provided and the scope of judicial review might be limited. For instance, with respect to adjudications of the Fair Trade Commission, the Tokyo High Court has exclusive jurisdiction and the finding of the Fair Trade Commission is binding on the Court so long as there is substantial evidence to support the finding under the Anti-trust Act (articles 85 and 80). Even though there are some administrative tribunals in Japan, the Constitution requires that the decision of these tribunals be subjected to judicial review (article 76, section 2). The preclusion of judicial review is not allowed.[19]

In a criminal case, the prosecutor has discretion to file charges. Petty crimes can be prosecuted in the Summary Court but serious crimes must be prosecuted in the District Court. When a defendant is prosecuted, the court will hold trial(s) to determine whether the defendant is guilty and will determine the sentence to be imposed if he or she is guilty. Contrary to the practice in Anglo-American countries, there are no jury trials in Japan. However, as will be explained below, in 2009, the government introduced the citizen judge system to allow six citizens to sit together with three professional judges to hear serious criminal cases. There

[19] The substantial evidence rule is generally viewed as permissible, since it will allow the Court to review at least whether there is substantial evidence to support the findings of administrative agency.

are no strict evidential rules, and judges have discretion to evaluate the trustworthiness of evidence and the testimony of the witnesses. Plea bargaining is not practised in Japan.

Trials shall be conducted and judgment declared publicly (article 82). When a court unanimously determines publicity to be dangerous to public order or morals, a trial may be conducted privately. However, trials of political offences, offences involving the press or cases wherein the rights of people as guaranteed in Chapter III of the Constitution are in question must always be conducted publicly. Therefore, both civil and criminal trials must be held in public and the court must announce its judgments in open court.[20]

If the parties are dissatisfied with the judgment of the District Court, they can file an appeal to the High Court. The High Court will find facts *de novo* and apply the law. If the parties are dissatisfied with the judgment of the High Court, they can further appeal to the Supreme Court. Yet, as stated above, the grounds for further appeal are limited.

The Supreme Court reviews the appeal mostly based on the briefs. It is rare to hold oral hearings. The judgment of the Supreme Court consists of conclusion and reasons. The opinion of the Court is announced under the name of the whole Court and not written by an individual Justice, but the individual Justices can write concurring opinions and dissenting opinions.[21]

The judgment of the Supreme Court binds the lower court with respect to a specific case before the courts. If the case is remanded to the lower court by the Supreme Court, the lower court must follow the judgment of the Supreme Court (Judiciary Act, article 4). However, as stated earlier, it has been assumed that Japan is a civil law country and the

[20] The public trial requirement has been held to not be applicable to cases in which the court is supposed to decide ancillary matters not directly related to the rights and obligations of the parties (so-called non-litigious cases). However, with respect to regular litigation, the phrase 'public order or morals' has been narrowly construed to refer to cases in which a public trial would endanger the public safety or sexual morality and in which it would therefore be appropriate to close the courtroom. In order to protect privacy and trade secrets, the government ultimately amended the Personal Matters Litigation Act and Unfair Competition Prevention Act to allow judges to exclude the public when examining witnesses and evidence in the courtroom.

[21] This is one major difference from the judgment of the lower courts, since they do not allow any individual concurring or dissenting opinions.

precedent is not legally binding,[22] even though an increasing number of critics came to argue that the precedents of the Supreme Court should be treated as legally binding to the lower courts in the similar cases.[23]

JUDICIAL REFORM

In the past, the judiciary has not played such a significant role in the Japanese society. The number of lawyers is quite small (there are some 27,000 attorneys for the total population of 127 million, in addition to some 3400 judges and 2400 public prosecutors) and the number of civil litigation is similarly quite small (some 180,000 new civil litigations are filed with the District Court, while some 475,000 new civil litigations were filed with the Summary Court in 2006). The litigation takes a long time (it may take ten years before the issue will be finally decided before the Supreme Court). In order to file litigation, the plaintiff must pay the filing fee based on the amount of damage the plaintiff is claiming. There used to be no legal aid for the poor. Even though the court fees must be borne by the losing party, the party must pay the attorney fees even when he or she wins the litigation (except for tort litigation, where the court usually orders the losing party to pay reasonable attorney fees). No lawyer accepts a case on the contingent fee basis. There is no class action system. The party can ask the court to order the production of relevant documents against the other party, but there are many exceptions and there is no mechanism of discovery. There is no civil jury. The amount of damage award is relatively low. There is no punitive damage. It is no wonder that many citizens do not want to file a suit and are willing to accept the settlement even when they did file suits.

Administrative litigation is much worse. As we saw in chapter four, the citizen could file a suit only against the administrative order seeking judicial revocation. The courts have adopted a very restrictive attitude towards allowing administrative suits, insisting on the tight standing requirement and narrow definition of administrative order.

With respect to criminal trial, the most striking was the conviction rate of 99 per cent. That is to say, if the prosecutor decided to file

22 Toshihiko Nonaka, 'Supreme Court Precedents and the Lower Courts in the Exercise of Judicial Review' in Yoichi Higuchi (ed), *Five Decades of Constitutionalism in Japanese Society* (Tokyo, Tokyo University Press, 2001) 279. See above, ch 1, n 46.

23 Sato, 311. For a critical view, see Higuchi I, 510–11.

prosecution, there is virtually no room for acquittal. Even though the Constitution protects the panoply of rights of suspects and defendants, the suspect is subjected to police questioning after arrest without effective assistance of counsel. Most suspects will thus make confessions and instead of challenging the guilt, most would simply ask the judges for lenient sentences. Since there is no criminal jury, admissibility and evidentiary value of testimony and evidence are relegated to the discretion of the professional judges. It is often useless to recant the confession and challenge the guilt before the judges, since they tend to believe the confession made during the questioning. The trial hearing is intermittent and the court usually holds public hearings once a month. The examination of documents plays a more important role than examination of witnesses. As a result, the long delays in some of the controversial cases has been a vexing problem.

Japan managed to maintain the social order with such a small role of the judiciary in the past. When there is a social problem, the citizen used to rely on bureaucrats for help and occasionally rely on politicians to put pressure on the bureaucrats. The administrative agencies have attempted to regulate the industries in order to make sure that no social problems will occur. As a result, there are so many regulatory statutes, requiring the permits and licences and authorizing the bureaucrats to regulate every detail of the business transactions. Until the 1980s, this model appeared successful as a way of rebuilding the country, making it competitive against international competitors. However, when the economic bubble burst in early 1990s, many came to believe that this over-reliance on the regulation by bureaucrats was stifling innovation and competition, and urging privatization and deregulation. Many citizens came to expect the judiciary to play a much larger role. In response, the government set up the Judicial Reform Council (JRC) and implemented its proposals in 2001.

As a part of the judicial reform in the 2000s, the legal education system was restructured (in 2004 law schools were introduced as graduate schools in order to provide professional legal education for those who wanted to become lawyers) and the new Bar examination system was introduced to increase the number of lawyers (it was expected that 3000 would pass the new Bar examination every year by 2010.) Legal aid was introduced to help the poor receive legal assistance.[24] The Administrative

[24] The Comprehensive Legal Aid Act was enacted in 2004 and the Japan Legal Aid Centre was established to offer free legal consultation to citizens and to provide

Case Litigation Act was amended to clarify the meaning of the standing requirement and to provide for suit for injunction and suit to oblige the administrative agency to act as requested.

From May 2009, the participation of citizens in the criminal trial was introduced. The absence of citizen participation had been the focus of criticism in the past and the JRC proposed the introduction of citizen participation as a way of introducing the common sense of citizens and to facilitate democratic participation into the government. Even though there are discussions as to whether the jury system or the mixed court system widely used in European countries is best suited to Japan, the JRC concluded that the combination of jury system and mixed court system is the best. The Diet passed the Citizen Judge Act (Act Concerning Criminal Trials with Participation of Citizen Judge) to allow six citizens randomly chosen from eligible voters to sit together with three professional judges to try each case involving serious crimes and decide the proper sentence.[25] Although the number of cases tried by the citizen judges is limited, the introduction of citizen judges is expected to alter the criminal trial by forcing the court to hold trials consecutively, to avoid technical jargons and to rely on oral testimony from witnesses.

Although various barriers to judicial access and the achievement of justice through the judiciary still exist, these reforms are surely the first step in the right direction. Further reforms are, however, surely needed to make the judiciary play far larger role in the Japanese society.

PART II: JUSTICIABILITY

THE CONSTITUTION AND THE JUSTICIABILITY REQUIREMENT

Although there is no explicit requirement that judges must be presented with a case or controversy, 'judicial power' vested in the courts by the Constitution has been construed to mean the power to adjudicate specific

financial aids for poor citizens. The Centre will pay the attorney fees for poor citizens when there is a possibility of winning the suit, but the citizens must pay back the expenses in general. There are no specific legal aid for public interest litigations.

[25] K Anderson and DT Johnson, 'Japan's New Criminal Trials: Origins, Operations and Implications' in A Harding and P Nicholson (eds), *New Courts in Asia* (Abingdon, Routledge, 2010) 371.

cases in accordance with the applicable law. Therefore, it has been assumed that a case or controversy before the court must exist before judges can exercise judicial power. Advisory opinions are thus not admitted in Japan.

However, the Judiciary Act grants 'other powers authorized by the statutes' to the courts, in addition to the power to adjudicate a case according to the law (article 3). The Local Government Act, for instance, allows local residents to file suits attacking illegal spending of local governments. Such taxpayer suits are generally regarded not as suits seeking redress against infringement of rights or legal interests of individual plaintiffs, but as suits seeking appropriate government action. In Japan, such a suit is generally called an 'objective action' in contrast to 'subjective actions' which are designed to seek redress for infringement of rights or legal interests of individual plaintiffs.

Since the Judiciary Act grants other powers authorized by statutes, virtually no academics have questioned the constitutionality of such provisions in the past. Yet, in light of the separation of powers principle, such statutory grant of non-judicial power to the courts could be called into question.[26]

In general, the case or controversy requirement demands that (1) the plaintiff must present a case capable of judicial resolution according to law; (2) the plaintiff has standing to sue; (3) the case is ripe for judicial resolution and (4) the case is not moot at the time of the judgment. The court has the power to adjudicate all cases except those exempted by constitutional provisions such as article 55 (the question of qualification of members of the Diet) or article 64 (impeachment of judges).[27]

SPECIFIC REQUIREMENTS

In order for the courts to exercise judicial power, there must be a case or controversy capable of resolution in accordance with the law. Therefore,

[26] Sato, 298–99 (there must be a constitutional limit on granting non-judicial power to the court and the Diet should not be allowed to grant the power unsuited to the judicial courts as a forum of legal principle).

[27] Even without explicit constitutional provision, some issues can be excluded by inference. The question of whether adequate procedure was followed in passing a statute in the House should be relegated to the autonomous decision of the House: Supreme Court, grand bench, 7 March 1962, 16 *Minshu* 445. The dissolution of the House by the Cabinet may be viewed as one such example, even though the Supreme Court concluded that it was a political question to be avoided. See below, n 50.

suits asking the court to decide on academic or policy questions cannot be adjudicated by the courts.[28]

The standing requirement demands that a plaintiff has sufficient legal interest in a suit and is particularly controversial in an administrative suit. The Administrative Case Litigation Act has demanded that the plaintiff has a 'legal interest' in seeking judicial revocation of an administrative action (article 9). The Supreme Court had held that the plaintiff must show that he or she has legal rights or legal interests protected under the relevant statutes in order to file a revocation suit.

The leading case on the issue of standing is the *Naganuma Case*.[29] In this case, local residents filed a suit seeking revocation of the decision of the Minister of Agriculture, Forests and Fisheries to reclassify a forest reserve for land development in order to construct an SDF anti-missile base. The plaintiffs argued the infringement of the right to live in peace, allegedly protected under the preamble of the Constitution, and claimed there were various harms that would be caused as a result of loss of the forest reserve, including the possibility of flooding. Although the Sapporo District Court admitted the right to live in peace as a basis for standing, the Sapporo High Court denied this right and granted standing based only on various possible harms. While there are no specific statutes which grant individual rights or legal interests to local residents, the Court construed the statute on forest reserves as giving protection against these harms as individual legal interests. The Supreme Court affirmed this judgment.

In the *Juice Regulation Case*,[30] the Supreme Court was faced with a suit filed by the Wives' Association and its member against the controversial approval of the use of the word 'juice' for beverages which were not 100 per cent natural. The Fair Trade Commission (FTC) approved a fair practice code for the Juice Associations concerning the use of word 'juice' but it did not require beverage containers to display labels stating 'no fruit ingredients' for beverages without any natural fruit ingredients. The Wives' Association, the biggest consumer advocacy group in Japan,

[28] Supreme Court, 3rd petty bench, 8 February 1966, 20 *Minshu* 196. A suit challenging the adequacy of economic policy: Supreme Court, 1st petty bench, 15 July 1982, 1053 *Hanreijihou* 93 and a suit challenging the appropriateness of branch closure of the courts: Supreme Court, 2nd petty bench, 19 April 1991, 45 *Minshu* 518, were not justiciable.

[29] Supreme Court, 1st petty bench, 9 September 1982, 36 *Minshu* 1679.

[30] Supreme Court, 3rd petty bench, 14 March 1978, 32 *Minshu* 211.

and its member filed a suit challenging this approval. The Act against Improper Premiums and Improper Representations provides that a person who is qualified to complain about decisions of the FTC has standing to file a complaint. The Court interpreted this language and held that it is only those whose own rights or legal interests are infringed or threatened with infringement, as distinguished from the mere loss of incidental benefits one can receive as a result of regulation for the public interests, that can file a complaint. Believing that the Act was intended to protect the interests of all consumers, it therefore concluded that the Act was not intended to vest an individual consumer with an individual right or legal interest to challenge the decision of the FTC, and that both the Wives' Association and its member did not have legal interest to file complaints under the Act or standing to file a revocation suit against the decision of the FTC.

The Court showed a different attitude in the *Niigata Airport Case*,[31] in which local residents sought revocation of a decision of the Transportation Minister to grant approval of an airline's regular service between Niigata airport and Seoul, South Korea. The Supreme Court construed the relevant statutes as vesting individual legal interests in local residents with regard to noise increases, since they required the minister to consider noise increases before granting approvals. The Court thus admitted that the local residents had standing to challenge the approval.

In contrast to the United States Supreme Court, which similarly demands the standing requirement but admits suits against administrative agencies where there is an 'injury in fact', the Japanese Supreme Court has clung to the doctrine which requires proof of infringement of rights or individual legal interests. Even when the citizen suffers from injury in fact, he or she cannot challenge the administrative action, therefore, unless he or she can rely on some of the statutes which could be construed as protecting the interests of the citizen as an individual right or legal interest. Since most of the administrative law statutes enacted by the Diet have no explicit clause allowing the citizen to file a suit in the court or any provision on judicial review, the citizen has difficulty in persuading the courts to construe regulating provision as protecting the interests of the citizen as a legal right or legal interest. As

[31] Supreme Court, 2nd petty bench, 17 February 1989, 43 *Minshu* 56.

a result, the standing requirement has prevented citizens from challenging administrative actions before the courts.[32]

The case or controversy requirement must be satisfied, both at the time of filing a suit and at the time of the judgment. If the rights and legal interests being pursued are lost during litigation, then the case becomes moot, ie, not real, and the courts must dismiss the suit.

For instance, the Supreme Court held in the *Asahi Case*[33] that the action became moot because the plaintiff died during the litigation. The plaintiff was a welfare recipient who had been seeking revocation of a decision of the Welfare Minister to reduce the amount of welfare benefits he received when his brother came to pay for his support. The Court held that the right to receive a welfare benefit under the Welfare Assistance Act is personal and could not be inherited by his heirs and therefore that the suit ended when he died. The Supreme Court also held in the second *Ienaga School Textbook Censorship Case*,[34] in which history professor Saburou Ienaga challenged a decision to reject approval for a school history textbook he had written from approval, that the action became moot when the standard for approval was modified and judicial revocation would not have led to approval in any case. In the *Naganuma Case*,[35] in which local residents filed a suit seeking judicial revocation of a decision of the Agriculture Minister to declassify forest reserve land for construction of an SDF missile base, the Supreme Court held that the action became moot when the government built alternative facilities to avoid possible flooding after the conversion of the forest reserve to an SDF missile base.

The Supreme Court further held in the *May Day Parade Case*,[36] in which an union, the organizer of a May Day gathering was seeking

[32] As a result of reforms in 2004, art 9 of the Administrative Case Litigation Act was amended and a new section was added. Now art 9, s 1, maintains the traditional definition of the standing requirement, while a new s 2 makes clear that the existence of standing can be found after examination of various statutes and regulations relevant to the decision. This section was meant to clarify the meaning of the standing requirement after the *Niigata Airport Case* and was not meant to expand the scope of standing.

[33] Supreme Court, grand bench, 24 May 1967, 21 *Minshu* 1043. Nevertheless, the Court went on to add its opinion on the merit, holding the decision of the Welfare Minister as constitutional. See below, ch 7, n 111.

[34] Supreme Court, 1st petty bench, 8 April 1982, 36 *Minshu* 594.

[35] Supreme Court, 1st petty bench, 9 September 1982, above n 29.

[36] Supreme Court, grand bench, 23 December 1953, 7 *Minshu* 1561. Nevertheless, the Court went on to add its opinion on the merit, holding the refusal to grant permit as constitutional. See below, ch 7, n 88.

judicial revocation of a decision of the Welfare Minister to refuse a permit to use the exterior garden of the Imperial Palace for a May Day parade, that the action became moot when the planned date of gathering passed during the trial. If the courts dismiss these kinds of cases for mootness, however, it will be impossible for citizens to challenge time-sensitive government actions. Even when similar cases are filed in the courts in the future, all such suits would be dismissed for mootness. In such cases, therefore, the courts should admit an exception to the mootness doctrine and should review the constitutionality (the doctrine of 'capable of repetition, yet evading review' recognized by the US Supreme Court).

The Administrative Case Litigation Act allows citizens to file suits seeking judicial revocation of 'administrative orders'. In other words, one is allowed to file a suit only after the administrative agency applies the statute in the specific case and issues an order. The Court has rejected suits seeking a declaration of unconstitutionality of a statute before application. Moreover, the Court has rejected suits for judicial revocation when they were filed before the agencies had applied the relevant statutes and had issued orders that had the effect of restricting the rights and legal interests of citizens or of imposing burdens on them. For instance, when a citizen filed a suit seeking judicial revocation of a redevelopment plan, the Supreme Court dismissed the suit, insisting that the plan was not an order and therefore the citizen could not seek revocation of the plan.[37] The redevelopment procedure is often used to redevelop inner city so that the government can order the property owners to exchange their properties and to allow more well-designed development. When the redevelopment plan is published, various restrictions are imposed on the owners of properties located in the redevelopment area. The Court believed, however, that these restrictions are imposed by the statute and are not the legal effect of the plan itself. The Court held that since the plan is merely a plan, the owners should not be allowed to file a suit until they are actually ordered to exchange their properties. This decision has been criticized as being too demanding since, in many cases, it is too late to file a suit once an agency issues a specific order based on a plan.

Yet, in a landmark 2008 decision, the Supreme Court overturned this

[37] Supreme Court, grand bench, 23 February 1966, 20 *Minshu* 271. See RW Dziubla, 'The Impotent Sword of Japanese Justice: The Doctrine of Shobunsei as a Barrier to Administrative Litigation' (1985) 18 *Cornell International Law Journal* 37.

precedent and held that publication of a plan of land redevelopment had the effect of restricting the power of the owners to build a house and other improvements on property included in the plan, thus having a legal effect on the rights of citizens. Therefore, the Court concluded that the owners should be allowed to challenge the plan in order to ensure an effective remedy.[38]

The 2004 amendment to the Administrative Case Litigation Act also allowed citizens to file suits for injunction and suits seeking a judgment obliging an agency to act in a certain way. There has been no precedent on the ripeness of these suits.

PART III: THE POWER OF JUDICIAL REVIEW

THE NATURE OF THE POWER OF JUDICIAL REVIEW

The Supreme Court is the court of last resort, with power to determine the constitutionality of any law, order, regulation or official act (article 81). What is the nature of this power to determine the constitutionality of law?

This issue was raised in the *National Police Reserve Case.*[39] When the government established the National Police Reserve, Diet member Mosaburou Suzuki filed a suit directly in the Supreme Court, virtually representing the opposition Japan Socialist Party (JSP). He sought a declaration of unconstitutionality and an injunction against the establishment and maintenance of the National Police Reserve. He argued that article 81 gave the Supreme Court dual roles: the role of the Supreme Court as a judicial court and as a constitutional court. The Supreme Court could accept a suit, according to him, without any case or controversy, and review the constitutionality of law as a constitutional court. Yet, the Supreme Court had already held in its decisions that article 81 merely affirmed the power of a judicial court to review the constitutionality of a statute in a case or controversy, as had been the practice of the United States Supreme Court. In this case, the Supreme Court reaffirmed this holding and rejected Suzuki's argument.

[38] Supreme Court, grand bench, 10 September 2008, 62 *Minshu* 2029.
[39] Supreme Court, grand bench, 8 October 1952, 6 *Minshu* 783.

Article 81 merely confirmed the power of the judiciary to review the constitutionality of a statute when exercising judicial power. Believing that this suit was filed without satisfying the case or controversy requirement, the Supreme Court dismissed it.

As a result of this decision, it was established that in order for the Court to review the constitutionality of a statute, there must be a case or controversy. The Supreme Court also held that not only the Supreme Court, but all the lower courts have the power of judicial review.[40]

The Court's view is generally supported.[41] However, as a result of this decision, in Japan it has been believed that a suit challenging the constitutionality of a statute before it has been applied in a specific case fails the case or controversy requirement. Although in the United States it is common to seek a declaration of unconstitutionality and an injunction against the application of a statute before it is to be applied to a specific case, such suits have not been admitted in Japan.

PROCESS OF CONSTITUTIONAL LITIGATION

It is necessary that cases or controversies must exist before the courts in order to exercise the power of judicial review. There is no 'constitutional suit' per se in Japan. One must file a suit in the District Court, therefore, in order to challenge the constitutionality of a statute or other governmental action. Otherwise, one must violate the statute and challenge the conviction when prosecuted, alleging the unconstitutionality of the conviction.

In order to challenge the constitutionality of a statute, one must file an administrative suit against an administrative agency seeking judicial revocation of the application of the statute in a specific case. Such a suit must follow the requirements of the Administrative Case Litigation Act.

Could a citizen file a civil suit seeking an injunction against the exercise of governmental power, alleging unconstitutionality? The Supreme Court held in the *Osaka International Airport Case*[42] that such a suit had to be filed as an administrative case and not as a civil case, since the citizen was challenging the exercise of governmental power. However, there used to be no provision with respect to administrative actions on seeking

[40] Supreme Court, grand bench, 1 February 1950, 4 *Keishu* 73.

[41] Kiyomiya, 371; Ashibe, 362; Sato, 333–34.

[42] Supreme Court, grand bench, 16 December 1981, 35 *Minshu* 1369.

injunction or mandamus against the government, and the courts have been very reluctant to accept such actions. With an increased call for such pre-enforcement suits, the Diet amended the Administrative Case Litigation Act in 2004 to provide for a suit for injunction and a suit for mandamus. Yet, it is still unclear to what extent the courts are willing to accept such pre-enforcement suits as administrative suits.

One can also file a civil suit seeking a damages award from the government alleging the unconstitutionality of a statute or its application under the Government Liability Act. In a tort action, the plaintiff must prove the illegality of governmental action and negligence on the part of public officials.

The Supreme Court can review and determine the constitutionality of 'any law, order, regulation or official act'. There have been some disputes as to whether a citizen can file a damages suit for legislative inaction. For instance, in the *Voting at Home Case*,[43] a physically handicapped voter sought damages against the government, insisting that the Diet had unconstitutionally abolished the system that had allowed physically handicapped voters to cast votes at home, and had failed to reintroduce such a system, thereby, in essence, depriving them of their right to vote. The Supreme Court admitted that a citizen can seek damages based on action of the Diet. Yet it held that the government should be liable only when the Diet violates the unequivocal language of the Constitution and concluded that in this case no such violation could be found. This holding was widely criticized as having the result of precluding tort actions against the Diet.[44]

The Supreme Court essentially reversed the holding of the *Voting at Home Case* in the *Overseas Voters Case*,[45] by holding that the government was liable when the Diet failed to provide an opportunity for voting to overseas voters and then failed to provide an opportunity to vote in election districts as opposed to via proportional representation. The Court reasoned that the government should be liable when the Diet clearly infringes constitutional rights or when the Diet fails to adopt essential measures to provide opportunities for citizens to exercise their constitutional rights.

In a constitutional challenge, one must assert the unconstitutionality of a statute in such a suit. Essentially, one can only assert the

[43] Supreme Court, 1st petty bench, 21 November 1985, 39 *Minshu* 1512.
[44] Sato, 350.
[45] Supreme Court, grand bench, 14 September 2005, 59 *Minshu* 2087.

unconstitutionality of a statute based on the infringement of the rights or legal interests of the parties. One cannot assert the infringement of rights of third parties as a basis for challenge. Yet the Supreme Court held, in the *Confiscation of Property of Third Parties Case*,[46] that there are some exceptions to this rule. In this case, the defendant attempted to illegally transport clothes to North Korea, and challenged the part of the sentence imposed on him that confiscated the clothes at issue owned by a third party on the ground that the third-party owner was not afforded any opportunity for hearing. Although the confiscation was imposed as a part of the sentence on the defendant, the Supreme Court held that it had the effect of depriving the third-party owner of the clothes of his property rights. Although there were some uncertainties as to whether the confiscation did result in an adverse effect on the defendant, the Supreme Court allowed the defendant to assert the unconstitutionality of the deprivation of property of third parties without affording them any opportunity for hearing.

Even when a constitutional question is presented to the court, the court has discretion to avoid ruling on the constitutional question if it can interpret the statute to conform to the Constitution or if it can decide the case on non-constitutional grounds. Indeed, the Supreme Court in a substantial number of cases has narrowly construed the scope of statutes to sustain their constitutionality. These decisions can be viewed as examples of such constitution-conforming interpretation.

If the dispute concerns a highly political question which is directly related to the government, then it may not be suited for judicial resolution. This is the political question doctrine.

The Supreme Court held in the *Sunagawa Case*,[47] in which the constitutionality of the Japan-United States Security Treaty and stationing in Japan of American military forces was challenged as a violation of article 9, that the issues raised were highly political and related directly to the national safety of the country. Thus, the Court held that such questions were not suitable for judicial decision unless the impugned actions were clearly unconstitutional. The Court first opined that the Japanese Constitution did not abandon the right of self-defence recognized under international law and it inquired whether the stationing of American military forces violated article 9, section 2. Since

[46] Supreme Court, grand bench, 28 November 1962, 16 *Keishu* 1593.
[47] Supreme Court, grand bench, 16 December 1959, 13 *Minshu* 3225.

it construed article 9, section 2, as prohibiting armed forces maintained by the Japanese government, it thus concluded that the stationing of American military forces was not a violation of article 9, section 2. The Court then examined whether the stationing of American troops violated article 9, section 1, and concluded that this raised a highly political question, because it directly implicated the fundamental issue of national defence. The Court held that such a political question is beyond the reach of the judiciary unless there is a clear violation of the Constitution. Ultimately, the Court concluded that the stationing of the American military forces was not clearly against the Constitution and therefore the court should not address the constitutional issue.

This decision was quite bizarre. Since the Court reviewed whether the stationing of American military personnel clearly violated article 9, this decision may be interpreted as upholding the constitutionality of this action on the merits. Yet, an overwhelming number of academics tend to view this decision as refusing to rule on the merits, invoking the political question doctrine.[48] After this decision, many lower courts tended to invoke the political question doctrine to avoid deciding on issues such as the constitutionality of the SDF.[49]

The Supreme Court once again invoked the political question doctrine in the *Tomabechi Case*,[50] in which one of the members of the House of Representatives challenged the dissolution of the House without a no-confidence vote as stipulated in article 69, and allegedly without a Cabinet decision to give advice and approval to the Emperor. The Supreme Court held that the dissolution of the House of Representatives raises a question of such a political nature, directly implicating basic questions regarding government, that the courts should not decide such a case. This decision is more straightforward and can be said to be relying on the political question doctrine.

While some support the doctrine,[51] many oppose it. Every constitutional question necessarily implicates highly political questions, critics argue, and there is no justification for refusing to rule on such

[48] Kisaburo Yokota, 'Political Questions and Judicial Review: A Comparison' in D Fenno Henderson (ed), *The Constitution of Japan: Its First Twenty Years, 1947–67* (Seattle, University of Washington Press, 1968) 141.

[49] See below, ch 8, n 25.

[50] Supreme Court, grand bench, 8 June 1960, 14 *Minshu* 1206.

[51] Kiyomiya, 340–41.

questions.[52] It is the national defence issue that is likely to raise the most volatile political questions.[53] Although many academics argue that the courts should not avoid the issue of article 9 because of the existence of political questions, since article 9 embodies the fundamental principles of the Constitution and is judicially enforceable, the courts will probably not be blamed for their unwillingness to decide the issue.

When the Supreme Court strikes down a statute, the ruling of unconstitutionality has a binding effect on the parties to the case in which the statute is at issue. Unlike a ruling of unconstitutionality under the Federal Constitutional Court of Germany, which has the effect of abolishing the entire statute, a ruling of unconstitutionality from the Supreme Court of Japan does not have that effect. The Supreme Court sends a copy of the judgment to the Diet, and it is the responsibility of the Diet to amend or abolish the statute that was held to be unconstitutional. Usually, the Diet quickly amends unconstitutional provisions. Yet, when the Supreme Court struck down the parricide provision in 1973, the Diet could not abolish the provision because of opposition from conservative members of the LDP. The provision was finally abolished in 1995, when the Criminal Code was totally rewritten in plain language.[54]

JUDICIAL REVIEW AND DEMOCRACY

Although courts are vested with the power of judicial review, judges are not elected by the people and do not have to seek re-election. Although there is a popular vote system for Supreme Court Justices, it has not functioned as an effective check against the judiciary. When unelected judges overturn a decision of the Diet, which is elected by the people, then the question is naturally raised why judges are allowed to do that in light of the democratic ideals of the Constitution.

The Supreme Court has never seriously considered this issue, since it has held only eight statutory provisions unconstitutional since the

[52] Urabe, 374–75.

[53] See above, n 27.

[54] See below, ch 7, nn 1 and 18. The prosecutors decided to prosecute the defendants under the general homicide provision instead of the parricide provision after the unconstitutional ruling. Although the parricide provision remained on the Criminal Code, it was not actually enforced.

end of Pacific War: the parricide provision of the Criminal Code;[55] the proper distance requirement for permits for new pharmacies under the Pharmaceutical Act;[56] the restriction on division claims by co-owners of a forest under the Forest Act;[57] the restriction on tort actions against a postal office pursuant to the Postal Act;[58] the absence of voting opportunities under the Public Office Election Act for citizens living abroad[59] and the discrimination against illegitimate children acquiring Japanese nationality under the Nationality Act.[60] In addition, two provisions of the Public Office Election Act on apportionment[61] were held to be unconstitutional. The Supreme Court also held the following to be unconstitutional: the punishment of a defendant for a crime not permitted as punishable under the Constitution after the end of occupation;[62] the application of mandatory mediation procedures for debt adjustment;[63] the confiscation of property of third parties without

[55] Supreme Court, grand bench, 4 April 1973, 27 *Keishu* 265. See below, ch 7, n 1.

[56] Supreme Court, grand bench, 30 April 1975, 29 *Minshu* 572. See below, ch 7, n 100.

[57] Supreme Court, grand bench, 22 April 1987, 41 Minshu, p 408. See below, ch 7, n 104.

[58] Supreme Court, grand bench, 11 September 2002, 56 *Minshu* 1439. The Postal Act contained provisions limiting the government's liability for mishandling mail. In this case, a creditor had sent a seizure order by special delivery mail, a particular kind of registered mail, but the postal office delivered it to the debtor's private post box and the creditor failed to secure the seizure. The creditor sought damages, but the Postal Act gives immunity to the government for handling registered mail even when the postal office causes damage with intent or by gross negligence. The Supreme Court held that this limitation of liability was unreasonable and unconstitutional.

[59] Supreme Court, grand bench, 14 September 2005, above n 45. See above, ch 2, n 16.

[60] Supreme Court, grand bench, 4 June 2008, 2002 *Hanreijihou* 3. See above, ch 2, n 17; below ch 7, n 21.

[61] Supreme Court, grand bench, 14 April 1976, 30 *Minshu* 223; Supreme Court, grand bench, 17 July 1985, 39 *Minshu* 1100. However, both of these decisions declined to invalidate the election results conducted under the unconstitutional provisions. See above, ch 2, nn 28 and 29.

[62] Supreme Court, grand bench, 22 July 1953, 7 *Keishu* 1562. See above, ch 1, n 59.

[63] Supreme Court, grand bench, 6 July 1960, 14 *Minshu* 1657. In this case, the Court applied the Mandatory Debt Adjustment Act to a dispute about a house and came to a decision without conducting an open trial. The Court reasoned, however, that courts must hold open trials in order to find facts and decide the rights and obligations of parties. The Mandatory Debt Adjustment Act should not have been applied in this case and the decision reached without an open trial was a violation of art 32 as well as of art 82.

affording an opportunity for hearing under the Code of Criminal Procedure;[64] the spending of public money on religious rituals of the Yasukuni Shrine[65] and the free provision of public property for the use of Shinto shrines.[66] [67] Yet, in all other cases, the Supreme Court rejected constitutional challenges. The Japanese Supreme Court has developed a very conservative constitutional jurisprudence.[68]

Why has the Supreme Court developed such a conservative jurisprudence? Vested with the power of judicial review, from the beginning the Supreme Court faced a tremendous number of litigations alleging constitutional violation. There is the reason for this. Unlike the previous Court of Judicature, the criminal defendant could not challenge the finding of facts or sentencing before the Supreme Court. As a result, a huge number of criminal defendants filed a constitutional challenge to the Supreme Court in order to attract its attention to review the finding of facts and sentencing. Many of the arguments were poorly written and the lawyers were not accustomed to constitutional arguments. Faced with such poor arguments, the Supreme Court came to reject all such argument, sustaining the constitutionality of all statutes. Perhaps, the Justices might have believed that the unelected Justices should not disturb the judgment of elected legislature unless the legislation was clearly unreasonable. Perhaps, the Supreme Court might have believed that it needed more time to build its prestige and acquire public trust before striking down statutes passed by the democratic Diet. The Court has, especially under the second Chief Justice Koutarou Tanaka (1950–59) who was a strong conservative Catholic and an avowed anti-communist, established a very conservative jurisprudence.

During the late 1960s, however, there were some hints of new development. The majority of Justices came to review the constitutionality of infringement of individual rights more carefully, as in the *All Postal*

[64] Supreme Court, grand bench, 28 November 1962, above n 46.

[65] Supreme Court, grand bench, 2 April 1997, 51 *Minshu* 1673. See below, ch 7, n 46.

[66] Supreme Court, grand bench, 20 January 2010: www.courts.go.jp/hanrei/pdf/20100120164304.pdf. See below, ch 7, n 47.

[67] Jun-ichi Satoh, 'Judicial Review in Japan: An Overview of the Case Law and an Examination of Trends in the Japanese Supreme Court's Constitutional Oversight' (2008) 41 *Loyola of Los Angeles Law Review* 603.

[68] D Fenno Henderson, 'Japanese Judicial Review of Legislation: The First Twenty Years' in D Fenno Henderson (ed), *The Constitution of Japan: Its First Twenty Years, 1947–67* (Seattle, University of Washington Press, 1968) 115.

Workers, Tokyo Central Post Office Case.[69] The liberal attitude of these Justices received strong criticism from the conservative politicians in the Diet. The Supreme Court became very sensitive to political accusation. After the Supreme Court overturned the *All Postal Workers, Tokyo Central Post Office Case* in the *All Agricultural and Forest Workers, Police Office Act Opposition Case,*[70] the Supreme Court steadfastly refused to interfere with politics. In order to maintain its status and independence, the Supreme Court established itself as a very conservative institution.

Looking back, since it is the Cabinet that has the power to choose the Supreme Court Justices, and since the government has been mostly occupied by the conservative parties, almost all the Justices have been selected by the conservative governments. Although the Chief Justice can recommend new candidates to the Prime Minister, it is unlikely that he or she will recommend someone who does not share the conservative ideology of the ruling party. Moreover, the majority of the Justices are chosen from former judges or prosecutors in order to make sure that these Justices can control the Supreme Court.

Furthermore, the Supreme Court usually accepts over 10,000 appeals and petitions every year and the number of constitutional litigations is quite small. The Justices are overwhelmed by the tremendous case load (each Justice will have to review 750 cases as a Justice responsible for the case and participate in 3500 cases as a member of the petty bench) and will not be able to concentrate on the constitutional issue. Since most of the Justices will retire within five or six years, they do not have sufficient time to develop their own constitutional philosophy. Moreover, influenced by the traditional societal commitment to harmony, even the Justices of Court may not be willing to oppose the government. All these factors might have contributed to the development of very conservative jurisprudence.

But the most fundamental reason for the unwillingness of the Supreme Court to review the constitutionality of a statute carefully and strike it down may lie in the perception of constitutional law by judges. For a judge trained in the civil law tradition, the Constitution looks more like a political principle than a legal rule to be applied by the judge. Most of the judges are positivists and believe in application of a rule embodied in

[69] Supreme Court, grand bench, 26 October 1966, 20 *Keishu* 901. See below, ch 7, n 115.

[70] Supreme Court, grand bench, 25 April 1973, 27 *Keishu* 547. See below, ch 7, n 118.

statutes to a case before them. For them, the Constitution does not look like statute to be judicially enforced.

On the other hand, the Supreme Court has showed its willingness to give protection to fundamental human rights by giving narrow construction to prohibited conduct. For instance, in the *Prison Inmates Newspaper Deletion Case*,[71] the Court narrowly construed a provision in the Prison Act, broadly authorizing a prison chief to delete inappropriate articles when he or she provided newspapers to prison inmates. The Court held that deletion was authorized only when there was a high possibility that the order and safety of the prison would be jeopardized, or the rehabilitation goals of prisoners would be undermined. Similarly, the Supreme Court, in the *Fukuoka Prefecture Youth Protection Ordinance Case*,[72] narrowly construed the unbridled ban on sexual intercourse with a youth as merely authorizing criminal punishment when adult persons deceive youths into sexual intercourse, or when adult persons have sexual intercourse with youths simply to gratify their sexual desires.

The Supreme Court has also showed its willingness to protect individual rights by employing the abuse of discretion doctrine on a non-constitutional basis. For instance, the Supreme Court held in the *Jehovah's Witness Kendo Refusal Case*,[73] that a public high school should not be allowed to expel a student who did not practice kendo—Japanese fencing—because of his religious belief against fighting. The Court believed that the expulsion should be a means of last resort and the school abused its discretion when it refused to provide the student alternative means to receive credit. The Supreme Court also held in the third *Ienaga School Textbook Censorship Case*,[74] that an order by the Education Minister to delete the description of biochemical experiments by Japanese military forces in China during the Pacific War as a condition of approving the history textbook submitted for review, was an abuse of discretion and was illegal, although it rejected the constitutional attack on the school textbook review system. The Court believed that the incident was common knowledge among historians and therefore there was no reason for ordering deletion.

[71] Supreme Court, grand bench, 22 June 1983, 37 *Minshu* 793.

[72] Supreme Court, grand bench, 23 October 1985, 39 *Keishu* 413.

[73] Supreme Court, 2nd petty bench, 8 March 1996, 50 *Minshu* 469. See below, ch 7, n 38.

[74] Supreme Court, 3rd petty bench, 29 August 1997, 51 *Minshu* 2921. See below, ch 7, n 54.

Many academics are critical of this extreme conservatism of the Supreme Court. They thus argue that the Court should play more of an activist role, defending individual rights against any encroachments.

It must be noted, however, that the general public had not cared much about such a conservative attitude of the courts toward constitutional litigation. Since most of the public had not expected the courts to play much active role in solving legal disputes in general, it is natural that they had not expected the courts to enforce the Constitution more vigorously. It is only minorities and lawyers who have supported their suits against the government who have expressed strong criticisms against the conservative jurisprudence of the courts. Yet, with the increasing call for judicial reform, many came to realize the necessity of the courts taking a more active role in also enforcing the Constitution against the government. Even the LDP came to admit the necessity of providing a more effective check by the judiciary against the political branch.[75]

In order to make the courts play a more active role in enforcing the Constitution, there has been a proposal to establish the Constitutional Court by amending the Constitution.[76] By giving the power to review the constitutionality without specific cases or controversies in response to request for constitutional opinion, this proposal will surely promote constitutional review. Yet, there is a serious question as to whether the mere establishment of a Constitutional Court will make the Court review the constitutionality of a statute more vigorously or make it more willing to strike down the statutes. More is definitely needed to ensure that the courts more actively enforce the Constitution.

CONCLUSION

Although the judiciary is vested with the judicial power to solve legal disputes, it has not played an active role in Japan. With the small number of lawyers and with the small amount of civil litigation, the Court simply has not played a large role in solving legal disputes. The Supreme Court has established a highly demanding 'case or controversy' requirement and rejected many administrative cases without reaching the merits. This has made it difficult for a citizen to challenge the actions of administrative

[75] LDP, 'Points for Constitutional Amendment': www.jimin.jp/jimin/jimin/2004_seisaku/kenpou/contents/05.html.

[76] See below, ch 9, n 24.

agencies. The conviction rate of over 99 per cent in criminal cases also casts doubt on whether the courts are properly checking the prosecutors.

With respect to power of judicial review, the Supreme Court has similarly fashioned very demanding cases or controversies requirement, and rejected many constitutional litigations for want of that requirement. It has also established a highly conservative constitutional jurisprudence and has rejected many constitutional attacks in deference to the judgment of the Diet.

This small role played by the judiciary is one of the most peculiar characteristics of Japanese society in general and the Japanese Constitution in particular. The Constitution has functioned largely, therefore, as a political norm rather than a judicial norm to be enforced by the judiciary. There is definitely an urgent necessity to reconsider this small role and to introduce reforms to facilitate the courts to exercise judicial power in general and the power of judicial review in particular. The recent judicial reform is surely a significant step. But more is needed to facilitate an increased active role for the courts in Japan.

FURTHER READING

HF Bolz, 'Judicial Review in Japan: The Strategy of Restraint' (1980) 4 *Hastings International & Comparative Law Review* 87.

Hideo Chikusa, 'Japanese Supreme Court: Its Institution and Background' (1999) 52 *SMU Law Review* 1719.

DJ Danelski, 'The Supreme Court of Japan: An Exploratory Study' in G Schubert and D Danelski (eds), *Comparative Judicial Behavior* (New York, Oxford University Press, 1969) 121–56.

Yasuo Hasebe, 'The Supreme Court of Japan: Its Adjudication on Electoral Systems and Economic Freedoms' (2007) 5(2) *International Journal of Constitutional Law* 296.

Hiroshi Itoh, *The Japanese Supreme Court: Constitutional Politics* (New York, Markus Wiener Publishing Inc, 1989).

Norikazu Kawagishi, 'The Birth of Judicial Review in Japan' (2007) 5(2) *International Journal of Constitutional Law* 308.

DS Law, 'The Anatomy of a Conservative Court: Judicial Review in Japan' (2009) 87 *Texas Law Review* 1545.

J Sanders, 'Courts and Law in Japan' in H Jacob, E Blankenburg, HM Kritzer, DM Provine and J Sanders (eds), *Court, Law & Politics in Comparative Perspective* (New Haven, Yale University Press, 1996) 315.

S Shizue Mckenna, 'Proposal for Judicial Reform in Japan: An Overview' (2001) 2 *Asia-Pacific Law & Policy Journal* 1.

Hidenori Tomatsu, 'Judicial Review in Japan: An Overview of Efforts to Introduce U.S. Theories' in Yoichi Higuchi (ed), *Five Decades of Constitutionalism in Japanese Society* (Tokyo, Tokyo University Press, 2001) 251.

6

The Protection of Fundamental Human Rights: Structural Issues

Introduction – PART I: FUNDAMENTAL HUMAN RIGHTS – Human Rights and Fundamental Human Rights – Structural Significance of Rights Protection–Classification of Rights – Who Is Entitled to Protection? – PART II: APPLICABILITY OF CONSTITUTIONAL RIGHTS – Applicability to Private Conduct of Citizens – Civil Rights Legislation – Part III: RESTRICTIONS ON FUNDAMENTAL HUMAN RIGHTS – Fundamental Human Rights and Public Welfare – Permissibility of Restriction – Conclusion

INTRODUCTION

THE JAPANESE CONSTITUTION has an elaborate Bill of Rights. In Chapter III: Rights and Duties of the People the Constitution lists certain rights and obligations of the people.[1] The rights of the people are guaranteed as 'fundamental human rights' in Japan. The people shall not be prevented from enjoying any of the fundamental human rights (article 11). The Constitution states that these rights shall be conferred upon the people of this and future generations

[1] The Constitution stipulates three obligations of citizens: the obligation of every parent to provide his or her child with education (art 26, s 2); the obligation to work (art 27, s 1) and the obligation to pay tax (art 30). Although the Constitution obliges public officials to respect and uphold the Constitution (art 99), it has been construed that the people are not obliged to support it. Since art 9 prohibits any armed forces, the Constitution does not have a provision mandating military service to the citizens. Conscription is believed to violate the prohibition of involuntary servitude in art 18 as well as art 9.

as eternal and inviolate rights (article 12). As stipulated in article 97, the fundamental human rights guaranteed by the Constitution to the people of Japan are 'fruits of the age-old struggle of man to be free; they have survived the many exacting tests for durability and are conferred upon this and future generations in trust, to be held for all time inviolate'.

This chapter will examine the structural issues of the protection of fundamental human rights, including the meaning of fundamental human rights and the significance of their constitutional protection. It will also examine the applicability of this protection and its possible limitations. The next chapter will be devoted to an examination of the content and application of specific rights guaranteed by the Constitution.

PART I: FUNDAMENTAL HUMAN RIGHTS

HUMAN RIGHTS AND FUNDAMENTAL HUMAN RIGHTS

Fundamental human rights are rights inherent in every human being. Every human being is entitled to human dignity and fundamental human rights derive from human dignity. All persons are entitled to such inherent rights as 'natural rights'.[2] Therefore, these rights are not only protected by the Constitution, they are inherently worthy of protection.

Although the Bill of Rights of the Japanese Constitution was very greatly influenced by the United States' Constitution, the strong contribution of German constitutional thought is apparent in the understanding of fundamental human rights. Accepting the leading German constitutional thought, fundamental human rights are thus believed to be a substantive restraint on the government, precluding government interference within the private sphere. In other words, they are substantive values. They also create the value hierarchy for all government actions, including those of the Diet. The most fundamental value is 'human dignity'. Every human being is supposed to have capacity to control and to discipline himself or herself based on reason. This faith in reason is the basis for human dignity.

[2] Miyazawa, 77–78, 81, 205; Ashibe, 78; Sato, 392–93. For a minority view, Matsui, 305–08 (fundmental human rights should be viewed as rights of citizens guaranteed for citizens to participate in the political process).

Unlike the German Basic Law, however, the Japanese Constitution does not have any clause specifically protecting human dignity. It simply provides that '[a]ll of the people shall be respected as individuals' in the first sentence of article 13 and also refers to 'individual dignity' in article 24, section 2, when it mandates the Diet to provide law on choice of spouse, property rights, inheritance, choice of domicile, divorce and other matters pertaining to marriage and the family, together with the essential equality of the sexes. Yet, it has been assumed that article 13 places individuals over the state or society, thus guaranteeing individualism as a constitutional principle, and that individualism mandated by article 13 requires the government to treat each individual as an individual human being, thus obliging the government to respect 'human dignity'.[3]

This is the most significant difference between the Japanese Constitution and the Meiji Constitution, since rights protected under the Meiji Constitution were a benevolent grant from the Emperor to his subjects. They were not rights conceptualized as being inherent in every human being or citizen.

Is there any distinction between human rights and fundamental human rights? The answer is no. All human rights are fundamental human rights.[4] Are all the rights listed in Chapter III fundamental human rights? The answer is again no. Although the welfare right protected under article 25 could be viewed as a natural right and a fundamental human right, since it is essential for human dignity, there are certain rights that do not deserve to be called fundamental human rights.[5]

STRUCTURAL SIGNIFICANCE OF RIGHTS PROTECTION

The rights under the Meiji Constitution were protected only within the confines of statutes. When the Imperial Diet, together with the Emperor, passed a statute restricting these rights, there was no way for citizens to complain about this unconstitutional infringement. The courts did not have the power to review the constitutionality of a statute. However, under the Japanese Constitution, the guarantee of rights is constitutional and the Constitution is the supreme law. If a statute passed by the Diet infringes the rights protected by the Constitution, then that statute is

3 Miyazawa, 78–79, 213–14.

4 Ashibe II, 46.

5 Ashibe, 80; Ito, 190 (excluding art 17 and art 40).

unconstitutional and void. Article 81 gives to the judiciary the power to review the constitutionality of a statute passed by the Diet, in addition to any 'order, regulation or official act'. All branches of the government are thus subject to the protection of individual rights and the courts can exercise their power to determine whether a restriction on individual rights is justified.

Some of the rights listed in Chapter III contain the 'institutional guarantee', which is not extended to individual citizens as an individual right. For instance, article 20 guarantees the separation of Church and State in addition to religious freedom. According to the Supreme Court, this guarantee is merely institutional and is not designed to grant an individual right.[6] Therefore, even where there are violations of this guarantee, no citizen is allowed to file a suit seeking declaration of unconstitutionality or damages. The protection of autonomy of the university under article 23 and the guarantee of the system of individual private property under article 29 are often cited as other examples of such institutional guarantees. Yet, there are very strong criticisms against the notion of institutional guarantee, since it would make it impossible to challenge violations of it as infringements of individual rights.[7]

Moreover, some of the rights protected in Chapter III may not be meant to grant individual rights, which can be invoked before the courts. For instance, the Supreme Court has held that the welfare right protected under article 25 is not an individual right which can be asserted in the courts.[8] The welfare right is, rather, a programme provision, which merely obliges the government to accomplish a goal. Critics claim that the welfare right should be recognized as an individual right.[9] Yet, most academics deny the right of citizens to file suit in the courts demanding the payment of welfare assistance solely based on article 25. The welfare right can be asserted before the courts only when it is transformed into a specific right by statute by the Diet.[10]

In Germany, fundamental rights protected under the Basic Law are generally believed to be subjective rights as well as objective principles,

[6] Supreme Court, grand bench, 13 July 1977, 31 *Minshu* 533 (*Tsu City Ground Breaking Ceremony Case*). See below, ch 7, n 41.

[7] Ashibe, 84; Sato, 398.

[8] Supreme Court, grand bench, 24 May 1967, 21 *Minshu* 1043 (*Asahi Case*). See below, ch 7, n 111.

[9] Ashibe, 254; Sato, 620–21.

[10] See below, ch 7, n 113.

and some follow this view in Japan. Some even argue that some of the individual rights provisions, such as the equality right, are not meant to grant subjective rights but rather to declare objective principles, which would entitle everyone to challenge the violation.[11] Also in Germany, the Federal Constitutional Court has admitted the constitutional duty of the government to protect constitutional rights against private infringement. In certain situations, the legislature is constitutionally obliged to impose criminal penalties against those infringing constitutional rights. Some follow this view and argue for the constitutional duty of the government to protect constitutional rights in Japan.[12] Yet, such a view is generally rejected because it would allow (even require) the government more powers to restrict freedoms, undermining the basic purpose of protecting those freedoms against government infringement.[13]

CLASSIFICATION OF RIGHTS

Aside from the equality right protected under article 14, most of the individual rights protected in Chapter III mandate that the government must not interfere with the rights and freedoms of individuals. Such rights may be called negative freedoms. If the government unreasonably infringes on these freedoms, then such infringement would be void and the courts would nullify the government action.

It is a custom among constitutional academics to distinguish, however, personal freedoms from economic freedoms. Freedom of thought and conscience (article 19), religious freedom (article 20), freedom of expression (article 21) and academic freedom (article 23) are generally called personal freedoms or mental freedoms. They are concerned with the freedom of the mind and its expression. On the other hand, the Constitution protects the freedom to choose one's occupation (article 22) and the right to property (article 29), and these provisions are generally viewed as protecting economic freedoms. Personal freedoms are seen as deserving stronger judicial protection than economic freedoms, because personal freedoms are essential not only for human dignity, but for democratic society, and because the danger of arbitrary infringement of

[11] Urabe, 51, 104–05.

[12] Go Koyama, *Kihonkenhogo no Houri* (Theory of Obligation to Protect Fundamental Rights) (Tokyo, Seibundou, 1998).

[13] Ashibe, 113.

personal freedoms is greater than the danger of arbitrary infringement of economic freedoms. While the government is allowed to restrict personal freedoms in order to prevent infringement of the rights of others and of other public interests, it is also allowed to restrict economic freedoms for the purpose of promoting the welfare state.

Some of the rights protected in Chapter III require the government to provide certain goods and services. The welfare right protected under article 25 is typical, since it requires government to secure a minimum standard of living. It is thus the custom among constitutional academics to view the welfare right protected under article 25 as a right of citizens to seek government services. The right to receive education under article 26, the right to work protected under article 27 and the rights of workers protected under article 28 are also examples of the right to demand government services. These rights are new rights, generally called 'social rights', since they are concerned with the social problems inherent in capitalist society.

The right to seek redress against infringement of rights under article 17 and the right of access to the courts protected under article 32 are rights entitling the citizen to seek judicial action. They are distinguished from social rights, however, because they are concerned with judicial process. They may also be classified as procedural rights.

The voting right protected under article 15 is generally called an 'active right', which entitles citizens to actively participate in the political process. The voting right is thought to be essential in guaranteeing freedom and as deserving of constitutional protection. Yet, the voting right has been viewed as having a dual nature: voting is both an individual right and a performance of official power. As a result, as we saw in chapter two above, it has been interpreted as allowing broader restriction of voting rights in order to secure the appropriate performance of official power.

Articles 31 to 40 protect the rights of criminal suspects and defendants. These rights are generally classified as protecting physical freedoms. They may be also viewed as procedural rights in contrast with other substantive rights.

WHO IS ENTITLED TO PROTECTION?

Since the Constitution protects the foregoing rights as rights of the people of Japan, all Japanese citizens are entitled to their protection.

Even minors, including infants, enjoy these fundamental human rights.[14] Of course, some rights are not extended to minors, such as the right to vote. Moreover, some restrictions are permissible for minors in order to protect them.

It has been assumed that fundamental human rights belong only to natural persons. However, the Supreme Court has held that there is no reason to deny fundamental human rights to corporations. In the *Yahata Steel Political Contribution Case*,[15] for instance, the Supreme Court held that private corporations enjoy human rights so long as these rights are not inappropriate for corporations. The Court concluded that private corporations have the right to make contributions to political parties. Since this case is concerned with a suit filed by shareholders against a company, and therefore does not involve infringement of constitutional human rights, the Court's holding is merely obiter dicta. Yet, the Supreme Court seems to have affirmed this position, as it has since held that mass media organizations enjoy freedom of expression.[16]

What, then, about non-citizens? Do they enjoy constitutional rights? Even though the Constitution only guarantees fundamental human rights to the people of Japan, it has been assumed that every human being, including non-citizens, is entitled to them. The Supreme Court thus held that a foreigner who entered Japan illegally was entitled to the protection of fundamental human rights.[17] The Supreme Court affirmed this holding in the *McLean Case*.[18] In this case, a foreigner, working as an English teacher, applied for renewal of his permit to stay in Japan, but the Foreign Minister refused it, primarily since McLean participated in rallies against the intervention of the US in the Vietnam War. The Supreme Court held that foreigners do not have a constitutional right to enter

[14] A foetus does not enjoy fundamental human rights. Although abortion is prohibited under the Criminal Code (arts 212 to 215), in practice the Mother's Body Protection Act makes it very easy to obtain an abortion (art 14).

[15] Supreme Court, grand bench, 24 June 1970, 24 *Minshu* 625.

[16] See below, n 37. The position of the Supreme Court has been supported by many: Ashibe, 87; Ashibe I, 162.Yet, some argue that only natural persons deserve fundamental human rights and corporations are entitled to constitutional rights as distinguished from natural rights. Yasuo Hasebe, 'Rights of Corporations, Rights of Individuals: Judicial Precedents' in Yoichi Higuchi (ed), *Five Decades of Constitutionalism in Japanese Society* (Tokyo, University of Tokyo Press, 2001) 73, 75–76; Tsujimura, 151–52.

[17] Supreme Court, 2nd petty bench, 28 December 1950, 4 *Minshu* 683.

[18] Supreme Court, grand bench, 4 October 1978, 32 *Minshu* 1223.

Japan or to stay in Japan. However, so long as foreigners are staying in Japan, they are entitled to protection of their fundamental human rights, including freedom of expression. However, the Court held that there is a special limit on freedom of expression of foreigners, since they should not be allowed to influence fundamental national policy-making, as this is to be left to Japanese citizens under the popular sovereignty principle. Moreover, the Court held that the Foreign Minister is allowed to consider the exercise of rights by foreigners as a factor in denying renewal of permits even when such rights are constitutionally protected. McLean's anti-US political activities may thus be considered as a justification for refusing renewal of his permit to stay. As a result, the Court concluded that there was no abuse of discretion on the part of the Foreign Minister.

According to this holding, foreigners are entitled to constitutional protection, yet some rights do not extend to them, such as the right to vote[19] or the welfare right.[20] Even when foreigners are entitled to certain rights, the government can refuse their entry or refuse renewal of a permit for any reason. Moreover, even when foreigners enjoy constitutional rights, the government can impose on them restrictions only applicable to foreigners, and the Supreme Court has been unwilling to invalidate these restrictions. For instance, the Foreigner Registration Act required foreigners staying in Japan to register on the foreigner registration list and mandated them to carry foreign registrations everywhere and to show them when requested by police officers. It then obliged foreigners to provide fingerprints every time they registered or renewed their registration. The fingerprinting requirement was especially upsetting for resident Koreans. They strongly protested the requirement, since they felt that they were being treated as criminals. They thus challenged the fingerprinting requirement as infringing the right to privacy as protected

[19] Supreme Court, 2nd petty bench, 26 February 1993, 1452 *Hanreijihou* 37 (a foreigner does not have a constitutional right to vote in national elections); Supreme Court, 3rd petty bench, 28 February 1995, 49 *Minshu* 639 (a foreigner does not have a constitutional right to vote in local elections, although the Diet might be able to grant voting rights to permanent residents).

[20] Supreme Court, 3rd petty bench, 25 September 2001, 1768 *Hanreijihou* 47 (exclusion of illegal foreigners from the welfare programme under the Welfare Assistance Act does not violate art 25 or art 14); Supreme Court, 1st petty bench, 2 March 1989, 1363 *Hanreijihou* 68 (limitation of eligibility to receive disability pension benefits under the National Pension Act to the Japanese citizens does not violate art 25 or art 14). However, it must be noted that the government grants welfare payment to foreigners legally living in Japan as a matter of administrative measures.

by article 13. The Court admitted in the *Foreigners Fingerprint Case*[21] that, under article 13, an individual has a right not to be forced to provide fingerprints, and foreigners also enjoy this right. Yet, the Supreme Court rejected the foreigner's constitutional attack, holding that fingerprinting is necessary for identifying foreigners and that it should be upheld as a reasonable restriction.[22] Despite article 14, the Supreme Court also showed its willingness to uphold these discriminatory provisions as reasonable in the *Foreigners Fingerprint Case.*[23] The Court found that there was a reasonable ground to require fingerprinting only to foreigners as distinguished from the Japanese citizens. The Court has also adopted similar tolerant attitudes towards discriminatory rules only applicable to foreigners.[24]

For instance, there are a number of policies that discriminate between foreigners and citizens. Foreigners are excluded from the ranks of national public workers, although there is no explicit provision about this aside from the Diplomat Act, which excludes non-citizens from becoming officers of the Foreign Ministry (article 7, section 1). It is the understanding of the government that public workers are exercising governmental power and that government jobs should thus be available only to citizens. The government has also adopted the same attitude towards local public workers. Although some of the local governments have openly ignored this policy and allowed foreigners such as resident Koreans to work for them, they have placed limits on promotion and have not allowed foreigners to hold management positions that involve political policy-making. When these limitations were challenged by a resident Korean in the *Foreigner Promotion Restriction Case*,[25] the Supreme Court held that, in light of the popular sovereignty principle, public

[21] Supreme Court, 3rd petty bench, 15 December 1995, 49 *Keishu* 842.

[22] The resident Koreans were later exempted from this fingerprint requirement in 1993 in response to the strong protest from the Korean government, and the Japanese government decided to abolish the fingerprint requirement altogether in 1999. Yet, after the intensified concern with national security against terrorists following the 9/11 attacks, the government amended the Immigration Control and Refugee Act in 2006 to mandate all foreign visitors to provide pictures and fingerprints when they enter Japan. Special permanent resident status holders such as resident Koreans are exempted.

[23] Supreme Court, 3rd petty bench, 15 December 1995, above n 21.

[24] Supreme Court, 2nd petty bench, 24 July 1959, 13 *Keishu* 1212 (foreign registration requirement does not violate equality rights of foreigners). See above, n 20.

[25] Supreme Court, grand bench, 26 January 2005, 59 *Minshu* 128.

workers who grant legal rights, impose duties on the public or who are involved in important policy-making functions, must be Japanese citizens. The exclusion of foreigners from promotion to such positions was thus held to be reasonable and not a violation of article 14.

This decision has been subjected to many criticisms. Moreover, some even argue that long-term resident foreigners such as permanent resident status holders, including resident Koreans, should be distinguished from temporary visitors and should be allowed broader constitutional protection.[26]

PART II: APPLICABILITY OF CONSTITUTIONAL RIGHTS

APPLICABILITY TO PRIVATE CONDUCT OF CITIZENS

The Constitution was meant to constrain the conduct of the national government and local governments. The Bill of Rights protected under the Constitution thus does not bind the conduct of private individuals and corporations.

The Supreme Court made this clear in the *Mitsubishi Plastic, Inc. Case.*[27] In this case, a university graduate was offered a job by Mitsubishi Plastic, Inc. but was refused employment as a full employee when his probationary period ended because the company found out that he was actively engaged in the student movement during his student days and he did not disclose this fact during his application and interview. The most important question raised in this case was whether the company was allowed to refuse full employment because of the political views and activities of employees. The student argued that the company was constrained by the Constitution and the company's refusal was an infringement of freedom of thought protected under article 19. Yet, the Supreme Court denied the applicability of the individual rights provision of Chapter III to private conduct of individuals and corporations.[28]

[26] Ashibe, 90. See also Tsujimura, 144 on distinguishing permanent residents from other visitors.

[27] Supreme Court, grand bench, 12 December 1973, 27 *Minshu* 1536.

[28] The Supreme Court affirmed this holding in subsequent cases: Supreme Court, 3rd petty bench, 19 July 1974, 28 *Minshu* 790 (*Showa University Case*, in which the private university dismissed a student for political activity); Supreme Court, 3rd petty

This does not mean that private companies are free to discriminate against people. Article 90 of the Civil Code prohibits juristic acts such as conclusion or termination of a contract that are against public order and good morals, and any juristic acts of a private corporation that are against public order and good morals are invalid. Similarly, when one infringes the rights and legal interests of others without justification, then the infringement can constitute a tort, thus allowing the victims to seek damages. The Supreme Court held in the *Nissan Motors Corporation Case*,[29] for instance, that the unduly unreasonable discriminatory practice of forcing female workers to retire at a younger age than male workers is against public order and good morals and is thus invalid. In this case, the Nissan Motors Corporation had an employment policy on mandatory retirement at the age of 50 for women and 55 for men. The Court found no reasonable justification to believe that women lose their working ability at a younger age than men and concluded that such a discriminatory practice was unjustified.

It has been argued that the courts should consider the value hierarchy established by the Constitution when they decide whether private conduct violates public order and good morals. Although the Constitution is not directly applicable, it has been argued that the value judgements of the Constitution should be indirectly applied in private law.[30] This is the theory of indirect third-party application of the Constitution dominant in Germany.

CIVIL RIGHTS LEGISLATION

This dispute is very significant since in Japan there is no comprehensive civil rights legislation that prohibits private discrimination and infringement of rights by individuals and private corporations.

There is a provision in the Labour Standards Act that prohibits discrimination as to working conditions, such as wage or working hours,

bench, 3 September 1991, 1401 *Hanreijihou* 56 (*Tokyo Gakuin High School Case*, in which a student of the private high school was expelled for violation of the school code against riding motorbikes); Supreme Court, 1st petty bench, 18 July 1996, 1599 *Hanreijihou* 53 (*Shutoku High School Case*, in which a student of the private high school was expelled for violation of the school code against using hair permanents).

[29] Supreme Court, 3rd petty bench, 24 March 1981, 35 *Minshu* 300.

[30] Miyazawa, 249–52; Ashibe, 107–14.

based on the nationality, creed or social status of workers (article 3) and discrimination as to wages because of the sex of the worker (article 4). Yet there is no statute prohibiting any other forms of discrimination and private infringements in general. Even with respect to sexual discrimination, while the Equal Employment Opportunity Act (Act to Provide Equal Employment Opportunity and Treatment for Men and Women in the Field of Employment), enacted in 1985 and amended in 1997, first to encourage and then to oblige private companies to provide equal employment opportunities to women, there is still no comprehensive legislation that prohibits sexual discrimination in other fields.

The government has shown some interest in enacting human rights protection legislation, which is designed to prohibit unreasonable private discrimination and to provide administrative assistance to victims of discrimination. The Human Rights Vindication Act Bill submitted to the Diet in 2002 purported to prohibit private discrimination, to establish the Human Rights Commission as an administrative body and to vest authority to help the victims of discrimination obtain redress. Yet, the Bill was also meant to govern discriminatory speech as well as infringement of privacy by mass media, thus triggering strong opposition from mass media organizations. Moreover, some conservative politicians expressed concern about the qualification of members of the Human Rights Commission, since its membership was not limited to citizens. As a result, the Bill failed in the Diet and the future prospects of the revised Bill are still uncertain, although the government has vowed to continue its effort to pass the Bill.

PART III: RESTRICTIONS ON FUNDAMENTAL HUMAN RIGHTS

FUNDAMENTAL HUMAN RIGHTS AND PUBLIC WELFARE

While the Constitution protects fundamental human rights, the constitutional guarantee cannot be unlimited. There are two provisions in the Constitution which suggest that fundamental human rights are subject to restrictions for the purpose of protecting the public welfare. According to article 12, '[t]he freedoms and rights guaranteed to the people by this Constitution shall be maintained by the constant endeavor of the people, who shall refrain from any abuse of these freedoms and rights and shall always be responsible for utilizing them for the public welfare'. And, according to article 13, '[a]ll of the people shall be respected as individuals. Their right to life, liberty, and the pursuit of happiness shall, to the extent that it does not interfere with the public welfare, be the supreme consideration in legislation and in other governmental affairs'.

Despite this, individual protection does not have limits, except according to article 22, section 1, which provides that '[e]very person shall have freedom to choose and change his residence and to choose his occupation to the extent that it does not interfere with the public welfare' and article 29, section 2, which provides that '[p]roperty rights shall be defined by law, in conformity with the public welfare', while section 1 protects property rights. The absence of further limitations in the Constitution may imply the refusal of the framers to allow restriction of these rights to protect the public welfare.

The Supreme Court has, however, construed article 12 and article 13 as indicating the possibility of public welfare restriction with respect to all the rights protected by the Constitution. The Supreme Court held, for instance, in the *Emergency Food Supply Order Case*[31] that, although freedom of speech protected under the Constitution cannot be curtailed unreasonably by the Diet, the public cannot abuse it and must use it for the public welfare. In this case, defendant was charged with a violation of the Emergency Food Supply Order, which imposed criminal punishment on persons who advocated the violation of the obligation of the farmers to sell major products to the government under the mandatory food distribution system. The defendant, a farmer who was frustrated by the government's policy, stood before the other farmers at a farmers' meeting and argued that they should resolve not to sell their crops to the government. The Court upheld the punishment as a means to secure the public welfare. Therefore, even freedom of speech was subject to restriction in order to secure the public welfare.

Similarly, the Supreme Court held in the *'Lady Chatterley's Lover' Case*,[32] that no abuse of individual rights was allowed in light of article 12 and article 13 regardless of whether the individual provisions

31 Supreme Court, grand bench, 18 May 1949, 3 *Keishu* 839. See below, ch 7, n 56.

32 Supreme Court, grand bench, 13 March 1957, 11 *Keishu* 997. See below, ch 7, n 73.

contained explicit limitations, and individual rights, including freedom of expression, were subject to restrictions in order to secure the public welfare. In this case, the publisher and the translator of the translation of 'Lady Chatterley's Lover' were prosecuted for publication of obscene materials in violation of article 175 of the Criminal Code. The Supreme Court upheld the punishment as a justified restriction on freedom of expression in order to secure minimal sexual morality as a public welfare.

Although there once was some opposition to the view of the Supreme Court on this matter of restrictions on constitutional rights, most academics came to support it.[33]

PERMISSIBILTY OF RESTRICTION

Thus, regardless of the existence of an explicit provision that allows restrictions to protect the public welfare, basically every right guaranteed under the Constitution can be restricted for the protection of the public welfare under articles 12 and 13.[34] However, this does not lead to the conclusion that a particular Diet statute restricting individual rights at issue before the courts is justified. The Court must be convinced that the restriction serves some legitimate public purpose and is the necessary means to accomplish this purpose.

The Supreme Court adopted a highly deferential attitude towards the Diet in its early decisions. In the *Emergency Food Supply Order Case*, for instance, the Supreme Court upheld the constitutionality of the ban on advocacy of illegal action without regard to what the defendant actually said and whether the speech was likely to cause illegal conduct. In the '*Lady Chatterley's Lover*' *Case*, the Supreme Court again upheld the constitutionality of the ban on publication of obscene materials as a means to protect the minimum standard of sexual morality. In neither case did the Supreme Court review to what extent the restriction was actually necessary. The Court has established very conservative jurisprudence from its inception.

[33] Miyazawa, 235–39; Ashibe, 98–99; Sato, 402–03.

[34] Equality rights are not subject to restriction based on protection of the public welfare; only unreasonable discrimination is held to violate the equality right. The ban on censorship in art 21, s 2, is absolute and there is no possibility of justifying it for the public welfare. The ban on torture in art 36 is also absolute and does not leave room for restrictions.

It is no wonder then that many were critical of the stance of the Supreme Court. During the 1960s, the Court began to show some willingness to keep permissible restrictions to a minimum. In the *All Postal Workers, Tokyo Central Post Office Case*,[35] the Court narrowly construed the permissible scope of criminal punishment of public corporation workers for engaging in a strike, while upholding the blanket ban on strikes. In Japan, although the right to strike of all workers is constitutionally protected under article 28, all public workers are prohibited from engaging in any strikes (eg National Public Workers Act, article 98, section 2). Any public worker who violates this ban can be subjected to disciplinary action. There is also a criminal ban on those who organize, solicit and assist illegal strikes, purporting to impose criminal punishment to union leaders who organize strikes (eg National Public Workers Act, article 110, section 1, item 17). The postal workers, public corporation workers at that time, were also prohibited from strikes under the Public Corporation Labour Relations Act but there was no criminal punishment. The government in this case attempted to impose criminal punishment on union leaders under the Postal Act, which imposed criminal punishment on those workers who refused to offer the postal service. Believing that the restriction of the rights of workers should be kept to the minimum, the Supreme Court limited the criminal punishment under the Postal Act as only applicable to strikes that are significantly illegal, such as strikes for achieving political aims, strikes accompanied with violence or strikes continued for an inappropriately long time significantly to disrupt the citizen's life. The Court remanded the case back to the lower court to find whether the defendants were punishable under this construction. The Court then applied this holding to local and national public workers. The Court also came to limit the permissible scope of criminal punishment on solicitation for illegal strikes to seriously illegal solicitation, denying punishment on solicitation, which usually accompanies with regular strikes, thus acquitting union leaders.

However, the Court showed no similar attitude towards restrictions of other individual rights and its stance on strikes was radically altered in the *All Agricultural and Forest Workers, Police Office Act Opposition Case*,[36] which practically overturned the *All Postal Workers, Tokyo Central Post Office Case* and upheld the constitutionality of criminal punishment for solicitation

[35] Supreme Court, grand bench, 26 October 1966, 20 *Keishu* 901. See below, ch 7, n 115.

[36] Supreme Court, grand bench, 25 April 1973, 27 *Keishu* 547. See below, ch 7, n 118.

of all illegal strikes. This dramatic change of stance by the Supreme Court is generally believed to be the result of changes in membership after strong criticism by conservative politicians against the liberalization of the Court. Thereafter, the Court showed extreme deference to the judgments of the Diet and upheld almost all restrictions on individual rights.

Occasionally, the Supreme Court relied on ad hoc balancing rather than on paying total deference to the judgments of the Diet. The *Hakata Station TV Film Production Order Case*,[37] is the good example. In 1968, protesters opposing the arrival of the USS Enterprise, a nuclear powered aircraft carrier at the Sasebo port, clashed with special mobile police force at the Hakata station. Protesters alleged that the police used brutal force during the clash but the prosecutors did not file any prosecution. They thus petitioned the Court to file charges. The Fukuoka District Court ordered four local television stations to produce the news films on the clash that had already been aired to the Court to find out whether there had been use of brutal force and who was responsible for such conduct. The broadcasting stations objected to the order, insisting that the use of news film for purposes other than broadcasting would have a significant chilling effect on future newsgathering, thus infringing their freedom of expression. In this case, the Court balanced the necessity of production of the TV films against the possible impact on freedom of expression, in order to find out whether the production order was justified. It rejected the constitutional attack, however, reasoning that the TV films were essential as potential evidence and their production would not cause serious threat to freedom of expression since they had already been aired.

The Supreme Court again used the balancing approach in the *Sarufutsu Case*,[38] in which a public worker was prosecuted for engaging in political activities in violation of the National Public Workers Act (article 102 and article 110, section 1, item 19). The defendant in this case, a postal worker, posted election posters for the socialist candidates and asked others to do the same despite the ban on political activities for all public workers in the Act. The Court held that, to decide constitutionality, it must balance the interest in prohibiting public officials' political activities

[37] Supreme Court, grand bench, 26 November 1969, 23 *Keishu* 1490.

[38] Supreme Court, grand bench, 6 November 1974, 28 *Keishu* 393. See below, ch 7, n 62.

against the interest in protecting public officials' freedom of expression. The Court concluded that the necessity of securing political neutrality as well as the appearance of political neutrality is a significant interest and any restrictions on freedom of expression of public workers are outweighed, thus concluding that the ban on political activities of public workers was justified. Although all the activities took place during off duty hours, outside of office and without using any official authority, the Court upheld the conviction.

Such use of ad hoc balancing is better than the blanket deference to the Diet found in the Court's early cases. Nevertheless, the result of this ad hoc balancing remained the same, upholding the constitutionality of restrictions on fundamental human rights. The Court tended to put much more emphasis on government interests and ignored the importance of individual rights, thus upholding even broad restrictions on individual rights.

As a result, as stated above, the Supreme Court has held only eight statutory provisions unconstitutional during more than 60 years of postwar history. Unconstitutional holdings are sporadic and it is hard to find any pattern or tendency in them. In all other cases, the Supreme Court has upheld the constitutionality of restrictions on individual rights by deferring to the judgments of the Diet or by employing ad hoc balancing.

There is a need to employ heightened scrutiny, to require more stringent standards for upholding restrictions, especially with respect to personal freedoms, which are essential not only to human dignity but to representative democracy. Most critics argue for the theory of constitutional double standards.[39] According to this theory, personal freedoms should be distinguished from economic freedoms and the courts should thus employ differentiated standards of review. The courts should employ a rationality test to see whether a restriction of economic liberties is rationally related to a rational purpose, with the presumption of constitutionality. Therefore, citizens who are challenging the constitutionality of a law must prove that the restriction is unrelated to any reasonable goal.

On the other hand, with respect to restriction of personal freedoms, such as freedom of expression, the theory of constitutional double standards holds that the courts must make sure that the restriction is

[39] Ashibe, 101–02, 181–84; Ashibe I, 213–45; Sato, 404–05.

necessary to promote a significant interest. Moreover, many argue that the courts should apply a more stringent standard of review, such as the 'clear and present danger test' or the 'compelling interest test' to see whether the restriction on freedom of expression based on content is justified, while the courts should employ a less stringent standard of review such as the 'least restrictive alternative test' to see whether the restriction is substantially related to an important purpose.

The Supreme Court indeed suggested the application of heightened scrutiny to restriction of personal freedoms, such as freedom of expression and application of a more lenient standard to review of restrictions of economic freedoms.[40] Yet it is doubtful whether the Court actually applies such heightened scrutiny to freedom of expression, since it has not struck down any legislation restricting freedom of expression, while it has sporadically struck down restrictions of economic freedom. Application of heightened scrutiny to personal freedoms is still an agenda the Court should accomplish.

CONCLUSION

The protection of fundamental human rights is one of the most significant principles of the Japanese Constitution. Under the Japanese Constitution, the people of Japan were granted inalienable human rights for the first time in history.

Despite these encouraging developments, the Supreme Court has developed a constitutional jurisprudence which allows the Diet to restrict these rights, ostensibly in order to protect the public welfare. Moreover, it has developed a practice of either deferring to the judgment of the Diet or of employing ad hoc balancing to uphold government restrictions. The Court has not inquired whether an impugned restriction is indeed designed to accomplish some legitimate, important purpose, or whether the restriction is actually necessary. Even when it employs ad hoc balancing, the Court tends to give more weight to government interests, ignoring the importance of individual rights and deferring judgment as to the necessity of broad restrictions. It is only in exceptional cases that the Court has shown its willingness to carefully scrutinize the

[40] Supreme Court, grand bench, 22 November 1972, 26 *Keishu* 586 (*Public Marketplace Act Case*); Supreme Court, grand bench, 30 April 1975, 29 *Minshu* 572 (*Pharmaceutical Act Case*).

constitutionality of restrictions, and to strike them down or to give them limiting construction. To what extent the Diet has restricted individual rights, and to what extent the Supreme Court has given them protection, is the focus of the next chapter.

FURTHER READING

LW Beer, *Human Rights Constitutionalism in Japan and Asia* (Honolulu, University of Hawaii Press, 2008).

R Goodman and I Neary, *Case Studies on Human Rights in Japan* (London, Routledge, 1996).

Shigenori Matsui, 'The Protection of "Fundamental Human Rights" in Japan' in R Peerenbloom, CJ Petersen and AHY Chen (eds), *Human Rights in Asia* (London, Routledge, 2006) 121.

I Neary, *Human Rights in Japan, Korea and Taiwan* (London, Routledge, 2002) 15.

7

The Protection of Fundamental Human Rights: Specific Rights

Introduction – PART I: EQUALITY – Equal Protection Doctrine – Suspect Classifications – Affirmative Action – Other Forms of Discrimination – PART II: PERSONAL FREEDOMS – Protection of Personal Freedoms – Freedom of Thought and Conscience – Freedom of Religion – Freedom of Expression – Academic Freedom – PART III: ECONOMIC FREEDOMS – Protection of Economic Freedoms – Right to Choose Occupation – Right to Property – PART IV: SOCIAL RIGHTS – Protection of Social Rights – Welfare Right – Right to Receive Education – Rights of Workers – Conclusion

INTRODUCTION

THE RIGHTS AND freedoms protected under the Japanese Constitution range from the equality right to personal freedoms such as freedom of thought and conscience, religious freedom and freedom of expression, to economic freedoms such as the right to choose one's occupation and the right to property, and even to social rights such as the welfare right, the right to receive education and the rights of workers. The Bill of Rights also covers democratic rights such as the voting right, which is dealt with above in chapter two and procedural rights such as due process, the right of access to the courts, the rights of suspects, including the right against unreasonable search, arrest and custody, the right to counsel, the privilege against self-incrimination and the rights of defendants, including the right to an open, speedy and fair trial.

In this chapter, we will examine some of these individual rights. Special focus will be placed on the extent to which these individual rights are actually protected in Japan and the degree to which the judiciary has given them constitutional protection. We will see that, despite their clear and detailed protection, individual rights are subject to various legislative restrictions, some of which are highly unreasonable. Although these restrictions are often challenged before the Supreme Court, the Supreme Court has most often deferred to the judgment of the Diet, upholding almost all restrictions. We will critically examine whether such conservative constitutional jurisprudence can be justified.

PART I: EQUALITY

EQUAL PROTECTION DOCTRINE

Article 14, section 1, guarantees the equality right by providing that '[a]ll of the people are equal under the law and there shall be no discrimination in political, economic or social relations because of race, creed, sex, social status or family origin'. The equality right requires that the government treats every person alike.

The Meiji Constitution had only a provision mandating equal opportunity for citizens to become civil servants (article 19) and did not have a general equality rights provision. In fact, the Meiji Constitution condoned class distinctions, through the existence of the House of Peers. The Japanese Constitution abolished this system by providing that '[p]eers and peerage shall not be recognized' (article 14, section 2). Moreover, it attempted to prevent the emergence of a new peerage via government grants of honour by providing that '[n]o privilege shall accompany any award of honor, decoration or any distinction, nor shall any such award be valid beyond the lifetime of the individual who now holds or hereafter may receive it' (article 14, section 3).

Although there once was a dispute as to whether article 14 was merely meant to require equal application of a statute, it is now settled that it also requires equal treatment in legislation. If the Diet passes a statute which does not treat individuals equally, then that statute is unconstitutional.

The leading case on the meaning of the equality right is the *Parricide Case*.[1] The Criminal Code used to have two homicide provisions: one for general homicide and the other for parricide. A defendant found guilty of homicide can be imprisoned for no less than three years, imprisoned for an unlimited term or given the death penalty. When there are mitigating circumstances, the court can reduce the sentence and can even suspend enforcement of the prison term. In other words, some defendants do not have to go to prison even when convicted. With respect to parricide, defendants were punished only by being imprisoned for an unlimited term or by being executed, leaving no room for suspension of enforcement even if there were mitigating factors. The defendant in this case was raped by her father and was forced to live as his wife, bearing several children. When she finally fell in love with another man, she was desperately afraid that her father would oppose the marriage. She then killed her father in despair and was prosecuted for parricide. The Supreme Court, overturning its precedent, held by a vote of 14 to 1 that the parricide provision was both unreasonable and unconstitutional. Yet the opinions of the Justices were split. Six Justices believed that treating parricide differently from other forms of homicide, by imposing heavier sentences, was itself unreasonably discriminatory. Eight Justices believed, however, that the sentences imposed on those convicted of parricide were unreasonably heavy in comparison with the sentences imposed on those found guilty of general homicide, even though the fact that the punishments for parricide and homicide were different was not in itself unreasonable. These eight Justices were troubled by the fact that the courts could not suspend the enforcement of sentences despite the existence of strong mitigating factors.

This case has made clear that different treatment does not infringe the equality right so long as it is not unreasonable, while unreasonable discrimination based on any classification should be held to be unconstitutional. Unlike other rights protected under the Constitution, therefore, the equality right is not subject to restrictions for the protection of the public welfare. The job for the courts is to decide whether a particular treatment is reasonable or not.

[1] Supreme Court, grand bench, 4 April 1973, 27 *Keishu* 265. Hidenori Tomatsu, 'Equal Protection of the Law' in PR Luney and Kazuyuki Takahashi (eds), *Japanese Constitutional Law* (Tokyo, University of Tokyo Press, 1993) 187, 188–91.

In deciding whether a particular classification is reasonable, the Supreme Court has found no difference between discrimination based on 'race, creed, sex, family origin, and social status' as explicitly listed in article 14 and other forms of discrimination. As discussed below, while most academics have suggested the courts should distinguish between forms of discrimination and employ a more vigorous standard of review to discrimination based on the grounds enumerated in article 14, the Supreme Court has not shared this view. Rather, it has viewed discrimination based on these enumerated grounds merely as examples of unreasonable discrimination and has thus applied a very lenient standard of review to many forms of discrimination. This is reflected in the fact that the Court has invalidated only the parricide provision of the Criminal Code and the discrimination against illegitimate children in the Nationality Act as unconstitutional,[2] while upholding all other instances of discrimination which were subject to constitutional challenges.

Most academics argue, however, that the listed grounds should be viewed as 'suspect' and that different treatment based on listed grounds should be viewed as unreasonable unless it survives heightened scrutiny.[3] There is still no consensus on what kind of scrutiny should be applied to such discrimination. Yet, there is consensus that the courts should employ at least some degree of heightened scrutiny with respect to discrimination based on the enumerated grounds.

SUSPECT CLASSIFICATIONS

According to these critics, article 14 specifically lists 'race, creed, sex, social status or family origin' as typical examples of 'suspect' classifications. The courts should employ heightened scrutiny when considering discrimination based on such listed grounds.

[2] Supreme Court, grand bench, 4 June 2008, 2002 *Hanreijihou* 3; see below, n 21. It must be noted, however, that the Supreme Court twice held that the apportionment provisions in the Public Office Election Act were unconstitutional violations of arts 14, 15 and 44 in terms of gross malapportionment. It has refused to invalidate the election results conducted under these unconstitutional statutes. See above, ch 2, nn 28 and 29.

[3] Ashibe, 129; Sato, 471.

Racial Discrimination

As yet there has been no court case on racial discrimination. No one argues that racial discrimination should be allowed under the Constitution.[4]

It must be noted that the Ainu are an aboriginal people in Japan and could be treated as a racial minority. They once had their own distinct language and culture. Most of the Ainu people lived on Hokkaido, the northern island of Japan. Yet, as a result of the assimilation policy of the Meiji Government, they lost their own language and culture. Specifically, the Meiji Government enacted the Former Barbarian Act in 1899 to treat the Ainu as primitive people who did not have any notion of individual rights. It thus vested the right to own property in individual Ainu people, ignoring their tradition of managing property communally. Many people could not manage individual properties and were thus forced to abandon them. In practice, the Act functioned to deprive the Ainu people of their property. It was not until 1977 that the government enacted the new Ainu Act (Act Concerning the Promotion of Ainu Culture and Promotion and Education of Knowledge of Ainu Tradition), which abolished the Former Barbarian Act, and attempted to preserve the distinct culture of the Ainu people. It could be argued that the Former Barbarian Act discriminated racially against the Ainu people and was unconstitutional. Yet, the Constitution does not guarantee any special rights or privileges to the Ainu as an indigenous people.[5]

Some other forms of discrimination may be cited as racial discrimination, such as discrimination against resident Koreans. Some argue that this discrimination has an ethnic basis. Yet, this discrimination is generally targeted against non-citizens. Resident Koreans are discriminated

[4] The Japanese Government ratified the Convention on the Elimination of All Forms of Racial Discrimination. Yet, the government filed reservations to a provision calling for criminal punishment for racial hate speech. As a result, there is no criminal provision in Japan punishing hate speech.

[5] However, one lower court invalidated the decision of the Land Expropriation Commission to take land sacred to the Ainu people for dam construction because it failed to consider the cultural significance of the property for the Ainu people. Sapporo District Court, 27 March 1997, 1598 *Hanreijihou* 33. MA Levin, 'Essential Commodities and Racial Justice: Using Constitutional Protection of Japan's Indigenous Ainu People to Inform Understandings of the United States and Japan' (2001) 33 *New York University Journal of International Law & Politics* 419.

against as non-citizens. Therefore, it is difficult to say that this is racial or ethnic discrimination.[6]

One of the most egregious forms of discrimination in Japan was the discrimination against the Buraku or 'village people'. Yet, as will be explained below, this discrimination was more a discrimination based on social status or family origin than on race or ethnicity, because the Buraku people are not a racial or ethnic minority.

Discrimination Based on Creed

As to discrimination based on creed, the Red Purge mandated by the Supreme Commander of Allied Powers (SCAP) during the postwar occupation, which meant to exclude communists and their sympathizers from public office, mass media and other major industries, was attacked as unreasonable discrimination based on creed. Yet, the Supreme Court upheld the purge, insisting that the order had an ultra-constitutional effect during occupation[7] and that the purge was based on specific conduct rather than on creed.[8] The National Public Workers Act now stipulates that citizens should not be subject to any discrimination based on 'race, creed, sex, social status, origin, political opinion or political affiliation' in their employment relations with the government (article 27).[9]

Sexual Discrimination

With respect to sex, women were not given the right to vote and were treated as incompetent under the Meiji Constitution. Family law under the Meiji Constitution was built on the power of the housemaster to control the house and the housemaster was given the power to decide residence and entry into the house. The power of the housemaster was

[6] See above, ch 2, pp 45–47; ch 6, pp 160–62.

[7] Supreme Court, grand bench, 2 April 1952, 6 *Minshu* 387; Supreme Court, 3rd petty bench, 3 December 1963, 156 *Hanreitimes* 205.

[8] Supreme Court, 3rd petty bench, 22 November 1955, 9 *Minshu* 1793.

[9] It must be noted that the Supreme Court rejected the constitutional attack on a refusal by a private company to hire a university graduate after a probation period because of his political views: Supreme Court, grand bench, 12 December 1973, 27 *Minshu* 1536 (*Mitsubishi Plastics Case*). See above, ch 6, n 27.

usually inherited by the first-born son. The Criminal Code contained a provision which punished adultery only with married women, thus allowing married men to have adulterous relationships with unmarried women. All of these instances of explicit discrimination against women were abolished after the Pacific War when the Japanese Constitution was enacted. Women were granted voting rights; women were also granted equal capacity to enjoy the same rights as men. Article 24 makes clear that '[m]arriage shall be based only on the mutual consent of both sexes and it shall be maintained through mutual cooperation with the equal rights of husband and wife as a basis' and that '[w]ith regard to choice of spouse, property rights, inheritance, choice of domicile, divorce and other matters pertaining to marriage and the family, laws shall be enacted from the standpoint of individual dignity and the essential equality of the sexes'. Therefore, outright sexual discrimination with respect to family matters no longer exists under the Japanese Constitution.

Yet, there remain some forms of sexual discrimination in Japanese law. For instance, the rape provision of the Criminal Code (article 177) was attacked as unconstitutional since it defines rape as forced sexual intercourse with 'women' over the age of thirteen.[10] Forced sexual intercourse with men would only constitute public indecent conduct, not rape, and the punishment is more lenient. Yet, the Supreme Court rejected a constitutional attack on this provision, holding that different treatment is reasonable since it is based on the difference between male and female physiques, and the fact that sexual assaults are most commonly committed by men against women.

The Civil Code has a provision that prohibits women from getting remarried for six months after divorce (article 733). This provision was inserted because of the conflicting paternity presumptions: the Civil Code presumes that the father of a child born after 200 days of marriage is the husband. It presumes, however, that the father of a child born within 300 days after divorce is the ex-husband (article 772, section 2). Therefore, if a woman is allowed to remarry shortly after divorce and bears a child, these presumptions would conflict. In one case, a woman who could not remarry her partner for six months sought damages alleging the unconstitutionality of the ban. The Supreme Court upheld this provision, however, in the *Waiting Period for Remarriage for Divorced Women Case*,[11] by

[10] Supreme Court, grand bench, 24 June 1953, 7 *Keishu* 1366.
[11] Supreme Court, 3rd petty bench, 5 December 1995, 1563 *Hanreijihou* 81.

holding that the Diet has broad discretion as to the conditions of marriage and that the prohibition is not utterly unreasonable, as it makes certain who is the presumed father of a child born after remarriage. There are many critics who were not persuaded. They argued that there is no need to prohibit re-marriage to protect the rights of children since paternity can be established through DNA testing. Even if there is a compelling need to protect the rights of a child, a ban for 100 days after divorce would be sufficient.[12]

Other provisions of the Civil Code could also be questioned in terms of sex discrimination. The Civil Code, for instance, allows marriage at the age of 18 for men but at the age of 16 for women (article 731). It may be hard to find any compelling justification for this age difference.[13] The Civil Code also requires a husband and wife to select one family name for themselves (article 750). Under the Meiji Civil Code, couples used to carry the name of the house. The current Civil Code is sexually neutral at least on its face. Yet, in more than 97 per cent of cases, the couple chooses the husband's family name. Wives are thus practically forced to abandon their family names. Some argue that such de facto discrimination should be held to be unconstitutional.[14]

Although sexual discrimination is specifically listed in article 14 of the Constitution, the decisions of the Supreme Court are quite tolerant of the unequal treatment of women.

Women have been subjected to many kinds of private discrimination, especially in the workplace, such as the refusal to provide employment and promotion opportunities and the provision of lower wages. Although the Diet has prohibited different treatment based on sex with respect to wages in the Labour Standards Act (article 4), there used to be no statutory ban on sexual discrimination in the workplace. The government enacted the Equal Employment Opportunity Act in 1985 to encourage provision of equal employment opportunities generally, and then amended it in 1997 to oblige employers to provide equal employment opportunities to women. Unfortunately, this statute has not

[12] Miyoko Tsujimura, 'Women's Rights in Law and Praxis: The Significance of Three Statistics from Politics, the Household, and Labor' in Yoichi Higuchi (ed), *Five Decades of Constitutionalism in Japanese Society* (Tokyo, University of Tokyo Press, 2001) 155, 161–62.

[13] *Ibid*, 161.

[14] *Ibid*, 162–64.

been vigorously enforced,[15] and there is no statute that prohibits private sexual discrimination in other arenas.

On the other hand, the Labour Standards Act used to have provisions protecting women in the workplace. It thus prohibited women from working late at night and strictly regulated overtime work. Although these provisions were supported by many as reasonable protective measures for women, an increasing number of women called for the abolition of these provisions because they hindered employment and promotion opportunities for women. As a result, many of these provisions were abolished in 1998. This abolishment was quite controversial even among women, because it allows employers to practically force women to work overtime or at night. Now, it merely regulates working conditions for the protection of pregnant women during pregnancy and after the child birth.

Discrimination Based on Family Origin or Social Status

As to family origin and social status, the most egregious discrimination based on social status was discrimination against the Buraku people.[16] The social caste system was established in the time of the Tokugawa Shogunate, placing samurai warriors at the top, farmers second, artisans third and merchants at the bottom. Yet, there were people, born in certain villages, called Buraku, who were engaged in professions in which most people did not want to engage, such as butchery. The Buraku people were regarded as 'filthy people' or 'non-humans' and were subjected to various forms of discrimination. Although the Meiji Government abolished this treatment after it abolished the social caste system in 1871, there remained strong public prejudice against Buraku people. Moreover, because of past discrimination, Buraku people were forced to live in poor neighbourhoods with insufficient infrastructure, neighbourhoods that provided poor education and employment opportunities. Even though government agencies no longer discriminate against Buraku people, it is generally agreed that such discrimination

[15] R Larsen, 'Note: Ryousai Kenbo Revisited: The Future of Gender Equality in Japan after the 1997 Equal Employment Opportunity Law' (2001) 24 *Hastings International and Comparative Law Review* 189.

[16] EA Su-lan Reber, 'Buraku Mondai in Japan: Historical and Modern Perspectives and Directions for the Future' (1999) 12 *Harvard Human Rights Journal* 297.

would be utterly unconstitutional.[17] It must be noted, however, that there still remains persistent private discrimination against Buraku people, especially in hiring and marriage. The Buraku people have demanded that the government enact civil rights legislation prohibiting private discrimination against people based on race or social status, yet the government has not enacted such legislation. As we saw in chapter six, the government's attempt to enact the Human Rights Vindication Act Bill also failed.

The parricide provision of the Criminal Code might be cited as another example of discrimination based on social status. As explained above, although the Supreme Court did not hold that the parricide provision was a form of discrimination based on social status, the Supreme Court struck it down, believing that the difference between sentences for general homicide and for parricide was highly unreasonable.[18] Yet, the majority of the Court did not hold that the imposition of heavier penalties for parricide was itself unconstitutional. The majority simply rejected the parricide provision because the penalty imposed was highly unreasonable in that suspension of enforcement of prison sentences was not allowed. The Supreme Court has therefore upheld as constitutionally reasonable the imposition of heavier penalties on a person causing injury resulting in the death of his or her parent than on a person causing injury resulting in the death of another person.[19]

Discrimination against illegitimate children can be also cited as discrimination based on social status. Article 900 of the Civil Code gave an illegitimate child only half of the share of a legitimate child in the estate of his or her father. Yet, the Supreme Court upheld this form of discrimination in the *Discrimination against Illegitimate Child Case*[20] as a reasonable exercise of the Diet's discretion. The Supreme Court held that the Diet had very broad discretion when creating the inheritance system. It therefore ruled that this different treatment was not unreasonable, as it was drafted in order to protect legal marriages. The Court also noted the

[17] The national government as well as local governments have attempted to improve the social conditions of Buraku people. See pp 183–84.

[18] See above, n 1. This provision was ultimately deleted in 1995. See above, ch 5, n 54. There is only a general homicide provision (art 199) in the current Criminal Code.

[19] Supreme Court, 1st petty bench, 20 November 1975, 797 *Hanreijihou* 153; Supreme Court, 3rd petty bench, 28 November 1975, 797 *Hanreijihou* 156; Supreme Court, 1st petty bench, 28 November 1996, 50 *Keishu* 827. This provision was also deleted in 1995.

[20] Supreme Court, grand bench, 5 July 1995, 49 *Minshu* 1789.

possibility of granting equal shares by will and the fact that illegitimate children were entitled to at least half the share compared with legitimate children.

Yet, the Supreme Court struck down discrimination against illegitimate children in the Nationality Act in the *Illegitimate Child Nationality Act Case*.[21] According to the Nationality Act, if a mother was a non-citizen, and if an illegitimate child was born without acknowledgment from his or her Japanese father, that child could receive Japanese nationality only if the mother married the father after birth, even if the Japanese father subsequently acknowledged the child. The Supreme Court concluded that it was no longer reasonable to require marriage as an essential condition for granting Japanese nationality. The Nationality Act was amended to grant the Japanese nationality to illegitimate child if acknowledged, the acknowledging father was a Japanese citizen at the time of birth, and the father is Japanese citizen or was a Japanese citizen when he passed away (article 3).

Other Suspect Classifications

There are potentially other suspect classifications. There is no consensus but foreigners,[22] homosexuals[23] or mentally or developmentally disabled persons may be asserted as possible candidates.

AFFIRMATIVE ACTION

Is affirmative action permissible? Since no widespread racial discrimination exists in Japan, the government has not established any racially-based affirmative action programmes. There is thus no serious discussion as to the permissibility of racially-based affirmative action.

After the Pacific War, government has introduced many measures to improve infrastructure for the Buraku. Some local governments have

[21] Supreme Court, grand bench, 4 June 2008, above n 2. See above, ch 2, n 17.

[22] The Supreme Court applied a very lenient standard, however, and upheld all discrimination against foreigners. See above, ch 6, pp 161–62.

[23] One lower court held the refusal to allow an overnight stay in the same room by a homosexual group in a public youth camping facility unreasonable: Tokyo High Court, 16 September 1997, 986 *Hanreitimes* 206. It must be noted that the Civil Code assumes that same-sex marriage would not be recognized in Japan.

also introduced measures to grant scholarships to Buraku children. These measures may be regarded as social affirmative action. Yet, because of strong criticism against such measures, the government now spends money on the Buraku as a part of general social welfare projects, and not as a policy specifically targeting Buraku people.

The government also encourages the hiring of women for government positions, including positions in public universities and for private companies as well. This is generally called 'positive action' in Japan. So far, this call for positive action has achieved modest success.[24] There is no court case on the permissibility of positive action programmes.

OTHER FORMS OF DISCRIMINATION

The Supreme Court has applied very lenient scrutiny to other forms of discrimination.

For instance, the Supreme Court upheld the difference between salaried workers and company owners or farmers with respect to tax deductions in the *Salaried Workers Tax Discrimination Case*.[25] With respect to salaried workers, the government obliges employers to withhold and pay employees' income tax (Income Tax Act, article 183, section 1). Unlike company owners or farmers, who must file tax returns by themselves, it is difficult for salaried workers to evade tax. Moreover, unlike for company owners or farmers, deductions were presumed by statute and no deductions were allowed even if the actual expenses exceeded the statutory presumption. In this case, one salaried worker challenged this difference as to deduction as unreasonable. Yet, the Supreme Court applied a very deferential standard to the tax statute and upheld it as reasonable.

The Supreme Court also applied a very deferential attitude with respect to discrimination in welfare and social security law. In the *Horiki Case*,[26] for instance, recipients of disability pension benefits challenged under article 14 their disentitlement to also receive child support benefits. The Supreme Court upheld the exclusion, since both benefits were regarded

[24] MC Luera, 'Comment: No More Waiting for Revolution: Japan Should Take Positive Action to Implement the Convention on the Elimination of All Forms of Discrimination against Women' (2004) 13 *Pacific Rim Law and Policy Journal* 611.

[25] Supreme Court, grand bench, 27 March 1985, 39 *Minshu* 247.

[26] Supreme Court, grand bench, 7 July 1982, 36 *Minshu* 1235. See below, n 112.

as measures to supplant income. The Court ruled that the Diet should be allowed very broad discretion to preclude the recipients of one kind of benefits from receiving similar benefits.

The National Pension Act obliges every adult citizen living in Japan to pay pension contributions and gives various benefits, including basic disability pension benefits, to disabled citizens. It used to exempt students from this obligation and, as a result, some students who did not contribute were refused basic disability pension benefits when they were injured and disabled. The Supreme Court upheld this exemption in the *National Pension Act Student Exemption Case*[27] as being constitutionally reasonable. The Court granted very broad discretion to the Diet and concluded that, considering that students do not have sufficient financial resources to pay contributions and that the risk of suffering injury is small, it was not completely unreasonable for the Diet not to mandate the students to contribute to the national pension.

The Supreme Court further rejected an attack against alleged discrimination against the poor. The Tax Evasion Control Act provides for a procedure to pay fines and avoid criminal prosecution but obliges the tax authority to file complaints with the prosecutor's office if the person charged does not have sufficient financial resources to pay fines. The Supreme Court upheld this different treatment, holding that (1) the different procedure is provided simply because it is meaningless to provide people with the opportunity to pay fines if they do not have sufficient financial resources, and that (2) the procedure is not meant to discriminate against the poor.[28] Article 18 of the Criminal Code provides that if the defendant cannot pay the imposed fine, the government can confine him, or force him or her to work so that he or she can earn the money to pay the imposed fine. The Supreme Court also upheld this procedure since the different impact of fines on the defendant was the natural result of the lack of wealth of the individual defendant and was inevitable.[29]

[27] Supreme Court, 2nd petty bench, 28 September 2007, 61 *Minshu* 2345. Supreme Court, 3rd petty bench, 9 October 2007: www.courts.go.jp/hanrei/pdf/20071012105252.pdf.

[28] Supreme Court, grand bench, 25 November 1953, 7 *Keishu* 2288.

[29] Supreme Court, grand bench, 7 June 1950, 4 *Keishu* 956.

PART II: PERSONAL FREEDOMS

PROTECTION OF PERSONAL FREEDOMS

The Japanese Constitution protects freedom of thought and conscience in article 19, freedom of religion in article 20, freedom of expression in article 21 and academic freedom in article 23. These freedoms are generally called 'personal freedoms' or 'mental freedoms'. They are primarily concerned with the internal mind and expression of thought and opinion.

Although these freedoms were protected under the Meiji Constitution, their protection was seriously limited. The government prohibited insult against the Emperor in the Criminal Code as well as defamation, regardless of truth. It also banned, via the Newspapers Act and the Publications Act, the publication of materials that would threaten the fundamental structure of the government ruled by the Emperor. The government also enacted the Public Order Preservation Act and prohibited any gathering which was likely to disturb public order. Under these regulations, socialists and communists were targeted first and, later, all liberal critics of the government were similarly targeted. Gradually, all criticism of the government came to be seriously curtailed and people lost the freedom not to support the governmental by the time of the start of the Pacific War. During wartime, the curtailment of personal freedoms was further intensified. Those who criticized the government were secretly detained by the secret police and tortured to force them to 'convert' their thoughts. All newspapers were placed under the tight control of the government and distributed false information provided by the government in support of the war.

Moreover, although the people were granted freedom of religion, this protection was granted only so far as it did not contravene the obligations of subjects to the Emperor. Shinto was not regarded as a religion; it was viewed as an obligation of subjects towards their Emperor. The Meiji Government wanted to use Shinto as a spiritual justification for the rule of the Emperor as a sacred, living god. As a result, any religious belief that placed God higher than the Emperor was strictly curtailed and the public was practically forced to believe in Shinto. Shinto shrines received special support from the government. By enshrining the soldiers who died for the Emperor, Shinto shrines, such as the Yasukuni Shrine, thus provided religious justification for war.

After the end of the Pacific War, the SCAP ordered the abolition of these statutes restricting freedom of expression, the immediate release of political prisoners and the abolition of the secret police. They also prohibited government endorsement of Shinto. The SCAP believed that protection of these freedoms was vital for democracy in Japan. The Japanese Constitution adopted this belief and continues to protect these freedoms. The government abolished the crime of insult against the Emperor and it also revised the defamation provision in the Criminal Code to give limited immunity.

It is generally believed that these freedoms are not only essential for human dignity, but are essential for democratic government under the principle of popular sovereignty. Therefore, it is generally agreed that these freedoms deserve stronger judicial protection than other freedoms, especially economic freedoms. The government should be allowed to restrict personal freedoms only when they cause some harm to others or to society. The presumption of constitutionality applicable to restriction on economic freedoms is not applied to restriction on personal freedoms. Moreover, the government has an obligation to prove that the restriction on personal freedoms is justified, that is to say, that it is the narrowly tailored measure to achieve compelling interests or is the least restrictive measure to achieve some important objectives.

FREEDOM OF THOUGHT AND CONSCIENCE

According to article 19, '[f]reedom of thought and conscience shall not be violated'. Freedom of thought and conscience guarantees freedom inside one's mind. This provision prohibits the government from banning a particular thought or from inflicting adverse consequences because of a particular thought.

This provision was inserted into the Constitution based on the historical oppression of socialism and of critics of the governmental structure ruled by the Emperor before and during the Pacific War.[30] The Red Purge conducted during occupation under the SCAP's orders

[30] RH Mitchell, *Thought Control in Prewar Japan* (Ithaca, Cornell University Press, 1976).

should have been held unconstitutional. Yet, as we saw in chapter one, the Supreme Court upheld it during the occupation because, at that time, the SCAP's authority was superior to the Constitution.[31]

A case that implicated freedom of conscience was the *Forced Apology Case*.[32] When a defendant was held liable for defamation, the court could order the defendant to publish an apology in major newspapers. In this case, the defendant challenged this order as an infringement of the freedom of conscience, since it forced him to admit that he was wrong even when he did not believe that he was wrong. The Supreme Court rejected the attack, however, holding that the forced publication of apology was not humiliating and was not meant to infringe freedom of conscience.

Freedom of thought was also invoked in a challenge against forced piano playing of the national anthem in the *Refusal to Play Piano for Kimigayo Case*.[33] 'Kimigayo' (which may be translated as 'May your reign last forever'), the national anthem, is a controversial song, since many people believe that this song praises eternal rule by the Emperor and is not suited to a democratic state based on popular sovereignty. When an elementary school principal ordered a music teacher to play the national anthem on the piano during an admission ceremony, she refused the order and was disciplined. She then challenged this disciplinary action as an infringement of freedom of thought. Yet, the Supreme Court found that the order of the principal was not meant to force the teacher to believe in a particular thought or to prohibit a particular thought and was not an infringement of her freedom of thought.

On the other hand, the Supreme Court invalidated the decision of a local Tax Attorneys' Association to require members to pay special dues in order to contribute to a political party in the *Tax Attorneys' Association Political Contribution Case*.[34] Affiliation with a local tax attorneys' association is statutorily mandated for tax attorneys. One member refused to pay the dues and was deprived of the right to vote for the members of the board. He then sought a judicial declaration of the non-existence of the obligation to pay the special dues, insisting on the infringement of freedom of thought. The Supreme Court upheld this claim, insisting

[31] See above, ch 1, n 58.

[32] Supreme Court, grand bench, 4 July 1956, 10 *Minshu* 785.

[33] Supreme Court, 3rd petty bench, 27 February 2007, 61 *Minshu* 291.

[34] Supreme Court, 3rd petty bench, 19 March 1996, 50 *Minshu* 615. See above, ch 2, n 33.

that the association should not be allowed to oblige its members to pay special dues in order to contribute to a political party.

FREEDOM OF RELIGION

Article 20 guarantees religious freedom by providing that '[f]reedom of religion is guaranteed to all' in section 1 and in section 2 that '[n]o person shall be compelled to take part in any religious act, celebration, rite or practice'. It also provides for the separation of Church and State by providing in section 1 that '[n]o religious organization shall receive any privileges from the State, nor exercise any political authority' and in section 3 that '[t]he State and its organs shall refrain from religious education or any other religious activity'. Article 89 in the section on public finance also stipulates that '[n]o public money or other property shall be expended or appropriated for the use, benefit or maintenance of any religious institution or association'.

Religious freedom is, of course, one of the fundamental rights in modern constitutions. The countries of the world are divided, however, over the relationship between religion and the government. The Japanese Constitution adopted the principle of separation between religion and government in order to secure religious freedom.

Religious Freedom

Religious freedom includes the freedom to believe in a particular religion, to engage in religious activities such as prayer, worship and religious education, or to create or join religious organizations. It also includes the freedom not to believe in any religion, not to be forced to attend or participate in religious ceremonies and not to join any religious organization. Religious freedom is absolutely protected, so long as it remains in the mind of the believer, but it is also subject to restrictions for public welfare when it is concerned with actual behaviour.

The leading case on religious freedom is the case of a priest who attempted to exorcize an evil spirit from a client and inflicted bodily injury causing death.[35] The priest was prosecuted under the Criminal

[35] Supreme Court, grand bench, 15 May 1963, 17 *Keishu* 302.

Code for injury causing death. The Supreme Court rejected the defence that this conduct was constitutionally protected and held that religious freedom did not give immunity to violation of criminal law.

On the other hand, when religious conduct does not cause any harm to others, it must be respected. The Supreme Court thus held that a public hospital could not force a Jehovah's Witness to undergo a blood transfusion over religious objection.[36]

The *Aum Shinrikyo Dissolution Case*[37] also presented a religious freedom issue. The Aum Shinrikyo, a religious cult, had the status of a religious corporation under the Religious Corporation Act. Its leader and his followers released deadly gas in Tokyo subways, killing 13 passengers and subway workers and injuring more than 5000 passengers and subway workers. Following the attack, the governor of the Tokyo metropolitan government, as well as a prosecutor, sought dissolution of the corporation because it engaged in unlawful conduct that disrupted the peace. The believers of the group opposed the dissolution on the grounds of religious freedom. Yet, the Supreme Court rejected the challenge, since the believers would not be prevented from gathering or believing in the religion even if the religious group's corporation were deprived of its status.

This does not mean that the Supreme Court has not shown willingness to protect religious freedom. The *Jehovah's Witness Kendo Refusal Case*,[38] for instance, was concerned with a public high school student, a Jehovah's Witness, who refused to practise kendo, Japanese fencing, on religious grounds and was refused advancement and ultimately expelled for repeating his refusal. The Supreme Court held that expulsion of a student must be a last resort and, in this case, the school should have allowed the student to take an alternative measure such as offering other physical education course or allowing the student to submit a report, since kendo is not essential and the student was otherwise successful. The Supreme Court held that allowing alternatives for students who refuse a course for religious reasons is not a violation of the separation of Church and State. Although the Supreme Court did not rule the expulsion unconstitutional, it is remarkable that the Supreme Court ruled it illegal. This case may be

[36] Supreme Court, 3rd petty bench, 29 February 2000, 54 *Minshu* 582.

[37] Supreme Court, 1st petty bench, 30 January 1996, 50 *Minshu* 199. T Leo Madden (trans) 'The Dissolution of Aum Shinri Kyo as a Religious Corporation' (1997) 6 *Pacific Rim Law & Policy Journal* 327.

[38] Supreme Court, 2nd petty bench, 8 March 1996, 50 *Minshu* 469.

also cited as one example of the accommodation of religion as part of the separation of Church and State principle.[39]

Separation of Church and State

The Constitution guarantees the separation of Church and State. It is generally believed among academics that the separation of Church and State was meant to protect religious freedom by mandating the separation of religion and government.

The relationship between the government and Shinto has been highly controversial. The Meiji Government did not treat Shinto as a religion as such, although it endorsed Shinto over other religions.[40] Shinto priests were treated as public officials and Shinto shrines were treated as public corporations. The government established the hierarchy of Shinto shrines. The Yasukuni Shrine was considered the foremost shrine in Japan; it enshrines the spirits of those soldiers who fought and died for the Emperor. Japanese soldiers died with the belief that they would meet together at the Yasukuni Shrine after death. Each prefecture has a Gokoku Shrine, a shrine to guard the safety of the country. There are many Memorial Stones or Memorial Towers all over Japan commemorating the spirits of dead soldiers. Shinto thus provided powerful religious justification for the Emperor's military actions. This endorsement of Shinto was later called State Shinto.

After Japan's defeat in the Pacific War, the SCAP believed that this special governmental support for Shinto contributed to the extreme militarism in Japan and ordered the dismantling of State Shinto by issuing the Shinto Directive in 1945, prohibiting any governmental support for Shinto. The Constitution followed this Shinto Directive and ordered the separation of Church and State. As a result, Shinto is treated as a religion and all the Shinto shrines, including the Yasukuni Shrine, are treated as religious organizations. Yet, after the end of occupation, the Japanese Government, led by conservative parties, came to permit government involvement with Shinto.

[39] Eiichiro Takahata, 'Religious Accommodation in Japan' (2007) *Brigham Young University Law Review* 729.

[40] Koichi Yokota, 'The Separation of Religion and State' in Luney and Takahashi (eds), *Japanese Constitutional Law* (Tokyo, University of Tokyo Press, 1993) 205, 208–11.

The leading case on the meaning of the separation of Church and State is the *Tsu City Ground-breaking Ceremony Case*.[41] In this case, Tsu City decided to build a gymnasium and held a ground-breaking ceremony before construction, inviting Shinto priests from the nearby Gokoku Shrine. The priests held the ceremony according to the Shinto rites and the city paid using public money. One of the city council members who attended the ceremony filed a suit under the Local Government Act seeking reimbursement from the mayor to the city for illegal spending. The majority of the Court asserted that the achievement of absolute separation is impossible and held that the connection between religion and government should be allowed so long as it remains within socially permissible limits in light of its purpose and effect. The ten-member majority concluded that the ground-breaking ceremony conducted by Shinto priests according to Shinto ceremonial rites was a customary ceremony and did not have the purpose of advancing Shinto or the effect of promoting Shinto. Consequently, public sponsorship of the ceremony was held not to violate the separation principle. The five-member minority, however, criticized the majority for adopting a far too lenient test and would have held that the public sponsorship of a religious ceremony is a violation of the separation principle. The minority concluded that the ground-breaking ceremony had a religious element and its public sponsorship was a clear violation of the separation principle.

Despite the sharp criticism by the minority in the *Tsu City Case*, the Japanese Supreme Court has followed the holding of the majority in subsequent cases and has applied the same purpose and effect test. It thus upheld (1) the SDF's involvement with joint-enshrinement of a deceased SDF solider at a Gokoku shrine in spite of opposition from his widow;[42] (2) public spending on removal of a memorial stone to another location, including providing free land at the new location and the participation of school board officials in the annual memorial services in front of the memorial stone;[43] and (3) provision of public money to an association

[41] Supreme Court, grand bench, 13 July 1977, 31 *Minshu* 533. Hiroaki Kobayashi, 'Religion in the Public Sphere: Challenges and Opportunities in Japan' (2005) *Brigham Young University Law Review* 683.

[42] Supreme Court, grand bench, 1 June 1988, 42 *Minshu* 277. EN Weeks, 'A Widow's Might: Nakaya v Japan and Japan's Current State of Religious Freedom' (1995) *Brigham Young University Law Review* 691.

[43] Supreme Court, 3rd petty bench, 16 February 1993, 47 *Minshu* 1687 (*Minoo Memorial Stone Case*).

of surviving families of deceased soldiers, an association that was deeply involved in the social movement to nationalize the Yasukuni Shrine and support the Prime Minister's official visit to it.[44] The Supreme Court also held that the attendance of public officials at a *daijosai*, the religious ceremony celebrating enthronement of a new Emperor, and public spending on it was not an unconstitutional violation of the separation principle.[45] All these involvements with Shinto were held as not having the purpose of advancing Shinto or the effect of promoting Shinto.

On the other hand, the Supreme Court applied the purpose and effect test in the *Ehime Tamagushi Case*[46] to conclude that public spending on *tamagushi* offerings at the Yasukuni Shrine and contribution of religious offerings to the local Gokoku Shrine by the governor of the Ehime Prefecture were unconstitutional violations of the separation principle. *Tamagushi*, a religious offering consisting of a twig of the *sakaki* tree (*Cleyera japonica*) covered with folded white paper, is a symbol of sacredness in Shinto. Unlike the ground-breaking ceremony, which is quite common for all citizens, not all persons pay for *tamagushi*. Apparently, the Supreme Court believed that paying for *tamagushi* had a stronger religious connection than the ground-breaking ceremony. The Court concluded that the public spending on *tamagushi* had the purpose of promoting Shinto and had the effect of giving the impression to the public that the Shinto shrines in question were special, thus violating the separation principle.

The Supreme Court also held in the *Sorachibuto Shrine Case*[47] that the free provision of public land for the maintenance of a shrine is unconstitutional. However, in arriving at this holding, the Court did not use the purpose and effect test. In this case, the shrine was originally built by villagers during the Meiji period on the grounds of a public school, and was then moved to an adjacent property provided by the local government. When it became necessary to use the property for rebuilding

[44] Supreme Court, 1st petty bench, 21 October 1999, 1696 *Hanreijihou* 96. The Supreme Court also dismissed the suit against the Prime Minister's official visit to the Yasukuni shrine because it did not infringe any legal interests of opposing citizens: Supreme Court, 2nd petty bench, 23 June 2006, 1940 *Hanreijihou* 122.

[45] Supreme Court, 1st petty bench, 11 July 2002, 56 *Minshu* 1204. See also Supreme Court, 3rd petty bench, 9 July 2002, 1799 *Hanreijihou* 101; Supreme Court, 2nd petty bench, 28 June 2004, 1890 *Hanreijihou* 41.

[46] Supreme Court, grand bench, 2 April 1997, 51 *Minshu* 1673.

[47] Supreme Court, grand bench, 20 January 2010: www.courts.go.jp/hanrei/pdf/20100120164304.pdf.

the school, the shrine was moved to a property belonging to one of the villagers. The owner of the property thereafter gave the property away to the town in order to avoid tax obligations, on the condition that the town would use the property for the shrine; the town accepted this condition. Ever since the town (now Sunagawa City) acquired it, the property had been used for the Shinto shrine for free, which was owned by the association of town residents and managed by resident believers. The Supreme Court held that the permissibility of free provision of public property for the use of religious facilities should be decided by considering various factors, such as the nature of the religious facility, the historical background of the provision, the specific manner of the provision and commonsense evaluation by the general public. The Court held that the Sorachitbuto Shrine was a Shinto religious facility and the free provision of public property for its use must be viewed as providing special benefit to a particular religion beyond the permissible limit.

This judgment is significant, since there still are many shrines on public properties. During the Meiji period especially, the government encouraged the donation of shrine properties and, as a result, many shrines were built on public properties and used for free. After the end of the Pacific War, the government prohibited any public assistance to Shinto and the Diet passed a statute calling for return of the shrine properties. Yet, there are still many shrines which have been allowed to remain on public properties for free. In the *Sorachitbuto Shrine Case*, the Supreme Court held that the removal of the shrine was not the only available remedy and, indeed, in the companion case involving the Tomihira Shrine,[48] it held that free surrender of public properties by Sunagawa City in order to avoid unconstitutional assistance to shrines should not be held unconstitutional. Therefore, a local government has the option of surrendering the property for free or collecting an appropriate rent for use in order to avoid a ruling of unconstitutionality. The Court's ruling is significant in terms of these implications as well as in its avoidance of the purpose and effect test. We will have to wait and see whether these cases are exceptional ones and the Supreme Court would be willing to apply the purpose and effect test in other cases, or that the Supreme Court has now modified the purpose and effect test in favour of the totality of circumstances test.

[48] Supreme Court, grand bench, 20 January 2010: www.courts.go.jp/hanrei/pdf/20100120161709.pdf.

Academics are divided on the adequacy of the purpose and effect test. Some support it, while insisting on a more vigorous application of the test to invalidate most of the government involvements challenged;[49] others reject it, in favour of a more rigorous test focusing on whether the challenged activities have any religious significance, thus holding any government involvement with any religious activities impermissible.[50]

Yet, most academics tend to accept more flexible understanding of the separation of Church and State principle when they face the governmental attempt to provide 'accommodation' toward religious freedom. The *Jehovah's Witness Kendo Refusal Case* may be cited as a typical case. The Supreme Court concluded in this case that allowing alternative measures for study to students who refuse to practise kendo because of religious belief is not a violation of the Church and State principle after applying the purpose and effect test. In other words, the public school cannot justify the unwillingness to provide exceptional treatment for some students because of their religious beliefs citing the separation of Church and State principle. Academics tend to support this conclusion, on the premise that the separation of Church and State principle was meant to protect religious freedom and it should be thus interpreted to provide adequate accommodation with religious exercise.

The Japanese people may have a unique attitude towards religion. Most people believe in Shinto—but most of them also believe in Buddhism. If we combine the number of Shinto believers and Buddhist believers, the number will be twice as large as the total population. Many go to a Shinto shrine on New Year's Day to pray for happiness, and these same people conduct funeral or memorial services every summer according to Buddhist practice. Some even want to have their wedding ceremonies in Christian churches although they are not Christians. Shinto is a native religion unique to Japan. It does not have a single superhuman God; it does not have sacred text. It is a religion based on belief in the existence

[49] Ashibe, 152–53; Ashibe III, 163.

[50] Urabe, 139. See BT White, 'Re-examining Separation: The Construction of Separation of Religion and State in Post-War Japan' (2004) 22 *UCLA Pacific Basin Law Journal* 29. There is a dispute as to whether the separation of Church and State principle precludes the participation of religious organizations in politics. The previous government was a coalition government between the Liberal Democratic Party (LDP) and the Komei Party, a political party supported by the Souka Gakkai, a religious corporation. Keiko Yamaguchi, 'Freedom of Religion, Religious Political Participation, and Separation of Religion and State: Legal Considerations from Japan' (2008) *Brigham Young University Law Review* 919.

of millions of gods and in Mother Nature, and consists mostly of religious ceremonies. These differences have often led some to believe that for Japanese people Shinto is not a true religion but a way of living.

Yet, in light of history, it is evident that Shinto should be regarded as a religion for constitutional purposes. Government involvement with Shinto should be diligently avoided, especially in light of the past history of endorsement of Shinto. No government involvement with Shinto should be allowed unless the government can prove that its involvement does not have the purpose of advancing Shinto, nor does it have the effect of promoting Shinto. The government should also be required to prove that no secular means (or at least non-sectarian means) were available to achieve its non-religious purpose.

FREEDOM OF EXPRESSION

Article 21 protects freedom of expression by providing in section 1 that '[f]reedom of assembly and association as well as speech, press and all other forms of expression are guaranteed' and in section 2 that '[n]o censorship shall be maintained, nor shall the secrecy of any means of communication be violated'.

Freedom of expression is generally believed to be essential not only for human dignity, but for a democratic society in which citizens have the right to govern themselves. Moreover, it is generally believed that this freedom is most vulnerable to arbitrary restriction, since the government is prone to restrict speech that is critical of it. As a result, it has been believed by constitutional academics that freedom of expression deserves stronger protection from the courts compared with other freedoms, especially economic freedoms.

Moreover, it has been agreed among leading academics that different standards of review should be applied depending on the type of restriction.[51] Censorship and prior restraint is the most dangerous method of restriction and is subject to the most exacting scrutiny. Even with respect to *post hoc* restraint, content-based restriction is distinguished from content-neutral restriction and a more stringent standard of review should be applied to the former because of the danger that the government will arbitrarily curtail critical speech. With respect to content-based restriction,

[51] Ashibe, 182–84; Ashibe II, 228–35.

the government must prove that it is the narrowly tailored means to achieve compelling interests or there is a clear and present danger of causing significant harms. With respect to content-neutral restriction, the government must prove that it is the least restrictive means to achieving some important objectives. The appropriate standard of review might also be different depending on the content of the speech. Many thus believe that political speech deserves stronger protection than commercial speech.

Prior Restraint and Censorship

Prior restraint is the most repressive measure against freedom of expression, since it excludes some forms of expression from public evaluation. Moreover, prior restraint often uses an abstract and ambiguous standard to exclude expression without affording the procedural protection which could be afforded by a *post hoc* restriction. The prohibition of censorship as stipulated in article 21, section 2, thus manifests an intolerance against such prior restraint.

Yet, in the *Customs Inspection Case*,[52] the Supreme Court narrowly construed prohibited 'censorship' to mean the system under which an administrative agency comprehensively reviews content before publication in order to prohibit publication if it believes the content harmful or dangerous. The case involved the constitutionality of customs inspections under the Customs Act, which allows a customs officer to inspect goods to be imported to find out whether they are prohibited. One category of prohibited materials is goods that violate good morality, including obscene materials. If customs officers find obscene materials, they must notify the importer and importation is precluded. The Court adopted a narrow definition of 'censorship' and held that the ban on such censorship is absolute, admitting no room for exception. The Supreme Court noted, however, that customs inspections are conducted after publication abroad, that they are conducted for the purpose of customs and are not intended to prohibit publication of harmful materials, and that there is room for judicial relief if the decision of the customs office is illegal. It thus concluded that customs inspections were not a prohibited form of censorship.

[52] Supreme Court, grand bench, 12 December 1984, 38 *Minshu* 1308.

The Court could have adopted broader definition of 'censorship', prohibiting all kinds of prior restraint on expression. According to the Court's interpretation, however, it is only prior restraint conducted by an administrative agency prior to publication in order to prohibit publication when it finds the content inappropriate or harmful that falls into the category of 'censorship' prohibited under article 21, section 2. Even though the ban on such censorship is held to be absolute, other forms of prior restraint are not covered by article 21, section 2. The Court has applied this narrow definition in subsequent cases.

The school textbook review system was also attacked as censorship. In Japan, textbooks are distributed to students for free at elementary and secondary schools. In order to publish a textbook, the publisher must receive approval from the government. The Ministry of Education, Science and Technology reviews submitted drafts of school textbooks and orders or recommends revision for approval. If a publisher refuses to accept revisions, the ministry will disapprove the book as a textbook. In the first *Ienaga School Textbook Review Case*,[53] history professor Saburou Ienaga sought damages against disapproval and also sought conditional approval for his Japanese history textbook for high school students. The Supreme Court rejected his constitutional attack, however, holding that school textbook review was not prohibited censorship, since it was possible to publish the book even if it was disapproved.[54]

Judicial injunction is also a form of prior restraint. However, the Supreme Court followed the definition delineated in the *Customs Inspection Case* and held in the *Hoppou Journal Case*[55] that judicial injunction does not fall under prohibited censorship. This case involved a judicial injunction issued by the court against the publication of a newspaper article critical of a candidate for governor. The candidate sought an injunction, insisting that the article was defamatory. The publisher then sought damages against the government, insisting the unconstitutionality of the

[53] Supreme Court, 3rd petty bench, 16 March 1993, 47 *Minshu* 3483. LW Beer, 'Freedom of Expression: The Continuing Revolution' in Luney and Takahashi (eds), *Japanese Constitutional Law* (Tokyo, University of Tokyo Press, 1993) 220, 243–45.

[54] In a subsequent decision on Ienaga's attack on school textbook censorship, the Supreme Court in the third *Ienaga School Textbook Review Case* affirmed the constitutionality of the school textbook review system, but it concluded that the order to delete the description of bio-chemical experimentation by the Japanese military in China during the Pacific War was inappropriate: Supreme Court, 3rd petty bench, 29 August 1997, 51 *Minshu* 2921. See above, ch 5, n 74.

[55] Supreme Court, grand bench, 11 June 1986, 40 *Minshu* 872.

injunction. The Supreme Court rejected the attack that the injunction constituted prohibited censorship under article 21, section 2. It held, however, that the injunction was a prior restraint against publication of comments critical of candidates for public office and should not be allowed in principle under article 21, section 1. It held that an injunction could be granted only where there was likelihood of serious irreparable harm resulting from publication, and only when the article was patently defamatory and there were no reasonable grounds to believe that the article was true. Applying this standard, the Court concluded that the article in question was patently defamatory and there were no reasonable grounds to believe it true and it thus upheld the injunction.

Advocacy of Illegal Conduct

Restriction based on content carries the possibility that the government is attempting to suppress expression it believes dangerous or harmful. As a result, many tend to believe that the courts should apply a more stringent standard of review against restrictions based on the content of the expression as compared with content-neutral restrictions.

The ban on advocacy of illegal conduct, such as an advocacy of revolution or overthrow of the government, is the most typical content-based restriction of political freedom. Yet, the Supreme Court held in the *Emergency Food Supply Order Case*[56] that such advocacy carries the danger of bringing about social harm and that the Diet could reasonably ban it. During the extreme food shortage after the Pacific War, the government maintained the mandatory food distribution system under the Food Supply Control Act and mandated that farmers sell their crops to the government at a designated price. It then prohibited any solicitation of violation of this obligation under the Emergency Food Supply Order. The defendant, a farmer who was frustrated by the government's policy, stood before the other farmers at a farmers' meeting and argued that they should resolve not to sell their crops to the government. The Supreme Court upheld his conviction under the Emergency Food Supply Order without regard to what he actually said or whether the speech had any danger of bringing about violation.

[56] Supreme Court, grand bench, 18 May 1949, 3 *Keishu* 839. See above, ch 6, n 31.

This judgment was subjected to strong criticism by academics. Yet, the Supreme Court affirmed this position in the *Riot against the Return of Okinawa Case*.[57] The defendant in this case was a leader of a radical student group which was critical of the return of Okinawa without removal of American military bases. He made a speech in front of protesters, urging them to attack and eliminate special police force members. The group consisting of roughly 400 radical students actually attacked the police station in the National Railroad (now JR) Shibuya Station, set fires and killed one police officer and injured several others. The defendant was prosecuted for solicitation of arson and riot for the purpose of accomplishing a political agenda, in violation of article 39 and article 40 of the Subversive Conduct Control Act. The Supreme Court upheld his conviction, holding that the solicitation was capable of provoking damage to public safety and it was reasonable for the Diet to ban such solicitation.

Election Campaigning

In Japan, the Public Office Election Act strictly regulates election campaigning. The Act allows election campaigning only between the day of the official announcement of the election (for instance, 12 days prior to the voting date for the election of members of the House of Representatives) and the day before voting day and prohibits election campaigning prior to that period (article 129). It also prohibits door-to-door canvassing (article 138) and practically bans distribution of any documents (article 142). As we examined in chapter two, the public is precluded from actively participating in elections because of these strict regulations. The most common election campaigning method is simply to repeat the names of candidates over vehicle-borne loudspeakers and to have people in these vehicles wave hands at voters and ask for votes.

Since the regulations only target expressive activities as part of election campaigning, they could be viewed as a form of content-based restriction. Yet, the Supreme Court has upheld the ban on election campaigning prior to official announcement of an election.[58] The Supreme Court has also upheld the ban on door-to-door canvassing, since it saw this as merely a restriction on the manner of speech and justified in order to

[57] Supreme Court, 2nd petty bench, 28 September 1990, 44 *Keishu* 463.

[58] Supreme Court, grand bench, 23 April 1969, 23 *Keishu* 235.

prevent election fixing, to protect the privacy of voters, to prevent the overspending of money on election campaigning and to prevent undue influence on voters.[59] The Supreme Court has also upheld the near total ban on the distribution of documents, since unrestricted distribution of materials might cause undue competition and might jeopardize the fairness of an election.[60] As a result, election speech is heavily regulated in Japan.[61] It is questionable whether such a sweeping ban on door-to-door canvassing as well as on distribution of documents can be justified.

Political Activities of Public Workers

Political activities of public workers are also banned by article 102 of the National Public Workers Act. The Supreme Court upheld its constitutionality in the *Sarufutsu Case*.[62] In this case, a postal worker posted election posters for a socialist candidate and asked others to do the same and was prosecuted. He was merely a regular postal worker and all his activities were conducted off duty, out of office, and without using his official authority. The lower court acquitted him, holding that the criminal punishment on every political activity of public workers regardless of the status of the public workers or the nature of the work was not the least restrictive alternative. Yet, the Supreme Court overturned this judgment and upheld the conviction. It held that a total ban on political activities is necessary to secure political neutrality as well as the appearance of political neutrality of public workers. The Court balanced the interest in banning political activities against the interest in freedom of expression of public workers and concluded that on balance the ban was reasonable.[63]

[59] Supreme Court, grand bench, 23 April 1969, *ibid*; Supreme Court, 2nd petty bench, 15 June 1981, 35 *Keishu* 205.

[60] Supreme Court, grand bench, 6 April 1955, 9 *Keishu* 819; Supreme Court, 3rd petty bench, 23 March 1982, 36 *Keishu* 339.

[61] Moreover, the government has construed posting on the internet as constituting distribution of materials. As a result, no candidate is allowed to renew his or her homepage during the election campaign period. The government is now considering the amendment, which would allow candidates and political parties to renew their homepages during the election period.

[62] Supreme Court, grand bench, 6 November 1974, 28 *Keishu* 393. See above, ch 6, n 38.

[63] The Supreme Court upheld a disciplinary action against an SDF officer who made comments critical of the government's defence policy: Supreme Court, 1st petty bench, 6 July 1995, 1542 *Hanreijihou* 134. It also upheld a disciplinary action

Defamation

Defamation gives rise to criminal liability as well as civil liability (there is no distinction between libel and slander). Article 230 of the Criminal Code prohibits the publication of defamatory statements which point out facts in public. This provision was inserted into the Criminal Code under the Meiji Constitution. It prohibited the publication of defamatory statements regardless of whether they were true. When the Japanese Constitution was enacted, there was a question whether article 230 could be squared with the constitutional guarantee of freedom of expression. The Diet thus amended the Criminal Code and added article 230-2, thus giving immunity to those who publish defamatory statements when they relate to matters of public interest, they are published with the sole purpose of advancing the public interest and it can additionally be proven that the statement is true.

The Supreme Court held that criminal liability for defamation was constitutional.[64] The Supreme Court initially construed article 230-2 literally and held that there would be no room for immunity if a defendant failed to prove that his statement was true. Yet, in the *Evening Wakayama News Case*,[65] the Court came to construe article 230-2 as also giving immunity where there are reasonable grounds to believe that the statement is true, even if the defendant cannot prove that the statement is true.

Defamation also gives rise to tort liability under article 709 of the Civil Code. The Supreme Court has also afforded the same protection in civil suits against defamatory statements[66] and has upheld the constitutionality of ordering civil damages against those who publish defamatory statements.[67]

Compared with the United States, where the truth of a defamatory statement is generally an absolute defence, it is only truth about a matter of public interest uttered for the sole purpose of advancing the public interest that is protected. Moreover, while in the United States the plaintiff (or prosecutor) must prove that a defamatory statement is false

against a lower court judge for political activity: Supreme Court, grand bench, 1 December 1998, 52 *Minshu* 1761 (*Teranishi Case*). See above, ch 5, n 16.

[64] Supreme Court, 1st petty bench, 10 April 1958, 12 *Keishu* 830.

[65] Supreme Court, grand bench, 25 June 1969, 23 *Keishu* 975.

[66] Supreme Court, 1st petty bench, 23 June 1966, 20 *Minshu* 1118.

[67] Supreme Court, grand bench, 4 July 1956, above n 32 (*Forced Apology Case*).

and the defendant had actual malice in the case of defamation against a public figure, in Japan it is always the defendant who must prove that a statement concerns a matter of public interest, that it is expressed with the sole purpose of advancing the public interest and that the statement is true or at least there are reasonable grounds to believe it is true. As a result, although the amount of damages awarded is generally limited because no punitive damages are allowed in Japan, the protection of defamatory speech is considerably limited.[68] It must also be noted that injunctions are available in exceptional circumstances, as is shown in the *Hoppou Journal Case*.[69]

Invasion of Right to Privacy

It is now settled that one can sue for invasion of privacy as a tort when private information is improperly disclosed.[70] The Supreme Court essentially admitted the existence of the right to privacy in the '*Reversed*' *Case*,[71] when it ordered an author to pay damages for publishing a non-fiction story entitled 'Reversed' about jury trial in Okinawa. The plaintiff had been prosecuted and convicted by a jury trial almost 12 years previously for injury resulting in death, since Okinawa was still governed by the United States' government. The nonfiction story was intended to emphasize the democratic importance of jury trial. This story disclosed the real name of the defendant. After serving his sentence, the defendant left Okinawa for Tokyo, got a job and married—without revealing his prior conviction. He was upset when NHK, the national public broadcasting corporation, decided to air a programme based on

[68] Beer, above n 53, 234–35; EM Smith, 'Note: Reporting the Truth and Setting the Record Straight: An Analysis of US and Japanese Libel Laws' (1993) 14 *Michigan Journal of International Law* 871.

[69] See above, n 55.

[70] The leading case was the '*After the Banquet*' *Case*. In this case, the famous writer Yukio Mishima was sued for invasion of privacy for publishing a fictional story modelled on the famous politician Hachirou Arita, which disclosed private details of Arita's sexual relationship with his wife, a famous restaurant manager. The Tokyo District Court admitted the possibility of seeking damages for invasion of privacy as a tort and awarded damages: Tokyo District Court, 28 September 1964, 15 *Kaminshu* 2317. Since this decision, it has generally been agreed that the right to privacy is infringed when information regarding one's private life is inappropriately published and that one can sue for damages for invasion of privacy as a tort.

[71] Supreme Court, 3rd petty bench, 8 February 1994, 48 *Minshu* 149.

this non-fiction story, which used his real name. After being contacted by NHK, he discovered for the first time that his real name had been used in the original book. He then sought damages against the author. The Court held that one has a legally protected interest in not having a prior conviction revealed unless there is a legitimate public interest in the crime, the case is concerned with a person of social influence or the case is concerned with public officials or political candidates. The Court concluded that no exceptional circumstances existed to justify the use of the defendant's real name and therefore awarded damages.

In the '*Fishes Swimming in the Stone*' *Case*,[72] the Supreme Court affirmed an injunction issued against the publication of 'Fishes Swimming in the Stone', a semi-autobiographical work by the famous writer Miri Yu. The story was first published as a magazine article and depicted the life of the author as a resident Korean, together with the struggles of one of her friends who had facial cancer. The woman after whom the story was modelled was deeply upset because her private information was revealed in the article and Yu had used many humiliating and cruel expressions to describe her appearance. She filed a suit seeking an injunction against publication of this article as a book and the Tokyo High Court granted the injunction on balancing the interest in freedom of expression against the right to privacy. The Supreme Court affirmed this holding, rejecting the constitutional attack. According to the holding of the High Court in the *'Fishes Swimming in the Stone' Case*, the court can grant an injunction against publication of private information based on a balancing of interests, a far more lenient standard than that delineated in the *Hoppou Journal Case.*

Obscenity, Child Pornography and Youth Protection

Article 175 of the Criminal Code prohibits the sale, distribution and public display of obscene materials as well as the possession of obscene materials for sale. The Supreme Court construed this ban on obscene materials as a measure to protect sexual morality and upheld it in the '*Lady Chatterley's Lover*' *Case*.[73] In this case, the publisher of a translation

[72] Supreme Court, 3rd petty bench, 24 September 2002, 1802 *Hanreijihou* 60.

[73] Supreme Court, grand bench, 13 March 1957, 11 *Keishu* 997. See above, ch 6, n 32.

of *Lady Chatterley's Lover*, by DH Lawrence, as well as the translator, the famous novelist Bin Ito, were prosecuted for violating article 175. The High Court had upheld the publisher's conviction but had acquitted Ito, in consideration of article 21. The Supreme Court held that it was constitutional to ban the publication of obscene materials in order to protect minimum standards of sexual morality. One of the essential characteristics of human beings, according to the Court, is the sense of feeling shame; and this sense of feeling shame dictates that sex should be a private matter. The publication of obscene materials, the Court held, thus undermines minimum standards of sexual morality and could thus be punished in order to protect public welfare. The defendants claimed that the publication of material that has high artistic or literary value should not be punished in light of article 21. However, even if the material has artistic or literary value, the Supreme Court held that it could still be viewed as obscene. Whether it is obscene should be decided based on whether the depiction of sexual activities improperly stimulates sexual desire, offends the normal sense of shame of good people and violates good sexual morality in light of common sense. Most academics viewed the Supreme Court's stand as bold, as the Court claimed it must be the guardian of good morality even when public sensibility was denigrated to the point that truly obscene material was not seen as obscene. The Court then concluded that *Lady Chatterley's Lover* was obscene, upholding the conviction of the publisher and quashing the acquittal of the translator.

The Supreme Court affirmed this holding in the '*Juliet*' *Case*[74] concerning the translation and publication of *Juliet*, written by the Marquis de Sade. However, this case was noteworthy because some of the Justices showed their willingness to limit the scope of prohibition. The majority held that even material that has high artistic or literary value could be obscene and concluded the material was obscene. The minority insisted, however, that the obscenity should be evaluated in context or against artistic or literary value. If material has sufficient artistic or literary value, then punishment may not be allowed.

The Supreme Court has maintained this position since deciding the '*Juliet*' *Case*. Although the Court has come to consider total context before finding material obscene,[75] it has still stuck to the position that the prohibition on publication of obscene materials is constitutional in

[74] Supreme Court, grand bench, 15 October 1969, 23 *Keishu* 1239.
[75] Supreme Court, 2nd petty bench, 28 November 1980, 34 *Keishu* 433.

order to protect sexual morality. It must be noted that the importation of obscene materials is prohibited by the Customs Act and the transmission of obscene messages is prohibited in the Telecommunication Act. Obscene broadcasting is also precluded by the Broadcasting Act.

Many countries prohibit the publication of obscene materials. Japan is not unique in this respect. Yet, the definition of obscenity in Japan is not limited to so-called 'hard-core' pornographic pictures.[76] It includes the publication of literature. It also includes the showing of sexual organs as well as pubic hair. On the other hand, unless sexual organs or pubic hair can be seen, a scene portraying sexual intercourse would not be regarded as obscene. With the changing public attitude towards nudity, the police have come to tolerate some pictures that show pubic hair. Yet, the police do not publicly admit that the publication of pictures depicting pubic hair is legal. The police also did not file charges when the complete translation of *Lady Chatterley's Lover* was published in 1996. It is remarkable that, in the *Mapplethorpe Case,*[77] the Supreme Court found an imported book of portraits by famous photographer Robert Mapplethorpe 'not obscene', although the book included some pictures of male sexual organs. The Supreme Court emphasized the artistic nature of the book and the fact that the pictures depicting sexual organs occupied only a small portion of the entire book.

It must be noted that the manufacture and publication of child pornography are prohibited by the Child Prostitution and Child Pornography Prohibition Act (article 7). The Supreme Court easily upheld the constitutionality of these prohibitions.[78] The ban does not cover computer graphic images or child pornography using an adult model posing as a child. The Act also does not ban the possession of child pornography for personal use or accessing child pornography. The government is planning to expand the scope of prohibition.

Most prefectures have youth protection ordinances, which prohibit bookshop owners from selling or distributing sexually explicit materials or materials promoting cruelty and brutality to those under the age of 18, if these materials are designated as 'harmful materials for youth' by the governor or if they satisfy the criteria published by the prefecture. These ordinances were justified as a paternalistic protectionist measure

[76] R Trager and Yuri Obata, 'Obscenity Decisions in the Japanese and United States Supreme Courts: Cultural Values in Interpreting Free Speech' (2004) 10 *U.C. Davis Journal of International Law and Policy* 247.

[77] Supreme Court, 3rd petty bench, 19 February 2008, 62 *Minshu* 445.

[78] Supreme Court, 3rd petty bench, 20 February 2006, 60 *Keishu* 216.

for the healthy development of youth. The Supreme Court, in the *Gifu Prefecture Youth Ordinance Case*,[79] upheld an ordinance imposing a ban on selling these materials to youth through vending machines, holding that it is common knowledge that these materials are harmful to the healthy development of youth.[80]

Content-Neutral Restrictions on Speech

Content-neutral restrictions can be divided into time, place and manner restrictions and regulation of symbolic speech.

The Anti-Public Display Act and local anti-public display ordinances enacted under this Act prohibit the public display of posters or advertisements on electrical poles, city trees or other public facilities (article 3). The Supreme Court upheld the constitutionality of the Act, holding that the protection of the beauty of the street and public places is a legitimate interest and the ban is reasonable.[81] Placing posters on the property of others, such as electrical poles owned by power companies, is also a violation of the Misdemeanour Act (article 1, item 33). The Supreme Court similarly upheld the constitutionality of the ban as a reasonable means of protecting the property rights of others.[82]

One controversial case was a criminal prosecution under article 130 of the Criminal Code for trespassing by anti-Iraq war protesters who entered the property of a housing complex for SDF officers in order to distribute anti-Iraq war documents. Although the District Court acquitted the defendant, holding that his conduct was not so grossly illegal as to deserve criminal punishment, the Supreme Court upheld the High Court decision, which overturned the District Court, holding that the punishment was reasonable in order to protect the privacy of the residents in the *Anti-Iraq War Protesters Trespassing Case*.[83]

[79] Supreme Court, 3rd petty bench, 19 September 1989, 43 *Keishu* 785.

[80] See also Supreme Court, 2nd petty bench, 9 March 2009, 63 *Keishu* 27.

[81] Supreme Court, grand bench, 18 December 1968, 22 *Keishu* 1549.

[82] Supreme Court, grand bench, 17 June 1970, 24 *Keishu* 280.

[83] Supreme Court, 2nd petty bench, 11 April 2008, 62 *Keishu* 1217. The Supreme Court also upheld the conviction of a person for trespass who entered an apartment building and distributed pamphlets describing the activities of a political party into the post box of each apartment, despite there being a ban on entering in order to distribute pamphlets: Supreme Court, 2nd petty bench, 30 November, 2009: www.courts.go.jp/hanrei/pdf/20091204185218.pdf.

With respect to punishment of symbolic speech, there are no court cases. The courts are likely to apply the same kind of lenient standard of review as the one that has been applied to content-neutral restrictions relating to the time, place or manner of speech.[84]

Demonstrations on Public Streets or in Public Parks

With respect to public demonstrations on public streets, local public safety ordinances regularly demand prior notification or prior permits for public demonstrations and deny permits if there is a risk that public safety might be endangered. They also impose various conditions even where a permit is given.

The Supreme Court held in the *Niigata Prefecture Public Safety Ordinance Case*[85] that the system of prior notification should be upheld, in contrast to a comprehensive prior permit system, and concluded that demonstrations could be prohibited when there was a clear and present danger to public safety. Yet, the Supreme Court in essence reversed this holding and upheld the prior permit system in the *Tokyo Public Safety Ordinance Case.*[86] The Supreme Court's current position is that public demonstrations are capable of turning into riots and that local governments can prohibit demonstrations if there is the possibility that public safety might be endangered.

The Supreme Court affirmed this holding in the *Tokushima City Public Safety Ordinance Case*[87] and held that a condition attached to a permit not to disturb traffic was not vague enough to invalidate it.

Public gatherings in public parks may present a similar issue. In the *May Day Parade Case*,[88] an application by a union for a permit to use the exterior garden of the Imperial Palace for a May Day parade was denied because of possible damage to the park. The applicant then filed a suit seeking judicial revocation of this denial. The Supreme Court rejected the constitutional attack because the case became moot when

[84] There is no statute punishing destruction or burning of the national flag in Japan. One lower court upheld the conviction for destruction of property of a defendant who took the Hinomaru, a national flag, displayed in national athletic events and burned it: Fukuoka High Court, Naha Branch, 26 October 1995, 1555 *Hanreijihou* 140.

[85] Supreme Court, grand bench, 24 November 1954, 8 *Keishu* 1866.

[86] Supreme Court, grand bench, 20 July 1960, 14 *Keishu* 1243.

[87] Supreme Court, grand bench, 10 September 1975, 29 *Keishu* 489.

[88] Supreme Court, grand bench, 23 December 1953, 7 *Minshu* 1561.

the planned date for the parade had passed. Yet, the Supreme Court added its opinion on the merits, rejecting the constitutional attack by holding that the denial was a result of reasonable exercise of discretion to manage public parks.

Gathering at Civic Centres

Although the government does not have a constitutional duty to build civic centres and make them available as public forums, the public has a right to use these facilities for expression as long as they remain open. The Local Government Act thus obliges the local government not to refuse their use by the public without legitimate reasons, and prohibits discrimination (article 244).

In the *Izumisano City Civic Center Case*,[89] the rejection of an application to use the centre for a gathering of a group opposing the construction of Kansai International Airport was challenged. The manager believed that the applicants were a radical group and had engaged in a series of bombings; the manager thus decided to refuse the group the use of the centre because of the danger of disturbing the public order and because of the possibility of resulting property management problems. The Supreme Court interpreted the provision in the Local Government Act to allow refusal only when there was a clear and imminent danger that the public safety would be jeopardized. Yet, applying this standard, it concluded that the refusal was justified in this case.

The Supreme Court showed a different attitude in the *Ageo City Welfare Center Case*.[90] An application to use the centre for funeral services of union leaders was refused in this case because of the fear that opposing radical groups might disrupt the activity. The manager refused the permit on the ground that there was the possibility of resulting property management problems. The Supreme Court held, however, that trouble must be specifically predicted based on objective facts and the centre should not be allowed to refuse use because of a fear of disruption by opposing groups unless the disruption could not be adequately handled by the police. The Court invalidated the refusal, holding that there were no circumstances to justify it in this case.

[89] Supreme Court, 3rd petty bench, 7 March 1995, 49 *Minshu* 687.

[90] Supreme Court, 2nd petty bench, 15 March 1996, 50 *Minshu* 549.

The *Ageo City Welfare Center Case* is significant, especially since the use of civic centres for the purpose of teachers' union gatherings has often been refused because of the fear that opposing right-wing radicals would come to disrupt such gatherings. The Court's holding will likely invalidate such refusals.

Freedom of Expression in Japan

Looking back, it can be said that from the beginning the Supreme Court has adopted a very deferential attitude towards speech regulation. Although the adoption of the interest-balancing approach in the 1960s might have indicated the possibility of change, the Supreme Court has not showed any significant change. The fact remains that the Supreme Court has never ever struck down any statute restricting freedom of expression as unconstitutional. The Supreme Court has been willing to impose punishment on those who advocated the illegal activity if there were dangers that such illegal activities might take place. Highly unreasonable statutes, such as the Public Office Election Act, that imposes a total ban on door-to-door canvassing and an almost total ban on distribution of materials during election campaigning, have been upheld as reasonable. Anyone who publishes criticisms against the government or government officials must be ready to prove before the court that the publication is on the matter of public interest, the publication is solely for the purpose of advancing legitimate purpose and the statement was true or at least there was a reasonable ground to believe it to be true. Anyone who publishes novels depicting sexual intimacies might be punished for the sake of preservation of sexual morality. Any public demonstration must be subject to prior permit requirement and could be prohibited if there is a danger that the public safety might be disturbed. Any kind of poster on public property, including electricity poles, trees and walls of public facilities is prohibited. Anyone who enters into the property of an apartment complex in order to distribute leaflets without permission could be criminally punished.

Japanese society places more weight on harmony of society than individual autonomy. Even though society prefers a consensus-building type of decision-making, strong dissent is not usually welcome for the sake of preservation of harmony. It is assumed that everyone should be ready to accept the decision of the majority, although often the majority will attempt to accommodate the voices of the minority. Those who insist on minority view would likely be viewed as weird or even as disruptive of the harmony of the group. In such a society, it is likely that it may be difficult to expect that everyone should respect the dissenting voice, no matter how unreasonable or even dangerous that voice would appear. It might be believed that freedom of expression should be subject to restrictions necessary to maintain the harmony of the society. That may be the reason why the Diet has imposed various restrictions on freedom of expression in Japan. The Supreme Court might have also shared the same ideology.

Since the government had been occupied by the conservative LDP for a long time, most often it was communists, socialists or liberal critics of the government that were likely to be punished for their speeches. Since there was no realistic chance of change of government, the conservative LDP government had more vested interests in restricting freedom of expression to ensure that their dominance was maintained. That may be another reason why freedom of expression has been subjected to various restrictions in Japan.

It is remarkable, however, that so many citizens have been willing to challenge these restrictions before the courts and this fact may suggest that Japanese society is changing to allow more dissent. Although their challenges have been rejected by the Supreme Court, these challenges often supported by many critics of the government might suggest that increasing numbers of citizens are now willing to respect freedom of expression. Now, with the change of government, the current government is supported by union organizations. It will be interesting to see whether this change of government has any effect on the protection of freedom of expression in Japan.

ACADEMIC FREEDOM

Academic Freedom

Article 23 provides that '[a]cademic freedom is guaranteed'.

Academic freedom protects professors and other researchers in institutions of higher education such as universities, guaranteeing the freedom to conduct research, publish results and teach views without interference. This freedom was inserted because of the prewar governmental ban on the theory of the Emperor as an organ of the state espoused by constitutional scholar Tatsukichi Minobe and the expulsion of some university economics professors because of their socialist views.

Academic freedom is, of course, subject to restrictions for the protection of public welfare. There are restrictions, for instance, on the use of animals for experiments (Act Concerning Protection and Management of Animals, article 41). There is also a restriction on stem cell research. The Act on Regulation of the Application of Cloning Technology to Humans thus prohibits placing in a woman's body an embryo that grew from the fusion of a sperm and an embryonic stem cell (article 3). Most people tend to support such a ban on human cloning; some even argue that human cloning violates human dignity as stipulated in article 13 of the Constitution.

University Autonomy

The protection of academic freedom includes the guarantee of university autonomy. Such a guarantee is necessary in Japan, since many universities are national or public, thus making these universities part of the government.[91] The university has autonomous authority in its personnel and property management decisions. The police are thus generally supposed to obtain permits from the university to enter its property except in cases of emergencies or serious crimes.

The leading case on university autonomy is the *Popolo Case*.[92] During a theatrical performance by the Popolo group at the University of Tokyo, participating students became upset when they discovered that some police officers had secretly attended the performance, and they took away their police identification cards by force. The defendant was thus charged with violation of the Act Concerning Punishment of Violent Conducts, which imposed criminal punishment on violence by groups, and challenged the legality of police conduct in attending social activities on campus without obtaining a permit from the university. The Supreme Court admitted that article 23 protects university autonomy. It rejected the constitutional challenge, however, holding that university autonomy did not extend to social and political activities on campus and was limited

[91] Private universities can enjoy the freedom of association guaranteed in art 21.
[92] Supreme Court, grand bench, 22 May 1963, 17 *Keishu* 370.

to academic and intellectual activities, concluding that activities of the Popolo group were not protected as part of university autonomy.

The Right to Learn and the Freedom to Teach

The Constitution does not have any explicit academic freedom provision for elementary and secondary schools. As will be examined below, the Constitution guarantees the right to receive education (article 26, section 1) and obliges every parent to provide 'ordinary education' to his or her children (article 26, section 2). It also mandates that compulsory education must be free. Yet, the Constitution is silent on who has the right to decide what to teach in these elementary or secondary schools.

The leading case on the role of the government in education is the *Asahikawa Achievement Test Case*.[93] In this case, public school teachers opposed to the standard achievement test conducted by the government used force in attempting to prevent the administration of the test and were prosecuted. The teachers attacked the prosecution on the grounds that the achievement test was illegal, since the government did not have any authority to interfere with education, the content of which should be decided by teachers, who have a right to teach children. They basically limited the power of the government to establish the public school system by building schools and hiring teachers and denied any power to decide on what should be taught in schools. On the other hand, the government insisted that it had broad authority to decide the content of education and that the achievement test was legal. The Supreme Court rejected both arguments. It placed the right of children to learn at the centre of education and admitted a limited right to teach for teachers under article 23. Yet, it also admitted the government did have limited authority to decide the content of education in order to assure uniformity throughout the country and to secure accuracy. The Court qualified this holding by stating that the government should not be allowed to indoctrinate children or otherwise impair children's right to learn. Applying this standard, the Supreme Court concluded

[93] Supreme Court, grand bench, 21 May 1976, 30 *Keishu* 615. Masayuki Uchino, 'The Struggle for Educational Freedom' in Higuchi (ed), *Five Decades of Constitutionalism in Japanese Society* (Tokyo, University of Tokyo Press, 2001) 115, 121–24.

that the achievement test was legal, thus rejecting the challenge of the teachers.

This issue is especially important because the educational system is highly centralized in Japan and is heavily regulated. Usually, it is a municipal government that has a responsibility to maintain public elementary and junior high schools, while it is a prefecture that has a responsibility to maintain public high schools. Teachers in these public schools are local public workers subject to regulation of the Local Public Workers Act. There are school boards in each municipality as well as in each prefecture that have authority to decide education mattes. Yet it is the Ministry of Education, Science and Technology that has ultimate control over these local school boards as well as the content of the education. The ministry has established the guideline not only on the organizational matters including the class size, but on the content of the education to be taught. The teachers are obliged to use the approved school textbooks and to follow the guideline for teaching the students. It is not only the public schools that are heavily regulated by the government. The government has enacted the School Education Act to oblige every parent to send his or her children either to public schools or to approved private schools (articles 16, 17, and 144) and the government has established the approval system for the private schools (Private School Act, article 31 and School Education Act, article 4). Private schools are also obliged to use the approved textbooks and follow the guideline although the government allowed more autonomy to such private schools.

However, since the government had been occupied by the conservative LDP, the ministry had often adopted the attitude of requiring education based on the conservative ideology, for instance, by ignoring the atrocities the Japanese military forces committed during the Pacific War or by attempting to promote patriotism towards the country. Teachers on the other hand often opposed this government policy. Many teachers belong to the Japan Teachers' Union, the strongest advocate of socialist ideology, and they strongly objected to any government attempt to control the content of education. Parents who shared the same ideology have supported their opposition. Therefore, there are many confrontations between the government and teachers and parents who are opposed to the government policy. The Court has thus granted some legitimate role for the government to decide the content of education, while placing limits on the government.

As stated above, the Supreme Court has upheld the constitutionality of textbook censorship in the first *Ienaga School Textbook Censorship Case*.[94] It has also rejected a challenge based on articles 23 and 26. The Supreme Court has also upheld the legality of the guidelines for learning[95] and affirmed the obligation of teachers to use approved school textbooks.[96]

PART III: ECONOMIC FREEDOMS

PROTECTION OF ECONOMIC FREEDOMS

One of the prominent characteristics of the Japanese Bill of Rights is the existence of two provisions on economic freedom. Yet, unlike the French Declaration of the Rights of Man and Citizens, these Japanese provisions carry with them explicit provisos that set limits on this protection. Thus, article 22 provides that '[e]very person shall have freedom . . . to choose his occupation to the extent that it does not interfere with the public welfare'. Article 29, section 1, provides that '[t]he right to own or to hold property is inviolable', while section 2 provides that '[p]roperty rights shall be defined by law, in conformity with the public welfare'. Article 29, section 3, also provides that '[p]rivate property may be taken for public use upon just compensation therefor'. Moreover, as will be explained below, the Constitution protects the right to receive welfare (article 25, section 1) and obliged the state to promote social welfare (article 25, section 2). The Constitution is thus committed to the 'welfare state' or 'social State'.

As a result, constitutional academics have posited that economic freedoms are subject to restriction not only to prevent harm to others, but to promote the welfare state.[97] This means that the government has broader power to regulate economic freedoms compared with personal freedoms. Moreover, they have argued that the Court should employ a less rigorous standard of review for restrictions on economic freedoms

[94] Supreme Court, 3rd petty bench, 16 March 1993, above n 53.

[95] Supreme Court, 1st petty bench, 18 January 1990, 44 *Minshu* 1.

[96] Supreme Court, 1st petty bench, 18 January 1990, 1337 *Hanreijihou* 3.

[97] Mutsuo Nakamura, 'Freedom of Economic Activities and the Right to Property' in Luney and Takahashi (eds), *Japanese Constitutional Law* (Tokyo, University of Tokyo Press, 1993) 255, 256.

than for restrictions on personal freedoms. The restriction on economic freedoms is presumed to be constitutional since such restriction is imposed by the democratic legislature and the citizen challenging the restriction of economic freedoms has to prove that the restriction is unreasonable, that is to say, that it lacks rational basis.

Moreover, most academics distinguish between restriction to prevent harms and restriction to promote social welfare and argue for differentiated standards of review: a somewhat careful standard of review for restriction to prevent harms and a more lenient standard of review for restriction to promote social welfare. The justification for this dichotomy can be found in the limitation of judicial capacity to evaluate the necessity of restriction in order to promote social welfare. They thus argue that restriction to promote social welfare should not be disturbed unless the restriction is proven to be 'clearly' unreasonable, while restriction to prevent harms could be struck down if it is found to be unreasonable. Many also argue that the courts should be more careful if the regulation is denying entry into business rather than regulating the manners of business activities, since the denial of entry into business is a more severe restriction compared with business manner regulation.

RIGHT TO CHOOSE OCCUPATION

The right to choose one's occupation, protected under article 22, includes not only the right to choose a particular occupation, but the right to engage in the chosen occupation. In this sense, article 22 protects all kinds of economic freedoms.

The leading case on the right to choose one's occupation is the *Public Bathhouse Act Case*.[98] The Public Bathhouse Act required a permit from the governor to operate a public bathhouse (article 2, section 1) and demanded as one of the conditions for the permit a proper distance from existing public bathhouses specified by municipal ordinance (article 2). In this case, the defendant was prosecuted for operating a public bathhouse in violation of the proper distance requirement. The proper distance requirement was noteworthy, since it was justified in the Diet not as a protectionist measure but as a public safety measure. It was highly controversial whether such a proper distance requirement

[98] Supreme Court, grand bench, 26 January 1955, 9 *Keishu* 89.

could be justified as a public safety measure. Yet the Supreme Court rejected the constitutional attack, holding that unrestricted competition might result in undue competition, and economic hardship for some public bathhouses might lead them to ignore sanitation standards, thereby endangering the health of users. In other words, the Supreme Court accepted the justification offered to justify the proper distance requirement as a safety measure. This decision prompted the insertion of similar proper distance requirement in other legislation.

The Supreme Court also applied a very deferential attitude in the *Public Marketplace Case*.[99] The Special Measures Act to Adjust the Public Marketplace required a permit for marketplace to rent or sell spaces for retail stores for specified products in certain cities (article 3, section 1) and denies a permit if the operation of marketplace would lead to excessive competition (article 5) and the local ordinance required certain distance from existing marketplace as a condition. In this case, the defendant company and its representative were prosecuted for operating a marketplace without getting a permit and this distance requirement was challenged. The Supreme Court distinguished public safety regulations and regulations designed to promote social welfare and applied a far more lenient standard of review to the latter. The Supreme Court held that, unless a regulation designed to promote social welfare was patently unreasonable, it should not be invalidated. The permit requirement and the distance requirement in this case were intended to adjust the locations of public marketplaces in order to promote the healthy development of the economy and were not patently unreasonable.

Interestingly, the Supreme Court adopted a very different attitude in the *Pharmaceutical Act Case*.[100] The Pharmaceutical Act required a permit for pharmacies or drugstores (article 4, section 1) and demanded a proper distance from existing pharmacies or drugstores specified by a local ordinance as a condition for the permit. After the *Public Bathhouse Case*, the proper distance requirement was inserted into the Pharmaceutical Act as a public safety measure and, in this case, the proper distance requirement was challenged as unconstitutional in a suit filed seeking judicial revocation of the denial of a permit. The Supreme Court inquired whether the proper distance requirement was 'a rational means to achieve an important public interest'. The Supreme Court questioned

[99] Supreme Court, grand bench, 22 November 1972, 26 *Keishu* 586.

[100] Supreme Court, grand bench, 30 April 1975, 29 *Minshu* 572.

whether the public interest could not be sufficiently protected by the regulation of business activities rather than denying permits because the permit requirement imposed a severe form of restriction on economic freedom and it could be justified only when the less restrictive means could not achieve the government objectives. The government argued that if the pharmacies or drugstores were allowed to open too close to existing pharmacies or drugstores, the rival businesses might engage in fierce competition, even ignoring consumer safety, resulting in harm to consumers. The Supreme Court was not persuaded. It held that there was no danger of compromising the safety of consumers, since drugs are heavily regulated by the government and the proper distance requirement was not necessary to protect public safety. It thus concluded that the permit denial was unreasonable and unconstitutional.

This case cast doubt on the constitutionality of other economic regulations, especially the proper distance requirement in the Public Bathhouse Act. Yet, the Supreme Court refused to follow this decision and upheld the proper distance requirement in the Public Bathhouse Act after re-characterizing it as a protectionist measure to protect existing public bathhouses, on which many people who do not have private baths in their houses depend.[101]

These decisions suggested a dichotomy between public safety regulation and social welfare regulation and the application of different standards of review as was suggested by academics. However, the Supreme Court showed an unwillingness to cling to this dichotomy in the *Liquor Sales License Case*.[102] The Liquor Tax Act required a licence to sell liquor (article 9, section 1) and this licence requirement was justified as a measure to secure payment of the consumption tax, by obliging liquor stores to pay sales tax to the revenue authority and collect tax from consumers. The Supreme Court upheld this licence requirement as reasonable, despite the fact that the requirement could not be placed within the dichotomy of public safety regulation and social welfare regulation.

Overall, the Supreme Court is willing to apply a far more lenient standard of review to restrictions on economic freedom enacted for the promotion of the welfare state. Many of these restrictions are protectionist, since they are intended to restrict competition in order to

[101] Supreme Court, 3rd petty bench, 7 March 1989, 1308 *Hanreijihou* 111; Supreme Court, 2nd petty bench, 20 January 1989, 43 *Keishu* 1.

[102] Supreme Court, 3rd petty bench, 15 December 1992, 46 *Minshu* 2829.

protect existing stores or small or medium-sized business from larger stores. Indeed, it appears that the Court tends to regard free competition as disruptive of the public interest. Despite the constitutional guarantee of the right to choose one's occupation, Japan's economy is highly regulated and tightly controlled by government bureaucrats.

There are hundreds of statutes requiring permits or approvals from the government for economic activities and the government has tremendously broad regulatory authority. In addition to this regulatory authority, administrative agencies often use 'administrative guidance', ie, non-legal advice and guidance, to direct businesses as well as citizens to follow their policies.[103] Bureaucrats tend to use this informal control mechanism rather than resorting to legal regulatory authority. Moreover, most major companies in Japan accept as executives former bureaucrats after early retirement, in order to maintain a good relationship with the government. This close relationship between the government and private industries has been the most prominent characteristic of the Japanese economy. Vested with such a broad regulatory power, administrative agencies could regulate almost all aspects of business. As was explained in chapter four, it is likely that such comprehensive economic regulation made it possible to create close relationships between bureaucrats and industries to promote economic development after the Pacific War, yet excessive reliance on the regulatory power of bureaucrats may stifle competition and prevent innovation. It is surely now an appropriate time to reconsider the role of bureaucrats in the market economy, even if the court should play only a minimal role in reviewing the constitutionality of economic regulation.

RIGHT TO PROPERTY

The right to property is protected by article 29, section 1. Yet, the content of the property right must be defined in conformity with the public welfare as stipulated in section 2. Although it could be argued that section 1 gives constitutional protection to property defined under section 2, it has been assumed by most academics that the property right is a natural right, existing prior to the Constitution. It has been also assumed that section 1 protects the system of individual property

[103] See above, ch 4, pp 107–108.

as an institution in addition to protecting individual property rights. According to this interpretation, it would be unconstitutional to change the economic system from capitalism to socialism, thereby denying individuals' property rights.

The leading case on the property right is the *Forest Act Case.*[104] Under the Civil Code, all joint owners of property can claim division of the property (Civil Code, article 256, section 1). Yet, the Forest Act had a provision which precluded a division claim of a jointly owned forest unless the claimant had more than half of the share of the forest. In this case, two brothers were each given a half share of a forest by their father and one of the brothers sought the division because of a dispute as to the management of the forest. He then challenged the constitutionality of the provision involved. The Supreme Court held that this provision was intended to prevent balkanization, thus contributing to the healthy management of the forest. Yet, it doubted whether a restriction on division claims could actually contribute to the effective management of the forest, because it could simply prolong the joint owners' management dispute. The restriction on the division claim of a forest was thus struck down. It is remarkable that the Supreme Court never referred to the dichotomy of public safety regulation and social welfare regulation and applied the rationality test to invalidate the statutory provision.

Yet, aside from the *Forest Act Case*, the Supreme Court has been quite reluctant to overturn statutes restricting property rights. The Supreme Court thus upheld (1) the limitation of liability of ship owners under the Act Concerning Limitation of Liability of Ship Owners;[105] (2) immunity granted to a person who filed for bankruptcy under the Bankruptcy Act;[106] (3) the requirement of permit by governors for refusal to renew leases of farm land under the Farm Land Act[107] and (4) a limitation on legitimate reasons a landlord can refuse renewal of a rental contract for the protection of tenants under the Land Lease Act.[108] Although some have attempted to give more protection to property rights,[109] the Court

[104] Supreme Court, grand bench, 22 April 1987, 41 *Minshu* 408.

[105] Supreme Court, grand bench, 5 November 1980, 34 *Minshu* 765.

[106] Supreme Court, grand bench, 13 December 1961, 15 *Minshu* 2803.

[107] Supreme Court, grand bench, 10 February 1960, 14 *Minshu* 137.

[108] Supreme Court, grand bench, 6 June 1962, 16 *Minshu* 1265.

[109] Kenji Yamashita, 'Property Rights and their Raison d'être in the Japanese Constitution' in Higuchi (ed), *Five Decades of Constitutionalism in Japanese Society* (Tokyo, University of Tokyo Press, 2001) 89. One can argue that the property right should be protected just as personal freedoms, or that at least property necessary for personal

seems to be unwilling to scrutinize the reasonableness of restriction on property right.

PART VI: SOCIAL RIGHTS

PROTECTION OF SOCIAL RIGHTS

Articles 25 to 28 protect the right to welfare, the right to receive education, the right to work and the rights of workers. Before the Great Depression, modern capitalism held that people should work and be responsible for supporting themselves. As a result, the government did not have any obligation to provide welfare assistance or to provide opportunities for work. Poverty and unemployment were simply social problems. Moreover, the relationship between employer and employee was regarded as a private matter to be regulated by contract. As a result, many workers had to work for long hours for lower wages. When workers came to unite and unions came to negotiate with employers under the threat of strike, many countries attempted to prohibit these strikes. That was exactly what the Meiji Government did.

The Japanese Constitution radically altered all of this by protecting the welfare right and the right to work, together with rights of workers. The government is thus now obliged to guarantee a minimum standard of living and to provide opportunities for work. Moreover, these provisions are generally viewed as applicable between the employer and employee. Since these rights are concerned with social issues, they are generally called social rights.

The most prominent characteristic of these social rights can be said to lie in the fact that every citizen is granted the constitutional right to demand that the government should fulfil the obligation to provide goods and services in order to solve social problems. Unfortunately, however, as will be explained below, the Supreme Court has seriously undermined this significance by denying that the welfare right can be invoked before the courts as an individual right. Although the reluctance

living should be granted stronger protection compared with property that is owned for investment or for capitalistic use, or that at least property which is necessary for personal development should be granted stronger protection compared with property which is not necessary for personal development.

of the Court to admit these rights as individual rights is understandable, and the Court should be deferential to the judgments of the Diet because of the inability and inadequacy of the Court to interfere with government decisions on welfare matters, there is no legitimate reason to deny the fact that they are protected as individual rights.

WELFARE RIGHT

Article 25 protects the welfare right in section 1 by providing that '[a] ll people shall have the right to maintain the minimum standards of wholesome and cultured living'. It also makes clear the government's obligation to accomplish the welfare state by providing in section 2 that '[i]n all spheres of life, the State shall use its endeavors for the promotion and extension of social welfare and security, and of public health'.

There were no provisions for welfare rights in the original draft prepared by the SCAP. It was added during the deliberation process in the Diet based on the proposal of the Socialist Party, and was meant to provide a minimum standard of living for all citizens, requiring the government to pay welfare assistance benefits. The Diet enacted the Welfare Assistance Act in 1950 to implement this constitutional welfare right.

The first case that implicated this right, however, was rather an inappropriate case, concerning a criminal prosecution. The Food Supply Control Act, enacted during an extreme food shortage, mandated that farmers sell major agricultural products to the government and maintained the government supply to all citizens by banning buying and selling in the market.[110] The defendant was prosecuted for a violation of this ban by buying rice through the black market. He then challenged this law against the welfare right since it made it impossible to live, insisting that the government supply was simply insufficient and almost all people had to buy food illegally. It was questionable whether the welfare right could properly be invoked in this context, since this case was not concerned with the failure of the government to provide the minimum standard of living. The Supreme Court rejected the attack, holding that the welfare right was not an individual right that could be invoked before the courts. In other words, even though the Constitution explicitly protects 'the

[110] Supreme Court, grand bench, 29 September 1948, 2 *Keishu* 1235.

right to maintain the minimum standards of wholesome and cultured living', the Supreme Court construed it as merely a political goal, not an individual right.

The Supreme Court reiterated this attitude in the *Asahi Case*.[111] Asahi was a welfare recipient under the Welfare Assistance Act and received hospital treatment. He was receiving 600 yen per month. When his brother began to support him for 1500 yen per month, the welfare office decided to cut the welfare payment and deducted his medical expenses for 900 yen from his brother's support payment. Asahi filed a suit seeking revocation of this decision, arguing its unconstitutionality. The Supreme Court dismissed the suit because the case became moot when Asahi died. The Court held that the right granted under the Welfare Assistance Act could be claimed only by a welfare recipient and could not be inherited by his surviving family, thus making this suit moot when Asahi died. However, the Supreme Court went on to add its opinion on the substantive merit. The Supreme Court upheld the impugned decision of the welfare office, holding that the welfare right was not an individual right that could be invoked before the courts and also granting very broad discretion to the Welfare Minister to decide the minimum standard of living. Although this holding is merely an obiter dictum, it clearly showed the reluctance of the Court to interfere with the welfare administration.

The *Horiki Case*[112] also implicated the welfare right in a somewhat different context. At issue was the constitutionality of a clause in the Child Support Benefit Act, which precluded the recipient of disability pension benefits from applying for child support benefits. As we saw, the Supreme Court granted the Diet a very broad discretion under article 14 in designing the social welfare system, holding that the Diet could reasonably conclude that the recipient of disability pension benefits should be excluded from receiving child support benefits, since both benefits were part of the measure to provide minimum income; the Court also rejected a challenge based on article 25.

Therefore, even though the welfare right is constitutionally protected, there has been some doubt as to whether it is indeed an individual right or merely a programme provision. Apparently, the Supreme Court is

[111] Supreme Court, grand bench, 24 May 1967, 21 *Minshu* 1043. See above, ch 5, n 33. Akira Osuka, 'Welfare Rights' in Luney and Takahashi (eds), *Japanese Constitutional Law* (Tokyo, University of Tokyo Press, 1993) 269, 278–80.

[112] Supreme Court, grand bench, 7 July 1982, above n 26.

unwilling to admit that the welfare right is an individual right guaranteed by the Constitution, despite the fact that the Constitution explicitly guarantees it as an individual right. Most constitutional academics are critical of the Court's interpretation: they believe that it should be protected as an individual right.

Even those who view it as an individual right have assumed, however, that it cannot be invoked before the courts unless it is implemented by statute.[113] It is only when the constitutional welfare right is implemented by the statute passed by the Diet and the individual right to seek welfare is guaranteed as an individual right, that the citizen can claim unconstitutional infringement of the welfare right when their applications are denied, when the payments were not sufficient or when their welfare payments are terminated.

However, even if the welfare right can be admitted as an individual right, the specific shape of welfare benefits has to be left to the very broad discretion of the Diet. Although some academics have argued that the government has a constitutional obligation to sustain the minimum standard of living regardless of the financial situation, it would be difficult for the courts to specify the minimum standard of living and order the government to prepare sufficient budget even in time of economic crisis. Although the amount of welfare benefits was significantly increased after the *Asahi Case*, welfare offices are said to be uncooperative towards applicants. They are criticized as being unwilling to start welfare payments, insisting on the ability to work or possibility of receiving support from family members. There are some 20,000 to 30,000 homeless people in Japan. Some of them choose not to apply for welfare benefits; however many are refused welfare benefits because they do not have an established home address or because they can still work to sustain themselves. Although the Constitution obliges the government to achieve the welfare state, Japan is far from achieving a guaranteed minimum standard of living.

RIGHT TO RECEIVE EDUCATION

Article 26, section 1, provides that '[a]ll people shall have the right to receive an equal education correspondent to their ability, as provided by

[113] Ashibe, 82, 254; Sato, 621–22. But see Osuka, above n 111, at 275–77.

law'. As stated above, all children have the right to learn and to attend school to receive an education. However, private schools are expensive and there is a critical need to ensure that every child can receive an education at a public school. In order to make sure that every child receives an education, article 26, section 2 provides that '[a]ll people shall be obligated to have all boys and girls under their protection receive ordinary education as provided for by law'. Moreover, such 'compulsory education shall be free'.

The School Education Act obliges every parent to send his or her children to school beginning at six years of age. Six years of elementary school and three years of junior high school are mandatory. No home schooling is allowed. Schools must be approved by the government and they must satisfy certain requirements in order to receive approval. The government must establish public elementary and secondary schools and admit a child if he or she wants to attend them. Compulsory education at public schools must be free. Yet, the Constitution does not guarantee that everyone will be admitted to high schools or universities.

As we saw above, in addition to requiring the government to provide public school education, some have construed this provision as protecting the right of the child to learn, the right of the parents to provide education to their children and the freedom of teachers to teach children.

RIGHTS OF WORKERS

The Japanese Constitution has two provisions on the rights of workers. Article 27 guarantees the right to work by providing in section 1 that '[a]ll people shall have the right . . . to work'. It also makes clear in section 2 that the government is permitted to regulate labour standards by providing that '[s]tandards for wages, hours, rest and other working conditions shall be fixed by law'. Section 3 prohibits the exploitation of children by providing that '[c]hildren shall not be exploited'. Finally, article 28 protects the rights of workers by providing that '[t]he right of workers to organize and to bargain and act collectively is guaranteed'.

The right to work guaranteed under article 27, section 1, means that everyone has the right to demand work from the government. However, since Japan is a capitalist country, the government cannot guarantee that everyone will be employed by private companies. Therefore, the right to work must mean the right to demand the government to provide work or at least the right to seek unemployment benefits if the government cannot provide work. The Employment Insurance Act thus grants the right to receive unemployment benefits.

In response to article 27, section 2, the Diet has enacted the Labour Standards Act to regulate standards for wages, working hours and other working conditions. In response to article 27, section 3, the Child Welfare Act sets limits on the employment of children.

The rights of workers protected under article 28 include three kinds of rights: the right to organize or to join the union, the right to bargain with employers and the right to a collective action, ie, the right to strike. They prohibit the government from imposing criminal punishment or civil liability on workers who exercise their labour rights. Thus, when workers are engaged in a lawful strike, the government is precluded from punishing them (Labour Union Act, article 1, section 2) and their employer is precluded from dismissing them or seeking damages for the strike (Labour Union Act, article 8). Moreover, this provision also requires the government to protect workers' union activities. The Diet has thus prohibited in the Labour Union Act unfair labour practices by employers, prohibiting the employers from imposing disadvantage on employees because of their union activities (it is only the employer that is precluded from engaging in unfair labour practices).

Yet, in actual practice, the unionization rate is quite low in Japan. Most unions are organized within individual companies and, as a result, union members have a very strong interest in the business goals of their employer companies. They are not willing to go on strike to deprive the company of profits. Even though the Labour Standards Act establishes maximum working hours, the employer can extend the limit by agreement with the union (article 36, section 1). This limit is not strictly enforced in Japan. *Karoushi*, death from overwork, has been a serious social issue. The constitutional protection of rights of workers has not functioned well to ensure good working conditions in Japan.[114]

Moreover, the Diet has deprived public workers of many labour rights. Some public workers, such as SDF officers, police officers and firefighters, are deprived of all three rights: they are denied the right to organize, the

[114] Hideki Mori, 'Workers' Rights in Japanese Labor Praxis' in Higuchi (ed), *Five Decades of Constitutionalism in Japanese Society* (Tokyo, University of Tokyo Press, 2001) 171.

right of collective bargaining as well as the right of collective action (eg SDF Act, article 64). Others have the right to organize worker groups (not unions) but are deprived of the right to conclude agreement and to engage in collective action (eg National Public Workers Act, article 98, section 2, article 108-2, and article 108-5). In other words, all public workers, either national or local, regardless of job or rank and including workers in public corporations, are prohibited from engaging in any strikes. Criminal punishment is also imposed on those who organize, solicit or assist such illegal strikes of national and local public workers (eg National Public Workers Act, article 110, section 1, item 17).

The Supreme Court in the *All Postal Workers, Tokyo Central Post Office Case*[115] showed its willingness to limit the scope of criminal punishment for violation of a ban on collective action. Postal workers were employees of a public corporation and strikes were prohibited under the Public Corporation Workers Labour Relations Act. Yet, there was no criminal punishment for illegal strikes. The defendants in this case were union leaders who were prosecuted for violating the Postal Act, which prohibited postal workers from refusing work when they urged other members to attend a gathering during work hours. The Supreme Court believed that public workers were also entitled to rights of workers protected in article 28; public workers have a right to strike under the Constitution. Although the Court allowed the limitation of these rights in light of the public welfare, it limited the permissible scope of limitation to a reasonable minimum after balancing the rights of workers against securing the public interest. It also held that criminal punishment for violations should also be limited to a minimum. Although the Court upheld the constitutionality of the ban on strikes for public corporation workers, it narrowly construed the Postal Act as criminalizing only seriously illegal conduct such as violent conduct, strikes for purposes other than legitimate union activity, or improperly prolonged strikes since the Public Corporation Workers Labour Relations Act did not impose criminal punishment for illegal strikes. The Court thus overturned the conviction below and remanded the case back to the High Court to apply these criteria to establish whether the punishment of the defendants could be justified.

While the Court upheld the total ban on strikes by public corporation workers, this was a landmark decision, since it showed the Court's

[115] Supreme Court, grand bench, 26 October 1966, 20 *Keishu* 901. See above, ch 6, n 35.

willingness to narrow the permissible scope of criminal punishment. The Supreme Court applied this judgment to a ban on strikes by local public workers in the *Metropolitan Teachers Union Case*,[116] in which union leaders were prosecuted for the solicitation of an illegal strike. It found the defendants 'not guilty' after limiting criminal punishment to grossly illegal strike and also limiting the punishment of solicitation to grossly illegal solicitation, giving immunity to those who solicited strikes with means which is ordinarily accompanied with usual strikes. In other words, the Court held that it is those union leaders who solicited grossly illegal strikes with gross illegal method beyond means ordinarily used with respect to strikes, that could be criminally punished. It also applied the same reasoning with respect to strikes by national public workers.[117]

Yet, the Supreme Court essentially overturned the *All Postal Workers, Tokyo Central Post Office Case* judgment in the *All Agricultural and Forest Workers, Police Office Act Opposition Case*.[118] The defendants were union leaders of all national agricultural and forest public workers and were prosecuted for soliciting an illegal strike by urging other members to participate in a gathering during working hours against the proposed amendment to the Police Office Act. Although the District Court acquitted the defendants by applying the limiting construction set out by the Supreme Court, the High Court overturned the judgment and the Supreme Court affirmed that judgment. The Court held that strikes by public workers were incompatible with the public nature of their jobs and seriously affected the common interest of the public, regardless of the type of job or rank. Moreover, since the labour relationship between the government and public workers must be regulated by statute, the Court continued, strikes by public workers would undermine the process of representative democracy, forcing the Diet to bow to the demands of unions through the threat of strikes. Finally, the Court stated that there is no limitation on strikes by public workers based on market mechanisms. As a result, the Court upheld the total ban. It further rejected the limiting construction of the *All Postal Workers, Tokyo Central Post Office Case* on the scope of criminal punishment as violating the principle of article 31, which requires a clear definition of any crime. It thus concluded that it was constitutional to impose criminal punishment on those who

[116] Supreme Court, grand bench, 2 April 1969, 23 *Keishu* 305.
[117] Supreme Court, grand bench, 2 April 1969, 23 *Keishu* 685.
[118] Supreme Court, grand bench, 25 April 1973, 27 *Keishu* 547.

organized, solicited or assisted illegal strikes regardless of the severity of illegality.

The Supreme Court applied the reasoning in the *Iwate Teachers Union Case*[119] to local public workers and in the *All Postal Workers, Nagoya Central Post Office Case*[120] to workers in public corporations to explicitly overrule the *All Postal Workers* judgment. As a result, all public workers, including public corporation workers, have been deprived of the right to strike. Despite repeated recommendations from the International Labour Organization, the Japanese Government has steadfastly refused to correct this total deprivation.

CONCLUSION

Although the Japanese Constitution has an elaborate Bill of Rights, the Supreme Court has developed a very conservative jurisprudence, which upholds almost every kind of restriction on fundamental human rights. The Constitution is the supreme law and any restriction on individual rights incompatible with its guarantee is unconstitutional and invalid. Yet, the Supreme Court is quite deferential to the judgment of the Diet and it is unwilling to closely review the necessity and reasonableness of restrictions. It is the most prominent characteristic of the protection of individual rights in Japan that the judiciary has played a very small role in enforcing them. As a result, individual rights are seriously restricted in Japan.

This does not mean, however, that the protection of individual rights is totally meaningless. The Supreme Court has held statutes unconstitutional on at least eight occasions. Moreover, the Supreme Court has occasionally given limiting constructions to a number of statutory prohibitions and has also struck down agency actions based on the abuse of discretion doctrine. Furthermore, even though the Supreme Court ultimately tends to uphold constitutionality, constitutional litigation has sometimes forced the government to change its policies. For instance, after the *Tsu City Ground-breaking Ceremony Case* was filed, many local governments came to refrain from conducting ground-breaking ceremonies by themselves.

[119] Supreme Court, grand bench, 21 May 1976, 30 *Keishu* 1178.

[120] Supreme Court, grand bench, 4 May 1977, 31 *Keishu* 182. The Court, while giving immunity from criminal punishment for mere participants in an illegal strike, concluded that the solicitation of leaders can be punished.

Although the Court dismissed a suit in the *Asahi Case*, as a result of the litigation, the government significantly increased levels of welfare payments. These examples indicate the possibility that these individual rights protections can function as political norms to constrain the conduct of the government. The opposing citizens file suits challenging constitutionality, hoping that mass media coverage of their litigation will produce sufficient public support to move the bureaucrats or politicians to alter their stances. Sometimes this strategy does work.[121]

It is doubtful, however, whether such protection is sufficient to guarantee individual rights. It is surely appropriate to reconsider the role the courts should play in protecting individual rights. At the very least, the courts should play a more active role in defending the personal freedoms essential for democracy under the Japanese Constitution.

FURTHER READING

L Beer, *Freedom of Expression in Japan* (Tokyo, Kodansha International, 1985).

J Breen and M Teewen, *Shinto in History: Ways of Kami* (Honolulu, University of Hawaii Press, 2000).

J Chan-Tiberghien, *Gender and Human Rights Politics in Japan: Global Norms and Domestic Networks* (Stanford, Stanford University Press, 2004).

CF Goodman, *The Rule of Law in Japan: A Comparative Analysis* (The Hague, Kluwer Law International, 2003).

A Gordon, *The Wages of Affluence: Labor and Management in Postwar Japan* (Cambridge, Harvard University Press, 1998).

H Hardacre, *Shinto and the State 1868–1988* (Princeton, Princeton University Press, 1989).

Masami Iwata and Akihiko Nishizawa (eds), *Poverty and Social Welfare in Japan* (Melbourne, Trans Pacific Press, 2008).

GJ Kasza, *One World of Welfare: Japan in Comparative Perspective* (Ithaca, Cornell University Press, 2006).

[121] One of the drawbacks of this strategy is the tendency of the litigants to employ arguments, which are likely to attract wide popular support, rather than arguments, which are most powerful legal ones to persuade the courts. The Justices know this strategy as well. Sometimes, they thus add the strong expectation to the Diet to change the law, even though they reject the constitutional challenges.

RJ Krotoszynski, *The First Amendment in Cross-Cultural Perspective: A Comparative Legal Analysis of the Freedom of Speech* (New York, NYU Press, 2006) .

Ikuo Kume, *Disparaged Success: Labor Politics in Postwar Japan* (Ithaca, Cornell University Press, 1998).

CS Littleton, *Shinto* (Oxford, Oxford University Press, 2002).

Yoshiko Nozaki, *War Memory, Nationalism and Education in Postwar Japan, 1945–2007: The Japanese History Textbook Controversy and Ienaga Saburo's Court Challenges* (London, Routledge, 2008).

DM O'Brien, *To Dream of Dreams: Religious Freedom and Constitutional Politics in Postwar Japan* (Honolulu, University of Hawaii Press, 1996).

M Weiner, *Japan's Minorities: The Illusion of Homogeneity* (London, Routledge, 1997).

MD West, *Secrets, Sex, and Spectacle: The Rules of Scandal in Japan and the United States* (Chicago, University of Chicago Press, 2007).

8

Pacifism and National Defence

Introduction – PART I: PACIFISM – Renunciation of War and the Ban on Armed Forces – Original Intent – Establishment of the National Police Reserve and the Self-Defence Force – PART II: THE SELF-DEFENCE FORCE – The Self-Defence Force and the Courts – The Limits of Military Action and Military Power – Defence Action and Emergency Situations – PART III: THE JAPAN-UNITED STATES MUTUAL SECURITY TREATY – The Japan-United States Mutual Security Treaty and American Troops – The Constitutionality of the Japan-United States Mutual Security Treaty – Military Cooperation with the United States – PART IV: THE CONSTITUTION AND INTERNATIONAL PEACE COOPERATION – The Gulf War and Enactment of the International Peace Cooperation Act – The Constitutionality of the Self-Defence Force's Peacekeeping Role – Conclusion

INTRODUCTION

THE JAPANESE CONSTITUTION is quite unique in providing a pacifism principle. It boldly renounces war powers and prohibits the government from maintaining armed forces. Many people believe that this pacifism clause is unique to Japan, since Japan totally renounced war powers and prohibited the maintenance of armed forces even for the purpose of self-defence. This principle of the Japanese Constitution aspires to absolute pacifism and is thought of by many Japanese people as an unprecedented and commendable accomplishment. Many people have accepted and supported this pacifism principle as a defining principle of the Japanese Constitution.

Yet, in reality, the government has established the Self-Defence Force (SDF) and also allows the United States to station its troops in Japan. The SDF is one of the top 10 militaries in the world, although the government does not call it an 'armed force' or 'military force'. Moreover, the SDF has been sent overseas in order to cooperate with the United Nations in peacekeeping operations and to engage in international peace cooperation.

In this chapter, we will see the original intent, historical development and current controversies surrounding Japan's national defence. This chapter also examines the controversies regarding the involvement of the SDF with international peace cooperation.

PART I: PACIFISM

RENUNCIATION OF WAR AND THE BAN ON ARMED FORCES

The first paragraph of the preamble to the Japanese Constitution makes clear that '[w]e, the Japanese people' have determined that 'we shall secure for ourselves and our posterity the fruits of peaceful cooperation with all nations and the blessings of liberty throughout this land, and resolved that never again shall we be visited with the horrors of war through the action of government'. This passage clearly shows that the commitment never to go to war was the major motivating factor for the enactment of the Constitution. The preamble also makes clear its commitment to pacifism in the second paragraph:

> We, the Japanese people, desire peace for all time and are deeply conscious of the high ideals controlling human relationship, and we have determined to preserve our security and existence, trusting in the justice and faith of the peace-loving peoples of the world. We desire to occupy an honored place in an international society striving for the preservation of peace, and the banishment of tyranny and slavery, oppression and intolerance for all time from the earth. We recognize that all peoples of the world have the right to live in peace, free from fear and want.

Premised upon this commitment to pacifism, the Constitution devoted an entire chapter to this issue (Chapter II: Renunciation of War), and provided in article 9:

> Aspiring sincerely to an international peace based on justice and order, the Japanese people forever renounce war as a sovereign right of the nation and the threat or use of force as means of settling international disputes.
>
> In order to accomplish the aim of the preceding paragraph, land, sea, and air forces, as well as other war potential, will never be maintained. The right of belligerency of the state will not be recognized.

As a result, there are no provisions on military or armed forces in the Japanese Constitution nor any provision concerning appointment of the commander-in-chief or addressing who has the power to raise the army or declare war. There are no provisions as to what the government should do if Japan is attacked by other countries.

ORIGINAL INTENT

Under the Meiji Constitution, the Emperor had supreme command of the Army and Navy (article 11). The Emperor determined the organization and peacetime standing of the Army and Navy (article 12) and declared war or made peace (article 13). Although article 12 could be interpreted to allow the assistance of Army and Navy ministers to the Emperor, thus practically giving the power to decide on the organization of the army and navy to the Cabinet, gradually the sovereign prerogative to command the military came to be interpreted very broadly to exclude the supervision of the Cabinet even with respect to organization of the military. Thus, the Emperor, with the assistance of the General Staff Office consisting of the Army Chief of Staff and Naval Chief of Staff, could command the military without supervision of either minister. Moreover, the positions of Minister of the Army and Minister of the Navy came to be reserved for serving military officers. Since Cabinet decisions were supposed to be unanimous, the Cabinet could not control the military over the objections of these ministers. The Army ultimately decided to invade China and other Asian countries with the strong support of the public.

Even after Japan was defeated in the Pacific War and the Supreme Commander of Allied Powers (SCAP) dismantled the Imperial Army and Navy, there was no plan to renounce war powers or ban the maintenance of armed forces. However, when MacArthur decided to draft the new constitution, one of the three basic principles to be incorporated into it clearly embodied this pacifism principle.[1] It is unclear where MacArthur got this idea,[2] yet he wanted to keep the Emperor and thought this provision essential for alleviating the hostility towards the Emperor in Asian countries and all over the world.[3]

The Japanese government was surprised to see the draft prepared by the SCAP since no one expected it. This provision in particular was undoubtedly most shocking.[4] No one ever imagined that the renunciation of war powers and the ban on the maintenance of armed forces should be a part of the new constitution.[5] Yet, ultimately, the government decided to accept the draft and enact the new constitution, accepting the pacifism clause.[6]

During the course of deliberations over the enactment of the new constitution in the Imperial Diet, no serious questions were raised as to article 9. The government came to defend article 9 as an ideal choice for Japan. It was passed despite opposition from the Japan Communist Party (JCP), which questioned the adequacy of abandoning war powers even for self-defence.[7] However, the phrase '[a]spiring sincerely to an international peace based on justice and order' was added to section 1 and the phrase '[i]n order to accomplish the aim of the preceding paragraph'

[1] See above, ch 1, n 20.

[2] MacArthur said that it was Kijurou Shidehara, the Prime Minister, who suggested this idea to him but there are disputes as to the accuracy of his statement. T McNelly, *The Origins of Japan's Democratic Constitution* (Lanham, University Press of America, 2000) 106; JE Auer, 'Article Nine: Renunciation of War' in PR Luney and Kazuyuki Takahashi (eds), *Japanese Constitutional Law* (Tokyo, Tokyo University Press 1993) 69, 71–72.

[3] McNelly, *ibid*, 125.

[4] JW Dower, *Embracing Defeat: Japan in the Wake of World War II* (New York, W.W. Norton, 1999) 377. Stunned by the draft, the government did not distribute the translated draft even among Cabinet members. However, the initial response from some Cabinet members was that the draft was simply unacceptable.

[5] The draft prepared by the Matsumoto Committee wanted the organization of the military to be regulated by statute and Diet participation with respect to the declaration of war.

[6] 'War, as a sovereign right of the nation, and the threat or use of force, is forever renounced as a means of settling disputes with other nations.

The maintenance of land, sea, and air forces, as well as other war potential, will never be authorized. The right of belligerency of the state will not be recognized'.

Draft for a Revised Constitution (17 April 1946). It is noted that the phrase 'even for preserving its own security' was deleted. The reason for the deletion is unclear. If that phrase had remained in the text of art 9, it would have been more evident that Japan had renounced the war power even for the purpose of self-defence.

[7] Dower, above n 4, 395.

was added to section 2. This amendment was proposed by Diet member Hitoshi Ashida and is therefore called the Ashida amendment. Although Ashida later came to argue that this amendment was meant to allow the government to maintain military forces for the purpose of self-defence, there was no clear indication of such an intent and the reason why this revision was accepted is not clear.[8]

The original intent behind article 9 was fairly straightforward. The Minister of Constitutional Amendment, Tokujirou Kanamori, remarked before the committee in the House of Peers that even though section 1 did not renounce the right of self-defence, section 2 would make it practically impossible to engage in a defensive war.[9] This remark suggested that, although Japan retained the right of self-defence and section 1 did not renounce war for self-defence, section 2 banned the maintenance of armed forces even for the purpose of self-defence. On the other hand, Prime Minister Shigeru Yoshida suggested in the plenary session of the House of Representatives on 29 June 1945, that section 1 renounced war for self-defence.[10] Reflecting on the fact that most of the recent wars were fought in self-defence, he emphasized the danger of allowing this justification to be used. It was apparent, therefore, that the government at least took the position that Japan could not have armed forces even for the purpose of self-defence under section 2, although Japan had the right of self-defence.[11] Yoshida strongly believed in the necessity of rebuilding Japan and he perhaps realized that heavy military spending would undermine the ability of the government to facilitate economic development. Article 9 was therefore viewed by some as potentially a tremendous asset for Japan.[12] The government thus enthusiastically defended this pacifism principle as an ideal principle to be adopted.[13]

[8] Shoichi Koseki (trans RA Moore), *The Birth of Japan's Postwar Constitution* (Boulder, Westview Press, 1998) 194–202; RB Finn, *Winners in Peace: MacArthur, Yoshida, and Postwar Japan* (Berkeley, University of California Press, 1992) 116.

[9] Dower, above n 4, 396.

[10] Koseki, above n 8, 193; Finn, above n 8, 115–16: Auer, above n 2, 72–73.

[11] Auer, above n 2, 74; KL Port, 'Article 9 of the Japanese Constitution and the Rule of Law' (2005) 13 *Cardozo Journal of International and Comparative Law* 127, 142–45.

[12] Finn, above n 8, 119, 121.

[13] In *Atarashii Kenpou no Hanasi* (*Outline of New Constitution*), a social science textbook distributed to junior high students, edited by the Ministry of Education, it was pointed out that there would be no more soldiers, battleships, or fighters and that there would be no more army, navy, or air force and the students were encouraged not to feel afraid. The textbook concluded: 'Japan decided to do the right thing, ahead of others. Nothing is stronger than doing the right thing'.

Public reaction to the new constitution, with the pacifism clause, was supportive.[14] After all, the people of Japan were totally exhausted by the war effort, had lost millions of people and had most of their homes burned down. The people were simply happy to learn that Japan would abandon war powers and that the people would never again have to face war.

Most academics tend to agree with this original intent. Many academics construe section 1 as renouncing all war powers including war powers for self-defence, and they construe section 2 as prohibiting the maintenance of armed forces even for the purpose of self-defence.[15] Although some construe section 1 as only renouncing war powers for the purpose of settling disputes with other nations, they still construe section 2 as prohibiting the maintenance of armed forces for all purposes, including self-defence.[16]

ESTABLISHMENT OF THE NATIONAL POLICE RESERVE AND THE SELF-DEFENCE FORCE

The government could not, however, follow its original pacifist intent. When the Korean War erupted in 1950, MacArthur was forced to move the armed forces stationed in Japan to Korea. Concerned with the reduced defence capability of Japan, he thus allowed Yoshida, the Prime Minister, to establish the National Police Reserve on 8 July. Yoshida thus decided to establish the National Police Reserve on 10 August, consisting of 75,000 officers. Although it was called a 'police reserve', it was equipped with heavily armed vehicles[17] and it was apparent to everyone that it was an armed force. This was the beginning of the rearmament of Japan.

The government decided to conclude the Japan-United States Mutual Security Treaty and allied with the United States in 1951 when concluding the San Francisco Peace Treaty with most of the nations of the world. It thus obliged the United States to assist Japanese defence and allowed the American government to station its troops in Japan even after the end of the occupation. The Japanese government decided to transform

[14] On general acceptance of the new constitution, see Dower, above n 4, 399–404.

[15] Ashibe, 57–61; Nonaka I, 167 (Takami).

[16] Tsujimura, 100.

[17] In order to avoid a possible conflict with the Constitution, tanks were called 'special vehicles'.

the National Police Reserve into the National Safety Force in 1952 when the Japan-United States Mutual Security Treaty took effect. This was also a critical move since the purpose of the National Safety Force was no longer to act as a 'police reserve'.

In 1954, the government enacted the SDF Act and converted the National Safety Force to the SDF, consisting of the Land Self-Defence Force, the Maritime Self-Defence Force and the Air Self-Defence Force. The government has been expanding the capabilities of the SDF ever since its creation.

These developments did not go unchallenged. When the government established the National Police Reserve, concluded the Japan-United States Mutual Security Treaty and established the SDF, the Japan Socialist Party (JSP), the largest opposition party at the time, strongly opposed them. In particular, when the government renewed the Japan-United States Mutual Security Treaty in 1960, more than five million people participated in the nationwide protest and more than 300,000 demonstrators surrounded the Diet building to try to stop the renewal approval.

Nevertheless, the SDF gradually came to be accepted among the majority of people, probably due to its emergency rescue missions during natural disasters.[18] With this shift in public opinion, the attitude of the major political parties to the SDF also significantly changed. The Liberal Democratic Party (LDP) has supported the SDF, while it has insisted on constitutional amendment to make clear that the maintenance of the SDF is not unconstitutional. The Komei Party used to oppose the SDF, but now supports the SDF, although it is somewhat more reluctant to support an increased role for the SDF. The Democratic Party of Japan (DPJ) is split. Even though some members of the DPJ

[18] According to a recent government survey, almost 80% of respondents had a favourable opinion of the SDF (15% had a good impression; 65% had a relatively good impression; 15% had a negative opinion). Cabinet Office Survey on Pubic Opinion on the SDF and National Defence (January 2009): www8.cao.go.jp/survey/h20/h20-bouei/index.html. Further, 65% of the respondents were happy with the current defence capacity; 14% wanted increased defence capacity and 10% wanted decreased defence capacity. Most respondents thought the primary function of the SDF was to participate in emergency rescue missions, not to carry out national defence (78.4% for emergency rescue and 70% for national defence) and most respondents wanted increased roles in emergency rescue rather than increased roles in national defence (73% for increased emergency rescue and 60% for increased national defence).

oppose the SDF, some members support it. There are some who even support constitutional amendment. The Social Democratic Party (SDP), a successor of the JSP, opposes the SDF, while the JSP once changed its stance to support the SDF when it formed a coalition government with the LDP. The JCP abandoned its stance of supporting the armed forces to defend the country and came to adopt a policy of gradual abolition of the SDF. The JCP argues for the termination of the Japan-United States Mutual Security Treaty and decreased defence capacity before termination, and will let the people to decide what defence capacity is needed after that, ultimately leading to total abolition of the SDF. There are thus still a considerable number of people who feel very strong attachment to article 9 and express strong opposition to the SDF.

The SDF currently has 228,536 soldiers,[19] including some 140,251 army officers, 42,432 navy officers, 43,652 air force officers, 50 destroyers and 350 aircraft, including over 200 F-15 fighter jets.[20] Japan has six Aegis vessels, together with a sophisticated Patriot air defence system and is ranked fourth in military spending internationally.

The SDF was once placed under the control of the Defence Agency in the Cabinet Office, but in 2007 the Defence Agency was elevated to one of the departments of the executive: the Ministry of Defence.

PART II. THE SELF-DEFENCE FORCE

THE SELF-DEFENCE FORCE AND THE COURTS

The Japanese government first attempted to justify the SDF using the argument that the 'war potential' prohibited under article 9, section 2, means 'military power capable of engaging in a modern war' and that the SDF did not meet such war potential since its capability is limited.[21] Then the government changed its stance and came to justify the SDF on the grounds that the Constitution, while prohibiting the maintenance of 'war potential', does not prohibit the maintenance of the 'minimum

[19] Ministry of Defence, Numbers of Personnel inside the Ministry of Defence and Self Defence Force: www.mod.go.jp/j/defense/mod-sdf/kousei/index.html.

[20] Ministry of Defence, Defence White Paper 2008: www.clearing.mod.go.jp/hakusho_data/2008/2008/figindex.html.

[21] Auer, above n 2, 75

force necessary to defend the country' and that the SDF is indeed the minimum force necessary to defend the country.[22] The basis for this argument is the assumption that the Constitution does not deny the right of self-defence recognized under international law and under the United Nations Charter. Apparently, the government believes that, since Japan has the right of self-defence, it should be allowed to maintain the minimum force needed to defend the country.

Yet, many are not persuaded. They have opposed the establishment of the SDF and its further expansions. Some of these critics have filed lawsuits to challenge the constitutionality of the SDF before the courts.

The first challenge was the *National Police Reserve Case.*[23]Diet member Mosaburou Suzuki, representing the JSP, which had opposed the establishment of the National Police Reserve in the Diet, filed a suit directly in the Supreme Court asking it to declare that all government conduct concerning the establishment of the National Police Reserve was unconstitutional. Yet, as explained in chapter five, the Supreme Court rejected the attack since it found no cases or controversies to satisfy the requirement for exercising the power of judicial review. The Supreme Court thus refused to review the constitutional challenge.

Ever since then, the Supreme Court has refused to face the question of whether the establishment of the SDF is constitutional. As we will see below, the Supreme Court held in the *Sunagawa Case*[24] that the Constitution does not deny the right of self-defence recognized in international law. Yet, it has refused to face the issue of whether article 9 of the Constitution allows the government to maintain the armed forces for self-defence.

In the *Naganuma Case*,[25] residents of Naganuma Village, Hokkaido, challenged the decision of the Agriculture Minister to reclassify the local forest reserve to land for development of the SDF's anti-missile base as an infringement of article 9. The Sapporo District Court, to the surprise of many, upheld the claims of the plaintiffs, holding the SDF unconstitutional as a violation of article 9, section 2 for the first time. The court found that the plaintiffs had a constitutional right to live in peace

[22] *Ibid*, 76.

[23] Supreme Court, grand bench, 8 October 1952, 6 *Minshu* 783. See above, ch 5, n 39.

[24] Supreme Court, grand bench, 16 December 1959, 13 *Keishu* 3225. See below, n 33.

[25] Supreme Court, 1st petty bench, 9 September 1982, 36 *Minshu* 1679.

and that the land re-designation threatened that right, thus concluding that the plaintiffs had standing to challenge the re-designation. It rejected the argument of the government that the court should not review the constitutionality of the SDF since the case presented a highly political question. It concluded that the SDF fell into the category of prohibited 'war potential'.

However, the Sapporo High Court overturned this judgment. It admitted that the plaintiffs had standing to challenge the re-designation, since they might potentially suffer damages from the loss of the forest reserve, including damage from possible flooding, but it rejected the argument that the plaintiffs had a constitutional right to live in peace. It held, however, that the case became moot because the plaintiffs' legal interest to challenge the re-designation was lost when an alternative facility was constructed to prevent possible damage from flooding after the suit had been filed. The court then held that it should not decide the constitutionality of the SDF, since this question was so highly political.

The Supreme Court affirmed the judgment of the High Court, holding that the case was moot. It thus dismissed the suit without reviewing the constitutionality of the SDF. The Supreme Court did not even invoke the political question doctrine to reject the constitutional challenge.

The *Hyakuri Base Case*[26] also presented the Court with the issue of the constitutionality of the SDF. The SDF was planning to build a base in the Hyakuri District of Omitama City, Ibaragi Prefecture. The original landowner sold the piece of land in question, which was located in the area planned for construction of the base, to residents who opposed the base. The buyer obtained temporary registration of the transfer of land on making a partial payment (in Japan, land title is registered with the government and any transfer of land is not effective against others unless the transfer is registered). The original owner then cancelled the contract, insisting that the buyer had not made the remaining payment and sold the property to the SDF for construction of the base. He thus filed a suit seeking the cancellation of the initial sale contract and requesting the deletion of the temporary registration. The opposing residents filed a counterclaim against the original landowner. The question presented was whether the sale of land to the government for the purpose of constructing the SDF base was constitutional. The Supreme Court denied, however, the applicability of the Constitution to a private contract, even one entered

[26] Supreme Court, 3rd petty bench, 20 June 1989, 43 *Minshu* 385.

into by the government, and decided that the sale contract between the landowner and the government concluded in order to construct the SDF base was not invalid.

The constitutionality of the SDF may be described as the single most controversial constitutional question in Japan. Even though it raises a highly political question regarding national defence, it is remarkable that the Supreme Court has consistently refused to face the issue.[27] Although many tend to believe that the SDF is unconstitutional and that the Supreme Court should declare it to be unconstitutional,[28] the Supreme Court has likely concluded that the issue is better decided by the political process and not by the judiciary.[29]

THE LIMITS OF MILITARY ACTION AND MILITARY POWER

As a result, the courts have never squarely addressed the constitutionality of the SDF or the limits of military power. The government has, however, adopted some limits on military action and military spending based on constitutional and policy considerations.

The SDF is thus allowed to have only defence capabilities. It does not have military weapons used mainly for attacks, such as Intercontinental ballistic missile (ICBM) The SDF is also only allowed to defend the country and is therefore not allowed to strike another country first, although the government argues that the SDF can strike another country if that country is about to strike Japan.[30]

The government has adopted an anti-nuclear policy. It would therefore prohibit manufacturing, possessing or allowing foreign countries to bring nuclear weapons into Japan's territory, although this is merely a principle

[27] Some of the opposing citizens requested that the courts issue an injunction against SDF spending. However, the Supreme Court dismissed the suit for not meeting the case or controversy requirement: Supreme Court, 3rd petty bench, 19 April 1977, 94 *Zeimusoshousiryou* 138. When a citizen refused to pay tax, insisting on the unconstitutionality of SDF spending and sought reimbursement when the government seized his bank account and deducted the tax in default, the courts rejected the suit as the citizen could not challenge the tax based on the unconstitutionality of SDF spending: Sendai High Court, 30 September 1983, 510 *Hanreitimes* 122.

[28] Ashibe, 61; Kiyomiya, 114. See also Port, above n 11, 160.

[29] Ito, 169, supports the stance of the Supreme Court, arguing that art 9 should be regarded as a political norm to be enforced by the political process rather than a judicial norm to be enforced by the judiciary.

[30] Auer, above n 2, 76.

based on policy and not a constitutional restriction.[31] This policy would seem to derive from the fact that Japan is the only country in the world that experienced the detonation of atomic bombs.

The government used to follow a policy of limiting the military budget to 1 per cent of GDP.[32] This limit on military spending serves to demonstrate that the SDF is merely the minimum force necessary to defend the country. The government changed this limitation policy in 1986 to give it more flexible limits in light of the international situation and domestic economic and fiscal situations. Yet, it has largely maintained the less than 1 per cent limit in the past decade.

As a result, although the courts are not willing to enforce article 9, article 9 has some powers to restrain the government; the existence of article 9 has contributed to the limitation of Japan's military power even though it has not prevented the government from establishing the SDF.

DEFENCE ACTION AND EMERGENCY SITUATIONS

According to the SDF Act, the Prime Minister can order the deployment of the SDF when Japan is attacked or when there is clear, imminent danger of armed attack (SDF Act, article 76). The Prime Minister must seek the approval of the Diet in accordance with the Armed Attack

[31] *Ibid*, 76. It must be noted, however, that the Japanese government trusts the United States government to consult with it before bringing in nuclear weapons when their vessels or submarines come to its military bases in Japan. The government thus does not ask the United States government whether the vessel or submarine is carrying nuclear weapons or attempt to investigate so long as the United States does not ask for consultation. Many suspect, therefore, that the United States must be secretly bringing in nuclear weapons when their carriers or submarines come to Japan. Some even argue that there is a secret agreement between both governments to allow the United States to bring in nuclear weapons. After the change of government, the DPJ Government established the expert committee to investigate the existence of secret agreements. The committee could not find the existence of a secret agreement at the time of renewal of the Japan-United States Mutual Security Treaty, but the Japanese government did not object to the understanding of the United States government that the arrival of nuclear vessels or submarine is exempted from the prior consultation obligation and came to accept that understanding, while officially denying it. The expert committee thus concluded that there was an implicit secret agreement between both governments not to clarify the issue: *Expert Committee Report on So-called Secret Agreements* (9 March, 2010): www.asahi.com/special/mitsuyaku/paper2.pdf.

[32] Auer, above n 2, 78.

Act. The SDF can use necessary force to defend the country when ordered (article 88). The Prime Minister, 'representing the Cabinet', is the supreme commander of the SDF (article 7). Yet, upon approval of the Prime Minister, the Defence Minister can order necessary action when there is a special need to protect life and property on the seas (article 82). Similarly, upon approval of the Prime Minister, and in order to prevent damage to life and property, the Defence Minister can order the interception of missiles if there is a possibility that they might hit Japan (article 82-2, section 1). Moreover, the Defence Minister can order such interception based upon guidelines approved by the Prime Minister if there is not sufficient time to seek approval of the Prime Minister (article 82-2, section 3).

According to the Armed Attack Act, the Cabinet decides the fundamental defence policy when Japan is attacked or when there is clear, imminent danger of armed attack (article 9, section 1 and section 6) and the Prime Minister must seek the approval of the Diet (article 9, section 7). If the Diet disapproves of the plan, the Prime Minister must terminate all orders based on the plan and must order the SDF to withdraw (article 9, section 11). If the plan is approved, the Prime Minister supervises the administrative agencies based on that policy by 'representing the Cabinet' (article 9, section 12).

PART III. THE JAPAN-UNITED STATES MUTUAL SECURITY TREATY

THE JAPAN-UNITED STATES MUTUAL SECURITY TREATY AND AMERICAN TROOPS

Japan concluded the Japan-United States Mutual Security Treaty in 1951 to allow the stationing of American troops in Japan even after the end of the occupation. The Japanese government needed the military power of the United States, especially its nuclear umbrella, to defend itself against possible invasions, particularly those by communist forces such as the Soviet Union. The United States government wanted Japan to be a barrier to the expansion of communism in the Pacific region and wanted to use the military bases in Japan as a means of keeping an eye on Asian countries. The Japanese government renewed the Treaty in 1960 and made it permanent by allowing it to be effective for ten years and by allowing each party to cancel after ten years with one year's advance notice. This was done over the strong objections of demonstrators outside of the Diet building opposing approval of the treaty.

Based on this Treaty, the United States has maintained military bases in Japan. Some 35,000 army, navy and air force officers and marines are stationed there. Most of them are located in Okinawa, an island far west of mainland Japan. Okinawa was placed under US occupation even after the occupation of the mainland was over. It was not until 1972 that Okinawa was finally returned to the Japanese government. A large portion of Okinawa is occupied by American bases. Since many people in Okinawa must endure the burdens that come with the existence of American bases, while at the same time relying on these bases for employment and living, there is always some tension in Okinawans' attitude towards the bases.

THE CONSTITUTIONALITY OF THE JAPAN-UNITED STATES MUTUAL SECURITY TREATY

The constitutionality of the Japan-United States Mutual Security Treaty was at issue in the *Sunagawa Case*.[33] In that case, those protesting the expansion of Tachikawa airport used by the American forces entered the airport during a protest and were prosecuted for violating the Special Criminal Act enacted as a result of the Japan-United States Mutual Security Treaty, which banned entry into the airport without authorization. They argued that the conviction violated article 9, section 2, since the Japan-United States Mutual Security Treaty and the stationing of the American troops were unconstitutional. The Tokyo District Court accepted the protestors' argument and held the Japan-United States Mutual Security Treaty and the stationing of American troops to be unconstitutional.

The government filed a special appeal directly to the Supreme Court and the Supreme Court quickly overturned this judgment and concluded that the Japan-United States Mutual Security Treaty as well as the stationing of American troops was not unconstitutional. The Supreme Court first affirmed that the Constitution did not deny the right of self-defence and that Japan has the power to defend itself through the

[33] Supreme Court, grand bench, 16 December 1959, above n 24.

use of force. It then interpreted article 9, section 2, as prohibiting only 'war potential' maintained by the Japanese government. The American troops stationed in Japan were thus not a prohibited 'war potential'. The Supreme Court then examined whether the decision to allow the American troops to be stationed in Japan violated article 9, section 1. It held that such a decision presented a highly political question, not suited for the courts to examine unless the unconstitutionality was undoubtedly manifest. It examined whether the stationing of American troops was patently unconstitutional and concluded that it was not. It thus refused to rule on the constitutionality of the stationing of the American troops under the Japan-United States Mutual Security Treaty.

Forty years later, the Supreme Court once again faced the issue in the *Land Lease Dispute Case* involving the American bases in Okinawa.[34] Pursuant to the Special Measures Act, the government had compulsorily taken over the authority to use the property of some Okinawan landowners for the use of American military bases. When this authority was about to expire, the government asked the governor of Okinawa to grant a permit to use the properties of the opposing landowners for the American military bases. In 1995, however, the governor of Okinawa refused to grant this permit. Frustrated with his refusal, the Prime Minister issued a request and then ordered the governor to grant the permit according to the provision of the Act. The governor of Okinawa then filed a suit challenging this order. The Supreme Court held that the courts should decide the constitutionality of the Special Measures Act on the assumption that the Japan-United States Mutual Security Treaty was constitutional since it was not evidently unconstitutional and invalid. The Supreme Court thus concluded that the Special Measures Act was constitutional and dismissed the suit filed by the governor.

As stated earlier, the *Sunagawa* decision was a bizarre decision. Since the Court at least inquired whether the stationing of the American troops clearly violated article 9, section 1, and concluded that it did not, the Court might have upheld the constitutionality of the Japan-United States Mutual Security Treaty. Yet, it has been construed by most academics that the Court refused to rule on the merits by employing the political question doctrine. Many tend to construe article 9, section 2, as prohibiting the government from allowing foreign military forces to be stationed in Japan and conclude that the Japan-United States Mutual

[34] Supreme Court, grand bench, 28 August 1996, 50 *Minshu* 1952.

Security Treaty as well as the stationing of American armed forces is unconstitutional.[35]

Although the Supreme Court as well as the government admits that the Constitution does not deny the right of self-defence, the government has adopted the position that the Constitution does not allow the collective self-defence recognized under the United Nations Charter.[36] If Japan has the right of collective self-defence, then it could conclude a mutual defence treaty and engage in military action if a partner country were attacked. However, according to the government, the Constitution only allows self-defence to be used to defend Japan.

This interpretation has imposed tremendous burdens on the government in cooperating with the United States. The Prime Minister, Shinzo Abe, was deeply dissatisfied with the traditional stance of the government and set up an advisory committee on collective self-defence in order to reconsider this position. In 2008, the committee ultimately reported, as was expected, that the government should reconsider the traditional stance and admit a limited collective self-defence right.[37] But the government has not altered its stance, at least not yet.

MILITARY COOPERATION WITH THE UNITED STATES

When the Japan-United States Mutual Security Treaty was first concluded in 1951, the United States probably did not expect Japan to play a leading role in the defence of the United States. With the economic recovery and with the resulting trade deficit with Japan, the United States gradually came to expect Japan to spend more on defence and to expand its mutual military obligations. However, since the Japanese government has adopted the position that the Constitution does not allow for collective self-defence, the Japan-United States Mutual Security Treaty has not been viewed as a treaty based on the right of collective self-defence. As a result, if Japan is attacked, the United States is committed by virtue of

[35] Nonaka I, 184–86 (Takami); Tsujimura, 113.

[36] EJ Southgate, 'From Japan to Afghanistan: The US-Japan Joint Security Relationship, the War on Terror, and the Ignominious End of the Pacifist State?' (2003) 151 *University of Pennsylvania Law Review* 1599, 1622.

[37] Anzenhoshou no Houtekikiban no Saikentou nikansuru Kondankai (Advisory Group for Reconsideration of the Legal Basis for National Security), *Report* (24 June 2008): www.kantei.go.jp/jp/singi/anzenhosyou/houkokusho.pdf.

the treaty to come to Japan's aid, while Japan does not have any obligation to assist the United States if the United States is attacked.[38] This basic stance has not changed.[39]

The United States government has also come to expect more active participation from Japan in its own defence and also for the maintenance of security in the Asia Pacific region. As a result, the Guideline for Cooperation between Japan and the United States, agreed to under the authority of the Japan-United States Mutual Security Treaty, was revised in 1997 and the Japanese government enacted the Vicinity Area Incidents Act (Act Concerning the Measures to be Adopted to Secure the Peace and Security of our Country in Response to Incidents in the Vicinity Area) in 1999 together with an amendment to the SDF Act that allows cooperative military action in response to emergency situations in the vicinity of Japan, if the lack of response might lead to a direct attack on Japan.[40] This concept of 'vicinity' is not a geographical one but a functional one and it could thus lead to cooperative action even in the Middle East. It is questionable whether the SDF's cooperation with the United States in such an area can be justified under the concept of Japan's right of self-defence.

[38] McNelly, above n 2, 160.

[39] The Japanese government, however, has a legal obligation to cooperate with the United States if the United States is attacked in the territories of Japan. This would oblige the Japanese government to engage in defensive action when American military bases or vessels are attacked within Japanese territory. The government has justified such defensive action on the grounds that such an attack would be tantamount to an attack against Japan. The trouble is that the mission of the American military forces stationed in Japan includes the maintenance of international peace and security in the Far East region. American aircraft thus participated in bombings in the Vietnam War and also participated in the Gulf War in 1991. There is the possibility, therefore, that Japan might be forced to participate in wars if American bases or aircraft are attacked by enemy countries within the territories of Japan.

[40] C Ajemian, 'The 1997 US-Japan Defense Guidelines under the Japanese Constitution and their Implications for US Foreign Policy' (1998) 7 *Pacific Rim Law & Policy Journal* 323; RA Fisher, 'Note: The Erosion of Japanese Pacifism: The Constitutionality of the 1997 US-Japan Defense Guidelines (1999) 32 *Cornell International Law Journal* 393; MJ Gilley, 'Comment: Japan's Developing Military Potential within the Context of Its Constitutional Renunciation of War' (2000) 14 *Emory International Law Review* 1681, 1707–12; Southgate, above n 36, 1616–19.

PART IV: THE CONSTITUTION AND INTERNATIONAL PEACE COOPERATION

THE GULF WAR AND THE ENACTMENT OF THE PEACE COOPERATION ACT

Japan is one of the top spenders on Overseas Development Aid (ODA). It used to be the top ODA spender but currently it ranks fifth in the world. Japan spends roughly US$13.5 billion every year.[41] Yet, despite this huge amount of ODA spending, Japan's contribution to world peace has not been appreciated.

This was quite apparent when Japan vowed to spend US$9 billion in support of the allied nations' attack against Iraq during the Gulf War in 1990. Japan was criticized as failing to support international peace by making military contribution.[42] This criticism hurt the pride of many Japanese people, especially since Japan enjoyed the status of a world economic leader. Backed by increasing citizen support, the government decided to enact a Bill to allow the SDF to engage in peacekeeping operations. Many citizens, however, are opposed to the idea of sending the SDF abroad since that move could potentially lead to military invasions like the invasions of Asian countries before the Pacific War. As a result of this opposition, the Bill failed in the Diet.

However, the government submitted another Bill, which ultimately passed the Diet as the International Peace Cooperation Act (Act on Cooperation with International Peacekeeping Operations of the United Nations) in 1992.[43]

[41] Ministry of Foreign Affairs, ODA: www.mofa.go.jp/mofaj/gaiko/oda/shiryo/jisseki.html.

[42] RB. Funk, 'Note: Japan's Constitution and UN Obligations in the Persian Gulf War: A Case for Non-Military Participation in U.N. Enforcement Actions' (1992) 25 *Cornell International Law Journal* 363.

[43] KF Royer, 'The Demise of the World's First Pacifist Constitution: Japanese Constitutional Interpretation and the Growth of Executive Power to Make War' (1993) 26 *Vanderbilt Journal of Transnational Law* 749; Akiho Shibata, 'Japanese Peacekeeping Legislation and Recent Developments in UN Operations' (1994) 19 *Yale Journal of International Law* 307; Shotaro Hamura and E Shiu, 'Renunciation of War as a Universal Principle of Mankind—A Look at the Gulf War and the Japanese Constitution' (1995) 44 *International & Comparative Law Quarterly* 426. See also S Madsen, 'Note: The Japanese Constitution and Self-Defense Forces: Prospects for a New Japanese Military Role' (1993) 3 *Transnational Law & Contemporary Problems* 549.

Under the International Peace Cooperation Act, as amended, the government can send the SDF to cooperate with international peacekeeping operations of the United Nations, to engage in humanitarian international aid, to engage in international supervision of elections and to provide necessary supplies for these purposes. The government argued that participation of the SDF should be allowed only when five principles are satisfied: (1) there must be an agreement to cease fire among the parties; (2) the participation must be supported by the consent of all relevant countries; (3) the SDF must remain neutral in the conflict; (4) the SDF will withdraw if any of the conditions for participation are undermined and (5) the SDF can use weapons only to defend its personnel. Considering the opposition, the government initially froze participation in peacekeeping operations that might have required the exercise of force, as in the case of supervision of ceasefires. However, the government ultimately unfroze this limitation in 2001 to allow Japanese participation in such operations as well.

The SDF has, since the enactment of the International Peace Cooperation Act, participated in many peacekeeping operations and international peace cooperation missions in Cambodia, Mozambique, Rwanda, the Golan Heights and East Timor.

Moreover, when the United States and allied forces attacked Afghanistan after the 9/11 terrorist attacks, Japan enacted the Anti-terrorism Special Measures Act (Special Measures Act Concerning Measures to be Adopted by our Country Regarding Activities of Foreign Countries in Order to Accomplish the Aims of the United Nations Charter in Response to the Terrorist Attack in the United States of America on September 11, 2001, and Related Humanitarian Measures to be Adopted Based on Resolutions of the United Nations) to allow the SDF to cooperate with allied forces by supplying fuel in the Indian Ocean in 2001.[44] When this Special Measures Act expired in 2007, the government enacted the New Anti-terrorism Special Measures Act (Special Measures Act Concerning the Implementation of Fuel Supply to Anti-terrorism Maritime Activities) to allow the SDF to supply fuel to the allied powers in the Indian Ocean for an additional year in 2008. This Act was passed by a two-thirds vote in the House of Representatives despite its rejection in the House of Councillors. With the prospect of the expiration of this new legislation, in December 2008 the government

[44] Southgate, above n 36, 1619–24.

again extended the Act for an additional year by a two-thirds majority vote in the House of Representatives, again despite rejection in the House of Councillors. With the change of government in 2009, however, the DPJ Government ended this mission in January 2010.

When the United States and allied forces attacked Iraq, Japan also enacted the Iraq Special Measures Act (Special Measures Act Concerning the Implementation of Humanitarian Reconstruction Support Activities and Security Maintenance Support Activities in Iraq) in 2003 to allow the SDF to engage in humanitarian assistance and to take measures to increase security in Iraq. The land SDF officers were sent to Samawa to provide medical assistance, to assist in the provision of water and to rebuild roads and schools. The air SDF officers were also sent to Iraq to transport allied forces military personnel. They have already withdrawn from Iraq.

Finally, in 2009, the Diet passed the Act to Punish and Prevent Piracy, despite rejection in the House of Councillors, in order to send the SDF to the coast of Somalia to guard not only Japanese ships but also foreign ships and to allow the SDF to fire if guarded ships were approached despite warnings. Such powers obviously extend far beyond the scope of self-defence.

It must be noted that, as a result of the amendment of the SDF Act in 2007, international peace cooperation is now listed as one of the inherent objectives of the SDF, while defending the security of Japan is still its primary purpose.

THE CONSTITUTIONALITY OF THE SELF-DEFENCE FORCE'S PEACEKEEPING ROLE

Very few people argue that the Constitution mandates eternal absolute neutrality, thus even prohibiting participation in the United Nations. Yet, many people believe that there is a necessary limit to participation in the military actions of the United Nations. The SDF is therefore not allowed to join United Nations forces organized under article 43 of the United Nations Charter.[45] The SDF is also precluded from participating in military actions based on resolutions of the United Nations Security Council under article 42.

[45] Ashibe, 64.

Although the majority of the public supports the participation of the SDF in the peacekeeping operations,[46] such participation has not been accepted without opposition. Considerable numbers of citizens still believe that the SDF is unconstitutional and that sending the SDF overseas is similarly unconstitutional. Even among those citizens who support the SDF, there is some question as to whether the SDF should be sent abroad, since the SDF has been justified only on the basis that it constitutes the minimum force necessary to defend the country. How can the SDF's participation in peacekeeping operations be justified in light of article 9?

The courts have been unwilling to review the constitutionality of SDF involvement in peacekeeping operations. When the government decided to spend US$9 billion for the support of allied powers during the 1990 Gulf War and to send mine sweepers of the maritime SDF to the Persian Gulf after the end of fighting, some citizens filed a suit challenging the government decision. The courts denied their standing and dismissed the suit.[47] Similarly, when citizens filed a suit seeking an injunction against sending the SDF to Iraq, the courts dismissed the suit for its failure to satisfy the standing requirement.[48]

The government argues that the SDF's participation in UN peacekeeping operations is not unconstitutional, since the SDF is not engaging in war for the purpose of solving international disputes.[49] It argues that so long as the five requirements for SDF participation listed above are satisfied, there is no risk that the SDF will be involved in combat. It also argues that the use of weapons does not fall into 'use of force' prohibited in article 9, section 1, so long as SDF officers are only using small weapons necessary 'to defend the life and person of oneself and other members who are present at the same place'. Yet, many still doubt

[46] Of respondents, 51.6% are happy with the current level of participation in international peace cooperation; 25.1% want more participation; 16% want less participation and 3.1% want no participation at all: The Cabinet Office, Public Opinion Survey on Diplomatic Relations (October 2008): www8.cao.go.jp/survey/h20/h20-gaiko/index.html. In total, 76% of the public supports SDF participation in international peace cooperation.

[47] Osaka High Court, 29 October 1991, 38 *Shougetsu* 761; Osaka District Court, 25 October 1995, 1576 *Hanreijihou* 37; Osaka District Court 27 March 1996, 1577 *Hanreijihou* 104; Tokyo District Court, 10 May 1996, 1579 *Hanreijihou* 62.

[48] Nagoya District Court, 14 April 2006, unreported.

[49] Hisashi Owada, 'Japan's Constitutional Power to Participate in Peace-Keeping' (1997) 29 *New York University Journal of International Law & Politics* 271.

whether sending the SDF overseas in order to cooperate with peace-keeping operations can truly be justified under article 9.[50]

While the government hopes that Japan will become one of the permanent members of the UN Security Council, these restraints are believed to be a serious hurdle for Japan. There are thus strong arguments for constitutional amendment to allow broader participation of the SDF in international peace cooperation.

CONCLUSION

The pacifism and national defence issue is the most controversial issue created by the Japanese Constitution. Although the text of the Constitution fairly clearly prohibits the maintenance of armed forces even for the purpose of self-defence, that clarity has not prevented the government from establishing the SDF or the conclusion of Japan-United States Mutual Security Treaty.

It is surely debatable whether the total renunciation of war powers and the total ban on armed forces as was suggested by the constitutional framers is appropriate in modern international politics. Many citizens especially feel a threat to security from North Korea, which proclaimed to have nuclear capability. One can thus question whether such a position is realistic. However, the text and original intent is fairly clear: article 9 prohibits the maintenance of armed forces even for the purpose of self-defence. There are doubts as to whether the SDF can be justified in light of this text and original intent of the Constitution.

Yet, although many academics criticize the unwillingness of the courts to review the constitutionality of the SDF and the stationing of American troops in Japan, this unwillingness is surely understandable and perhaps defensible in light of the difficulty of finding a discernable limit to national defence short of an absolute ban on any armed forces.

[50] Ashibe, 65; Nonaka I, 192–93 (Takami). The Nagoya High Court held that the SDF's activities in Iraq violated the Special Measures Act and art 9 of the Constitution, since Baghdad can be seen as a war zone and the transportation of soldiers by the Air Self-Defence Force can be construed as a military action. The Court dismissed, however, the damages claim and injunction on the grounds that the plaintiffs had no legal interest in the matter and therefore had no standing. The unconstitutional holding is thus merely an obiter dictum. Nagoya High Court, 17 April 2008, unreported.

Moreover, it is possible, even if article 9 is not judicially enforced, that its mere existence might have some restraining power over politics.[51]

However, the existence of the SDF, despite the relatively clear provision prohibiting armed forces even for the purpose of self-defence, may undermine the rule of law and the basic assumptions of constitutionalism. As a result, some have argued that the Constitution should be amended to make it clear that the government can establish the SDF.[52] Many Japanese people do tend to support the SDF; yet a majority of the public is also not willing to amend article 9.[53] Unless article 9 is revised or the SDF is abolished, article 9 will continue to raise this thorny constitutional issue in Japan for some time to come.

FURTHER READING

J E Auer, *The Postwar Rearmament of Japanese Maritime Forces 1945–1971* (New York, Praeger, 1973).

CF Goodman, *The Rule of Law in Japan: A Comparative Analysis* (The Hague, Kluwer Law International, 2003) 147–66.

JO Haley, 'Waging War: Japan's Constitutional Constraints' (2005) 14 *Constitutional Forum* 18.

PJ Katzenstein, *Cultural Norm & National Security: Police and Military in Postwar Japan* (Ithaca, Cornell University Press, 1996).

JP Keddell, *The Politics of Defense in Japan: Managing Internal and External Pressures* (Armonk, M.E. Sharpe, 1993).

M Mochizuki (ed), *Toward a True Alliance: Restructuring US-Japan Security Relations* (Washington, DC, Brookings Institution Press, 1997).

Yasuaki Onuma, 'Japanese War Guilt, the 'Peace Constitution', and Japan's Role in Global Peace and Security' in MK Young and Yuji Iwasawa (eds), *Trilateral Perspectives on International Legal Issues: Relevance of Domestic Law and Policy* (Irvington, Transnational Publishers, 1995) 523.

[51] LW Beer, 'Peace in Theory and Practice under Article 9 of Japan's Constitution' (1998) 81 *Marquette Law Review* 815.

[52] See below, ch 9, pp 270–72.

[53] Of respondents, 66% do not want to amend art 9, while only 23% support amendment of article 9. Asahi Shinbun (2 May, 2008): www.asahi.com/national/update/0502/TKY200805020272.html.

D van Hoften, 'Note: Declaring War on the Japanese Constitution: Japan's Right to Military Sovereignty and the United States' Right to Military Presence in Japan (2003) 26 *Hastings International & Comparative Law Review* 289.

9

Constitutional Amendment and Reforms

Introduction – PART I: CONSTITUTIONAL AMENDMENT – Procedure for Constitutional Amendment – Limits on Constitutional Amendment – PART II: AMENDING THE JAPANESE CONSTITUTION OR ENACTING A NEW CONSTITUTION – Past Attempts – Current Proposals – Pacifism Principle – Conclusion

INTRODUCTION

MOST OF THE written constitutions of the world have provisions allowing for amendment. Even the Meiji Constitution had an amendment provision, although the Constitution itself was viewed as sacred and eternal. The current Japanese Constitution was enacted in accordance with the Meiji amendment provision. The contemporary Japanese Constitution also has a provision for constitutional amendment.

Most constitutions are designed to be difficult to amend, requiring either a special majority of the legislature, a special popular vote for ratification, or both. In other words, the Constitution is entrenched. The Japanese Constitution requires a two-thirds majority of each House in the Diet to propose an amendment, as well as the majority support of the public at a ratification vote on the constitutional amendment.

The issue of constitutional amendment has been the focus of debate in Japan ever since the end of the occupation. Many politicians have called for total amendment or enactment of a new constitution. Nevertheless, no amendment has been passed thus far, not even a minor one. What is the focus of debate? Why has no constitutional amendment been made?

What are the prospects for constitutional amendment in Japan? What are the reform agendas? This chapter will investigate these questions.

PART I: CONSTITUTIONAL AMENDMENT

PROCEDURE FOR CONSTITUTIONAL AMENDMENT

According to section 1 of article 96 of Chapter IX: Amendments, 'amendments to this Constitution shall be initiated by the Diet, through a concurring vote of two-thirds or more of all the members of each House and shall thereupon be submitted to the people for ratification, which shall require the affirmative vote of a majority of all votes cast thereon, at a special referendum or at such election as the Diet shall specify'. Amendments when so ratified, according to section 2, 'shall immediately be promulgated by the Emperor in the name of the people, as an integral part of this Constitution'.

Therefore, the amendment process can be divided into two stages: the first stage is the initiation and submission of the amendment by the Diet for popular ratification and the second stage is ratification by the people.

First, the amendment must be initiated and submitted by a two-thirds majority of each House for ratification. There is no primacy of the House of Representatives in this situation. Moreover, the Constitution requires a two-thirds majority of 'all the members of each House'. There is a split of opinion: some construe this to mean the total number of members designated by statute,[1] and others interpret it as meaning the total number of existing members.[2] Despite the split, however, there is a consensus that those who abstained or who cast invalid votes must be included. A two-thirds majority vote of all valid votes is thus not sufficient.

While it is accepted that the Cabinet can introduce a legislative Bill to the Diet, some would not allow the Cabinet to introduce a constitutional amendment Bill.[3] The reasons for this position are as follows: (1) because the authority to initiate constitutional amendment is a part of the power

[1] Higuchi I, 377; Tsujimura, 530.
[2] Kiyomiya, 400; Ashibe, 377; Sato, 35.
[3] Higuchi I, 377; Ashibe, 276–77.

of the sovereign right of the people, it would be more appropriate for members of the Diet, who are chosen by the people, to introduce a Bill and initiate the process and (2) given the fundamental difference between ordinary legislative process and the constitutional amendment process, it would be more appropriate to limit the introduction of a Bill to Diet members since the power to initiate the constitutional amendment is specifically given to the Diet. This means it is only Diet members who are capable of introducing a constitutional amendment Bill to the Diet.

Secondly, the amendment must be ratified by the affirmative vote of a majority of all votes cast thereon, at a special referendum or at such election as the Diet shall specify. Ratification requires majority support of 'all votes cast thereon', including invalid votes.[4] A majority of all valid votes is thus not enough. The Diet has the option of holding a special referendum or seeking ratification at an election. It has been assumed that the Diet should seek ratification at a general election of the members of House of Representatives, and not in a by-election or an election of members of the House of Councillors.

Although the Diet was supposed to enact a statute on popular ratification of constitutional amendments, the controversies surrounding the amendment issue delayed the enactment of the necessary statute. This is because those who are opposed to constitutional amendment are opposed to the enactment of the referendum statute for fear that it will ultimately pave the way for constitutional amendments. Nevertheless, the Diet finally successfully enacted the Popular Referendum Act (Act Concerning the Procedure for Amendment to the Japanese Constitution) in 2007, almost 60 years after the enactment of the Constitution, backed by increasing popular sentiment favouring constitutional amendment.

According to this Act, an eligible citizen over the age of 18 can cast a vote in a popular referendum for constitutional amendment. (This provision was predicated on the possible amendment of the Public Office Election Act to allow every citizen over the age of 18 to participate in elections; only citizens over the age of 20 will be able to vote until that amendment is passed.) The Act also allows the majority of legal votes to approve an amendment Bill, with no requirement for minimum participation. Thus, even if the participation rate is extremely low, a constitutional amendment Bill can be approved by the majority of legal votes. There are strong criticisms of this Act.

[4] Higuchi I, 378; Hashimoto, 671.

LIMITS ON CONSTITUTIONAL AMENDMENT

There are, of course, potential political hurdles to approving constitutional amendments. But is there a legal limit on constitutional amendment itself?

Although there is a split in opinion, many argue that there must be legal limits on permissible constitutional amendment.[5] Since the power to amend the Constitution, they insist, is the power granted by the Constitution to the people, that power should not be allowed to alter the fundamental principles of the Constitution. What then are the fundamental principles of the Japanese Constitution that lie beyond the reach of constitutional amendment? Many argue that the popular sovereignty principle, the protection of fundamental human rights and the pacifism principle are the fundamental principles of the Constitution.

Therefore, it goes beyond the permissible limit to change the popular sovereignty principle and grant sovereign power back to the Emperor. Yet, there are some uncertainties regarding the limit on amendments to the protection of fundamental human rights and the pacifism principle. It is implausible to argue, for instance, that any changes to individual rights are beyond the permissible limits of constitutional amendment. It is probable that an amendment to create new rights would be acceptable, and minor revisions to or restrictions on individual rights would likely be similarly acceptable. On the other hand, most would likely say that the repeal of article 21 protecting freedom of expression is beyond the permissible limit, since freedom of expression is essential to democracy and to the principle of popular sovereignty. There is also a split of opinion as to the limit on constitutional amendment to the pacifism principle. Some argue that the pacifism principle is the most fundamental constitutional principle and should not be allowed to be amended. Others argue that section 1 of article 9, the renunciation of war, is the key provision of the pacifism principle, prohibiting war for invasion, and should not be amended, but that section 2, the ban on armed forces, is merely instrumental to the key principle and could be amended, for instance, to allow the maintenance of armed forces for the purpose of self-defence.[6]

[5] Kiyomiya, 410; Ashibe, 379–80; Sato, 40.
[6] Ashibe, 380.

Some of the constitutions of the world exclude certain provisions from constitutional amendment or prohibit certain constitutional amendments.[7] The preamble of the Japanese Constitution proclaims the popular sovereignty principle and provides that '[w]e reject and revoke all constitutions, laws, ordinances, and rescripts in conflict herewith'. This provision might thus be interpreted to preclude any constitutional amendment of the popular sovereignty principle. Therefore, some academics argue that amendment of the popular sovereignty principle is prohibited. Since the popular sovereignty principle is beyond the permissible scope of constitutional amendment, this argument may be cited as an additional argument against amendment of the popular sovereignty principle.

Could the provision on constitutional amendment itself be amended? Because of the difficulty of constitutional amendment, there has arisen an argument to amend article 96 and lower the two-thirds majority support requirement in each House or to abolish the popular ratification requirement. If this kind of amendment is allowed, then the revised amendment provision would allow whatever other amendments might be proposed. Many thus tend to argue that the amendment power is a power granted by the power of the people to enact the Constitution and therefore amendment to the amendment provision should not be allowed.[8]

What would happen if a constitutional amendment beyond the permissible limits were made? Such an amendment should be viewed as illegal and void in light of the existing Constitution. Yet, so long as the new provision was supported by the people, it would probably be justified as the enactment of a new constitution rather than as an amendment to the old constitution. Indeed, the Japanese Constitution itself was enacted in accordance with the constitutional amendment provision of the Meiji Constitution, but it altered the sovereignty principle and was thus beyond the permissible limit of the Meiji Constitution. Therefore, the enactment of the Japanese Constitution is itself best viewed as the enactment of a new constitution disguised as an amendment to the old constitution.

[7] The 1958 French Constitution, for instance, provides that '[t]he republican form of government shall not be the object of any amendment' (art 89).

[8] Ashibe, 380–81; Sato, 40.

PART II: AMENDING THE JAPANESE CONSTITUTION OR ENACTING A NEW CONSTITUTION?

PAST ATTEMPTS

The Japanese Constitution took effect on 3 May 1947 and MacArthur gave the Japanese government an opportunity to review the Constitution in January 1947, in accordance with the decision of the Far Eastern Commission. Although there were some voices calling for the establishment of a committee to examine the necessity of constitutional amendment, those voices never attracted strong support and in April 1949 Yoshida Shigeru, the Prime Minister, ultimately declined the invitation for constitutional amendment.

However, after the end of occupation, the dissatisfaction of conservative politicians with the Constitution intensified and many conservative politicians came to argue for wholesale amendment or the enactment of a new constitution. Many conservative politicians insisted that the Japanese Constitution was imposed by the occupation forces and was contrary to the traditions of Japanese society. They argued that Japanese society should be based on the power of the Emperor and that the Japanese Constitution excessively protected the rights of individuals without regard to the public welfare and without paying sufficient attention to public obligations. But it was the renunciation of war and the ban on armed forces in article 9 that upset so many conservative politicians. They argued that article 9 should be amended to allow Japan to have a military to defend the country. As a result, they alleged that either wholesale amendments to the current constitution or the enactment of a new constitution was necessary.

In the 1955 election, Ichirou Hatoyama, the Prime Minister of the Japan Democratic Party, made constitutional amendment a major part of his platform. Yet, many citizens opposed constitutional amendment with the slogan, 'defend the Constitution'. As a result, the conservative forces could not obtain the necessary two-thirds majority in the Diet. In October, 1955, leftist forces joined hands to create the Japan Socialist Party (JSP) in order to defend the Constitution and to oppose the Japan-United States Mutual Security Treaty. In response to this movement, the Japan Democratic Party and the Japan Liberal Party converged into the

Liberal Democratic Party (LDP), with a party platform strongly arguing for the amendment of the Constitution.

In 1956, the LDP government submitted a Bill to establish a constitutional commission to discuss the amendment issue and the Diet passed the Act on the Constitutional Commission despite strong opposition from the JSP. Based on this Act, the government established the Constitutional Commission in 1957. Yet, the JSP refused to participate and most constitutional academics were critical of the move. As a result, the membership of the Commission was clearly tilted towards those who were in favour of constitutional amendment.

It took almost seven years before the Commission submitted its final report and, in the end, it could not report back any specific amendment proposals.[9] Meanwhile, strong opposition erupted against the renewal of the Japan-United States Mutual Security Treaty and the Shinsuke Kishi Government had to step down in 1960, although it ultimately managed to renew the Japan-United States Mutual Security Treaty. Hayato Ikeda, the new Prime Minister, vowed to focus on economic development rather than on constitutional amendment and thus in 1960 abandoned the idea of constitutional amendment. The government had already changed its official interpretation of article 9 to allow the government to maintain the Self-Defence Force (SDF). It must have felt that constitutional amendment was not necessary to justify the SDF.

Thereafter, although sweeping amendments or the enactment of a new constitution remained on the LDP party platform, each government vowed that they were not interested in seeking constitutional amendment. The issue of constitutional amendment thus had not attracted much public attention from 1960 to 1990, even though some of the conservative politicians occasionally called for substantial constitutional changes or enactment of a new constitution.

The Gulf War in 1990 altered all this. Although the Japanese government decided to spend billions of dollars supporting the multinational forces attacking Iraq, many countries called for the contribution of personnel rather than just a monetary contribution. Japan was already one of the leading economies in the world and this criticism hurt the pride of much of the Japanese public. They thus came to support the participation of

[9] Kenzo Takayanagi, 'Some Reminiscences of Japan's Commission on the Constitution' in D Fenno Henderson (ed), *The Constitution of Japan: Its First Twenty Years, 1947–67* (Seattle, University of Washington Press, 1968) 71.

the SDF in peacekeeping operations and international peace cooperation. However, article 9 seems to be a barrier to effective participation of the SDF and many members of the public came to support constitutional amendment to article 9. As a result, during the 1990s, multiple proposals were made concerning constitutional amendments.

The absence of constitutional amendments to the Japanese Constitution has also prompted the public to believe in the necessity of constitutional amendment more generally. Since no amendment has been made to the Constitution in over 60 years since its enactment, many citizens came to believe that the Constitution was outdated or had failed to keep in touch with changing social and international circumstances. As a result, by the late 1990s, the majority of the public had come to support the idea of constitutional amendment.

Moreover, some of the influential members of the Democratic Party of Japan (DPJ) came to share this view. Ichirou Ozawa, one of the previous leaders of the LDP, was a particularly strong advocate for constitutional amendment before joining the DPJ in 2003. Yukio Hatoyama, another influential leader of the DPJ, was also a strong supporter of constitutional amendment. Although the DPJ itself had never been a strong supporter of constitutional amendment, the attitude of some of its leaders revealed the changing attitudes of this opposition party.

In 1999, both the House of Representatives and the House of Councillors set up constitutional commissions to review the issue of constitutional amendment. They called witnesses and sent observers to survey the constitutions of the world. Their reports were published in April 2005.[10] Meanwhile, in May 2004, the *Yomiuri* newspaper, which has the largest circulation in Japan, published the third draft of its own proposed constitutional amendments.[11] The ruling LDP also published its draft of a new constitution in October 2005.[12]

Looking back, it is interesting that no constitutional amendment has ever been achieved under the Japanese Constitution. The amendment procedure of the Japanese Constitution is definitely demanding, but it is

[10] Constitutional Commission of the House of Representatives, *The Final Report*: www.shugiin.go.jp/index.nsf/html/index_e_kenpou.htm; Constitutional Commission of the House of Councillors, *The Final Report*: www.sangiin.go.jp/eng/report/ehb/ehb_index.htm.

[11] *Yomiuri* newspaper, 2004 Preliminary Draft of the Constitutional Amendment: www.yomiuri.co.jp/feature/sian2004 (hereinafter cited as Yomiuri draft).

[12] LDP, Draft of the New Constitution: www.xn—x41az7v.jp/k010/051122jimin-sinkenpousouan.pdf (hereinafter cited as LDP draft).

less demanding than the procedure of other countries such as Canada, where the consent of all provinces is required for certain amendments. Yet, although the LDP has held power since 1955, except for a short period from 1993–94, it has not enjoyed the two-thirds majority in both Houses necessary to initiate a constitutional amendment. As a result, wholesale revision of the Japanese Constitution or enactment of a new constitution, let alone an amendment to article 9, has not been achieved. But why not even a minor one? It might be that minor amendments to the Constitution, such as an amendment to article 89 indicating that the government funding of private universities is permissible, would be more acceptable to the public. Those who opposed to amendment to article 9 opposed to any amendment, even a not-so-controversial one, such as the amendment to article 89, because they feared that any amendment might ultimately pave the way to the amendment to article 9. They have been thus unwilling to agree to even a minor amendment to the Constitution. Moreover, since the government has interpreted the government funding of private universities as permissible even under the current article 89, not many people felt the compelling necessity to amend the Constitution. Probably, this applies to other minor amendment proposals as well. These factors have prevented any constitutional amendment from being adopted since the enactment of the Japanese Constitution in May 1947.

CURRENT PROPOSALS

There are many contemporary proposals for constitutional amendment.[13] Yet, the most influential are the draft new constitution published by the

[13] These include the proposal of the Japan Conference, a conservative think-tank and network for constitutional amendment. Japan Conference, Shinkenpou Seitei de Nihon Saisei e (Toward Resurrection of Japan by Enactment of the New Constitution): www.nipponkaigi.org/1200-kenpo/1210-01qanda.html (hereinafter cited as Japan conference proposal). Former Prime Minister Yasuhiro Nakasone also published a draft of the new Constitution. Sekai Heiwa Kenkyuusho (Institute for World Peace), headed by Yasuhiro Nakasone, Draft of the New Constitution (2005): www.kenpoukaigi.gr.jp/seitoutou/20050128nakasonekaikenan.htm (hereinafter cited as Nakasone proposal). Keizai Douyuu Kai (Japan Association of Corporate Executives) also published its opinion on constitutional amendment: Japan Association of Corporate Executives, Kenpoumondaichousakai Ikensho: Jiritsushita Kojin, Jiritsushita Kuni ninarutameni (Opinion to Constitutional Commission: Toward Accomplishment of Autonomous Individual and Independent State) (April 2003): www.doyukai.or.jp/policyproposals/articles/2002/030421a.html (hereinafter cited as JACE opinion).

LDP ('LDP draft') and the proposal for constitutional amendments published by the Yomiuri newspaper ('Yomiuri draft'). The LDP draft is especially instructive since, unlike other proposals by the LDP in the past, it is relatively modest[14] and can be viewed as an attempt to attract the majority support of the public. This section will examine some of the issues raised by these proposals, while the issue of article 9 will be looked at more extensively in the next section.

Some observe that the wording and phrases of the Japanese Constitution seem like direct translations of English and are not written in what is seen as the more poetic or majestic Japanese style. Some note that the preamble of the Japanese Constitution does not seem to proclaim what kind of country Japan should aspire to be. These critics thus conclude that the new constitution should be written in a more 'beautiful' Japanese style[15] and should embody the ideal goals to which the country should aspire.[16] Many also argue that the preamble should mention the tradition and heritage of Japan and declare the necessity of paying respect to this history and culture, thus making it possible for the public to have patriotic feelings towards the country.[17] Yet, those who oppose the amendments argue that the Constitution is a legal text and should not be written using language found in poems or novels. They also point out that the very concept of constitutionalism is of foreign origin, and any constitutional provision must necessarily be a translation of a foreign concept.[18] They also argue that it is wrong to specify in the Constitution the goals of society that happen to be preferred by the majority, even if those goals appear ideal.[19] Moreover, they argue that it is dangerous to refer to tradition and heritage, since such references can

[14] It is modest even compared with the LDP Summary of Issues by the Committee on Constitutional Amendment (10 June 2004): www.kyodo-center.jp/ugoki/kiji/jimin-ronten.htm (hereinafter cited as LDP summary).

[15] LDP, Important Points for Constitutional Amendment (2004): http://www.jimin.jp/jimin/jimin/2004_seisaku/kenpou/index.html (hereinafter cited as LDP points).

[16] LDP points, above n 15; JACE opinion, above n 13.

[17] LDP points, above n 15; JACE opinion, above n 13.

[18] Tooru Mouri, 'Kokuminshuken Genri to Kaikenron' (Popular Sovereignty Principle and Argument for Constitutional Amendment) in Zenkokukenpoukenkyuukai (National Association of Constitutional Studies)(ed.), Kenpoukaiseimondai (Issue of Constitutional Amendment) (Tokyo, Nihonhyouronsha, 2005) (hereinafter cited as Issue) 20, 23.

[19] *Ibid.*

be used to force the public to become patriotic, thus infringing freedom of thought.[20]

Unlike the old proposals, which attempted to elevate the Emperor to the position of head of state and to grant him some political prerogatives, most of the current proposals remain committed to the popular sovereignty principle. Therefore, the Emperor is declared to be a symbol of the state and of the people, but without political power.[21] No attempt has been made to alter the popular sovereignty principle.

With respect to the structure of the government, some argue for a mechanism to allow the public to directly choose the Prime Minister.[22] Yet, those opposed to such popular selection argue that it is dangerous to allow the public to select the Prime Minister, since such popular selection would give him or her excessive power, possibly even permitting a dictatorship.[23]

With respect to the judiciary, some have proposed the establishment of a constitutional court, which would hear exclusively constitutional cases. Those in favour of this amendment are convinced that the Supreme Court is not properly exercising the power of judicial review and that it is better to establish a constitutional court like the Constitutional Court of Germany, which has exclusive jurisdiction on constitutional issues. For instance, according to proposed article 93 of the Yomiuri draft,[24] the constitutional court would be the only court that would have exclusive power to decide whether a statute or other government act conformed to the Constitution. The Constitutional Court would be staffed by a Chief Justice and eight Associate Justices (article 96). The Chief Justice would

[20] Kazuhisa Saito, Kokumikyoutsuu no Ishiki toshiteno Aikokushin to Koukyoushin (Patriotism and Public Virtue as Common Consciousness of the Nation) in Issue, above n 18, 244.

[21] LDP draft, above n 12; Yomiuri draft, above n 11. The Nakasone proposal declares that the Emperor is the head of state, but this is unusual. Nakasone proposal, above n 13, art 1.

[22] The Nakasone draft provides that the purpose of a general election lies in the election of the members of the House of Representatives and the selection of the candidate for Prime Minister, and mandates political parties must nominate their candidates for Prime Minister at the time of election. Nakasone proposal, above n 13, art 74. The LDP draft, above n 12, will authorize the Prime Minister to supervise administrative agencies as part of his own power.

[23] Nobuhiro Okada, Shushou Kousenron to Leadership no Seiji (Argument for Public Election of Prime Minister and the Politics on Leadership) in Issue, above n 18, 172.

[24] Yomiuri draft, above n 11.

be appointed by the Emperor based upon nomination by the House of Councillors (article 9, section 2) and the Associate Justices would be appointed by the Cabinet based upon nomination by the House of Councillors (article 96). The term of office for Constitutional Court Justices would be eight years and Justices would not be reappointed. The Constitutional Court would have jurisdiction if (1) the Cabinet or one-third of the members of the House of Representatives or House of Councillors petitioned the Court to hear a case; (2) the constitutional issue raised in a specific case was referred to the Court by the Supreme Court or lower courts; or (3) a party petitioned the Constitutional Court to review the constitutionality of a judgment of the Supreme Court (article 94). A declaration of unconstitutionality from the Court would bind all government organs (article 95).[25] Yet, those who oppose this scheme argue that the reasons for the unwillingness of the Supreme Court to engage in judicial review, let alone to strike down statutes, lie in the ideology of the judges and not in the system, which allows the Court to examine constitutionality only in specific cases. They also argue that the establishment of a constitutional court would not solve this problem.[26]

As to individual rights, many propose the inclusion of the new rights, such as the right to privacy or the right to enjoy a good environment.[27] Yet, the right to privacy is already given constitutional protection without an express provision,[28] and there are some doubts as to whether the right to a good environment can and should be given to all individuals as a constitutional right.[29]

Moreover, some have argued for the insertion of more explicit limitations on individual rights and the corresponding duties of

[25] For similar proposals, see the Nakasone proposal, above n 13, arts 91–94; JACE opinion, above n 13.

[26] Shigeki Nakajima, Kenpou Saibansho (Constitutional Court) in Issue, above n 18, p 176.

[27] The Yomiuri draft, above n 11, adds the personality right (art 20); right to enjoy a good environment (art 30); the rights of victims of crime (art 47) and the right to access government information (art 50). The LDP draft, above n 12, adds the right to privacy (art 19-2) and the rights of victims of crime (art 15-3). It also obliges the government to protect the environment (art 25-2).

[28] Masahiro Usaki, Mass Media to Privacy (Mass Media and Privacy) in Issue, above n 18, 203.

[29] Kiyotaka Maehara, Kankyouken, Kankyouhogogimu (Environment Right and Duty to Protect the Environment) in Issue, above n 18, 236.

citizens.[30] Those in favour of such amendment believe that the current constitution protects individual rights without sufficiently emphasizing the necessity of respecting public values or societal harmony. They thus criticize the Constitution for allowing what they see as egoistic and self-centred assertions of individual rights at the expense of the public welfare. They are convinced that the Constitution should be amended to make clear that citizens have a responsibility to respect public welfare and that citizens should be constitutionally required to bear additional duties.[31] Those who oppose these proposals argue, by contrast, that such limitation is unnecessary and that the Constitution is not a document designed to enumerate the obligations of citizens.[32]

Some of the proposals attempt to amend the amendment procedure itself in order to make it easier to amend the Constitution. For instance, the LDP draft[33] would allow constitutional amendment by initiation and submission to the public by the majority in each House, and by ratification via a popular majority vote (article 96). Similarly, the Yomiuri draft[34] would allow constitutional amendment either by initiation and submission for approval by majority vote in each of the Houses, and by ratification of the majority of the people, or by a two-thirds vote in each of the Houses (article 116). As explained above, such a proposal is likely to be criticized as going beyond the permissible limit of constitutional amendment.

Some of the proposals attempt to require people to 'respect and uphold' the Constitution.[35] Currently, the Japanese Constitution obliges

[30] The LDP draft, above n 12, thus provides that rights and freedoms accompany obligations and duties and oblige the people to exercise rights and freedoms only within the public interest and public order (art 12). The Yomiuri draft, above n 11, also obliges the public to respect the rights and freedom of others and to accommodate the safety of the state, public order, a healthy environment and other public interests (art 17). The LDP summary, above n 14, proposed adding a duty to support the family as well as a duty to cooperate with the government for national defence and in times of emergency.

[31] The LDP draft, above n 12, art 20, s 3, also proposes amending the principle of separation of Church and State in art 20 so that it prohibits only religious activities of the government beyond social custom or tradition, which have a religious purpose and the effect of assisting a particular religion. The LDP summary, above n 14, also proposes reconsidering the family law provisions of art 24 so that they respect family values. This would allow preservation of traditional family values over egalitarian goals of art 24.

[32] Osamu Ishimura, Kenpoukaiseiron no Shusi to Jinken (Argument for Constitutional Amendment and Human Rights) in Issue, above n 18, 14.

[33] LDP draft, above n 12.

[34] Yomiuri draft, above n 11.

[35] Yomiuri draft, above n 11, preamble; LDP summary, above n 14.

public workers to 'respect and uphold' the Constitution (article 99)—in other words, to pledge obedience to the Constitution and refrain from publicly criticizing it—but it has been construed that the general public is not obliged to respect and uphold the Constitution. Nevertheless, some critics of the Japanese Constitution argue that such obligations should be extended to the general public. Those opposed to this extension argue, however, that the Constitution is the law enacted by the people to restrain the government, and therefore the people should not be forced to respect and uphold it.[36]

PACIFISM PRINCIPLE

Without doubt, the focus of debates on constitutional amendment is article 9. Indeed, it is not unsurprising to note that those in favour of constitutional amendments generally support amending article 9, and those who are opposed to constitutional amendments or who argue for the necessity of defending the Constitution generally oppose amending article 9.

Most of the current proposals attempt to preserve section 1 of article 9, but seek to revise section 2 by explicitly providing that the government should be allowed to have military forces to defend the country and by providing that the Prime Minister is the military commander-in-chief.[37] Many also attempt to insert a new section into article 9 or to insert a new article on cooperation with international peace efforts by allowing Japan's military forces to participate in international peace cooperation.

The LDP draft thus proposes keeping section 1 of article 9 and adding a new article 9-2 on national defence and on international peace cooperation. The draft provides in section 1 that '[i]n order to defend

[36] Mouri, above n 18, 24; Hitoshi Nishihara, Kaikenron no Mezasu Kokka to Kojin no Kankei (The Relationship between the State and Individuals Envisioned by the Arguments for Constitutional Amendment), in Issue, above n 18, 26

[37] Under the current constitution, the executive power is vested in the Cabinet and the Prime Minister can thus command the SDF only by 'representing the Cabinet'. See above, ch 4, pp 95–96. This means that the Prime Minister must have a Cabinet decision to order the SDF. There is a question whether there is sufficient time to call a Cabinet meeting in an emergency and whether it is practical to demand Cabinet decisions on all orders of the Prime Minister. In order to vest the power to command the armed forces in the Prime Minister himself or herself, however, the constitutional amendment is necessary.

the peace and independence of our country and to protect the safety of the country and its citizens, the Self-Defence Military, which is to be commanded by the Prime Minister as commander-in-chief, should be established' and in section 2 that '[i]n order to perform activities to fulfil the duties under the preceding section, the Self-Defence Military must be subject to Diet approval and other necessary control'.[38] It also provides in section 3 that '[t]he Self-Defence Military is authorized to perform as defined by law international cooperative activities in order to secure the peace and security of the international society and activities to protect public order and to protect lives and safety of citizens in times of emergency in addition to activities permitted under section 1'.

The Yomiuri draft, on the other hand, maintains section 1 of article 9 as a new section 1 of article 11 under the new Chapter III on national security. It then replaces the current section 2 of article 9 with a new section banning the manufacture, maintenance and use of weapons of mass destruction. It then adds a new article 12 allowing the establishment of military forces for defending the peace, independence and security of Japan (section 1), while giving the power to command the military to the Prime Minister (section 2) and providing that military service is not mandatory (section 3). Additionally, the Yomiuri draft adds a new Chapter IV on international cooperation. The draft's article 13 declares the aspiration to wipe out human disasters due to military conflict, international terrorism, natural disasters, environmental pollution, economic shortages and regional disorder in specified areas. It also obliges the government to actively cooperate with activities of established international aid organizations and with other international activities to provide humanitarian aid and to maintain or restore peace and security. Under article 14, the draft further authorizes the government to send public workers and military personnel to participate in such international cooperation efforts.

On the whole, those who are opposed to amendments to article 9 have been critical of the government's decision to establish the SDF and to conclude the Japan-United States Mutual Security Treaty. They believe that article 9 renounces war powers, including the power to wage war in self-defence and also prohibits the maintenance of armed forces even for

[38] C Pence, 'Comment: Reform in the Rising Sun: Koizumi's Bid to Revise Japan's Pacifist Constitution' (2006) 32 *North Carolina Journal of International Law and Commercial Regulation* 335.

the purpose of self-defence. They have thus argued for the abolition of the SDF and abolition of the Japan-United States Mutual Security Treaty. They strongly object to amending article 9 to allow the government to establish military forces or to align itself militarily with the United States.[39]

Even those who do accept the SDF and the Japan-United States Mutual Security Treaty may question the necessity of constitutional amendment, since the government has insisted that the SDF and the Japan-United States Mutual Security Treaty are constitutional even under the current article 9. What are the reasons for these amendments, they ask, if these measures are already constitutional?

Many citizens would support a constitutional amendment to allow the SDF to participate in international peace cooperation. In particular, those who want Japan to become one of the permanent members of the United Nations Security Council strongly argue for these amendments.

Yet, sending the SDF abroad runs the risk of involvement in military action. Moreover, an amendment to article 9 will be sure to attract a strong negative reaction from other Asian countries, which suffered tremendous damage at the hands of the Japanese military before and during the Pacific War.[40] Those opposed to amendments to allow military participation in international peace cooperation would thus argue that Japan's contribution should be limited to non-military contributions and that there is no need for constitutional amendment.

CONCLUSION

The government has now successfully enacted the Popular Referendum Act to pave the way for constitutional amendment. The LDP, as well as many members of the DPJ, are in favour of constitutional amendment. However, when Shinzo Abe, the Prime Minister fought the 2007 House of Councillors election, insisting that the issue of constitutional amendment was on the political agenda, the result was a devastating election loss for the LDP. His successor as Prime Minister, Yasuo Fukuda, as well as his successor, Tarou Aso, did not therefore place much emphasis on constitutional amendment. Moreover, even though

[39] For instance, Toshihiro Yamauchi, Heiwashugi to Kaikenron (Pacifism Principle and the Argument for Constitutional Amendment) in Issue, above n 18, 7.

[40] MJ Kelly, 'The Article 9 Pacifism Clause and Japan's Place in the World' (2007) 25 *Wisconsin International Law Journal* 491.

Ichirou Ozawa, the former leader of the DPJ, and Yukio Hatoyama, the first DPJ Prime Minister, have been strong supporters of constitutional amendment, many members of the DPJ are opposed to constitutional amendment. It would be difficult for the DPJ to come to consensus as a party on the issue of constitutional amendment. Naoto Kan, the current Prime Minister, also supports the constitutional amendment but apparently he believes that it is not among the urgent agendas. Furthermore, the attack on Iraq and the subsequent participation of the SDF in the rebuilding of Iraq have raised serious concerns among the public about the role of the SDF. Although a majority of the public still supports some sort of constitutional amendment, the majority also opposes amendments to article 9.[41] In light of this, it is unlikely that the government will soon start to work toward constitutional amendment. Even if the government were to propose amendments, it would probably only approve those amendments that would create new individual rights or that would make minor changes to existing provisions. Major changes to the fundamental principles of the Japanese Constitution, enactment of a new Constitution, or even an amendment to article 9, seem unlikely.

The Japanese Constitution has survived more than 60 years of history since its enactment, despite repeated calls for total revision or the enactment of a new Constitution. On the whole, it may be said that the Japanese Constitution has received wide support from the public. Various reforms may be needed, yet almost every reform could be accomplished by means of constitutional interpretation. In that sense, it is doubtful that any constitutional amendment is actually necessary.

FURTHER READING

JP Boyd and RJ Samuels, *Nine Lives?: The Politics of Constitutional Reform in Japan* (Washington, East West Center, 2005).

GD Hook and G McCormack, *Japan's Contested Constitution: Documents and Analysis* (London, Routledge, 2001).

[41] A recent poll indicates that 51.6% of citizens support constitutional amendment in general, while only 36.1% oppose amendment. With respect to art 9, however, only 38% support amendment, while 21% would prefer the original intent and the remaining 33% would support a flexible interpretation allowing the SDF. *Yomiuri* newspaper (3 April 2009): www.yomiuri.co.jp/politics/news/20090403-OYT1T00006.htm.

Index